SALADIN **AHMED**   SAMI **KIVELÄ**   JASON **WORDIE**

Abbott™

BOOM!
STUDIOS

BOOM! STUDIOS

ABBOTT, October 2018. Published by BOOM! Studios, a division of Boom Entertainment, Inc. Abbott is ™ & © 2018 Saladin Ahmed. Originally published in single magazine form as ABBOTT No. 1-5. ™ & © 2018 Saladin Ahmed. All rights reserved. BOOM! Studios™ and the BOOM! Studios logo are trademarks of Boom Entertainment, Inc., registered in various countries and categories. All characters, events, and institutions depicted herein are fictional. Any similarity between any of the names, characters, persons, events, and/or institutions in this publication to actual names, characters, and persons, whether living or dead, events, and/or institutions is unintended and purely coincidental. BOOM! Studios does not read or accept unsolicited submissions of ideas, stories, or artwork.

For information regarding the CPSIA on this printed material, call: (203) 595-3636 and provide reference #RICH – 799130.

BOOM! Studios, 5670 Wilshire Boulevard, Suite 400, Los Angeles, CA, 90036-5679. Printed in USA. First Printing.

ISBN: 978-1-68415-245-2
eISBN: 978-1-64144-107-0

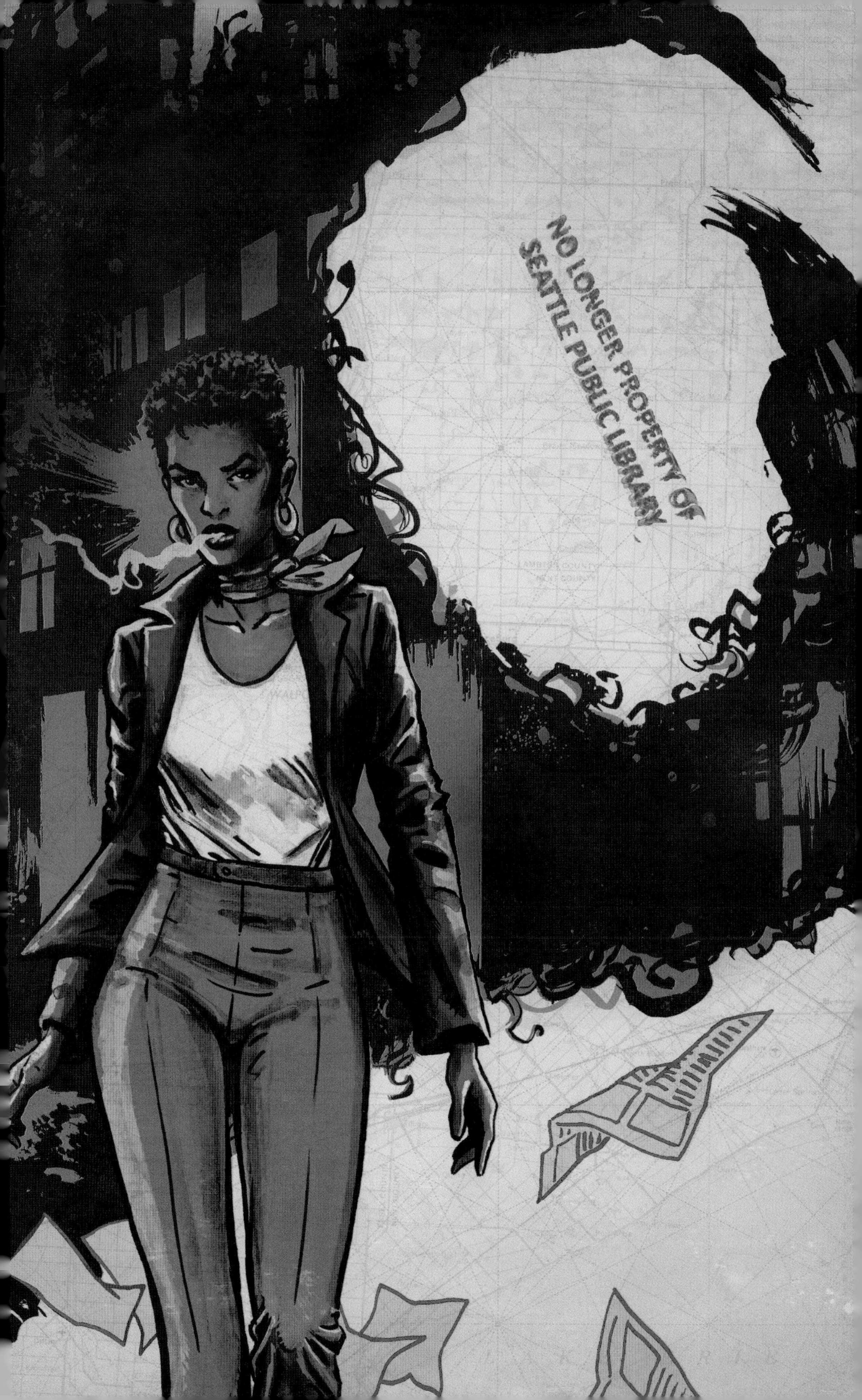

“JOURNAL
DETEC
FOR THE

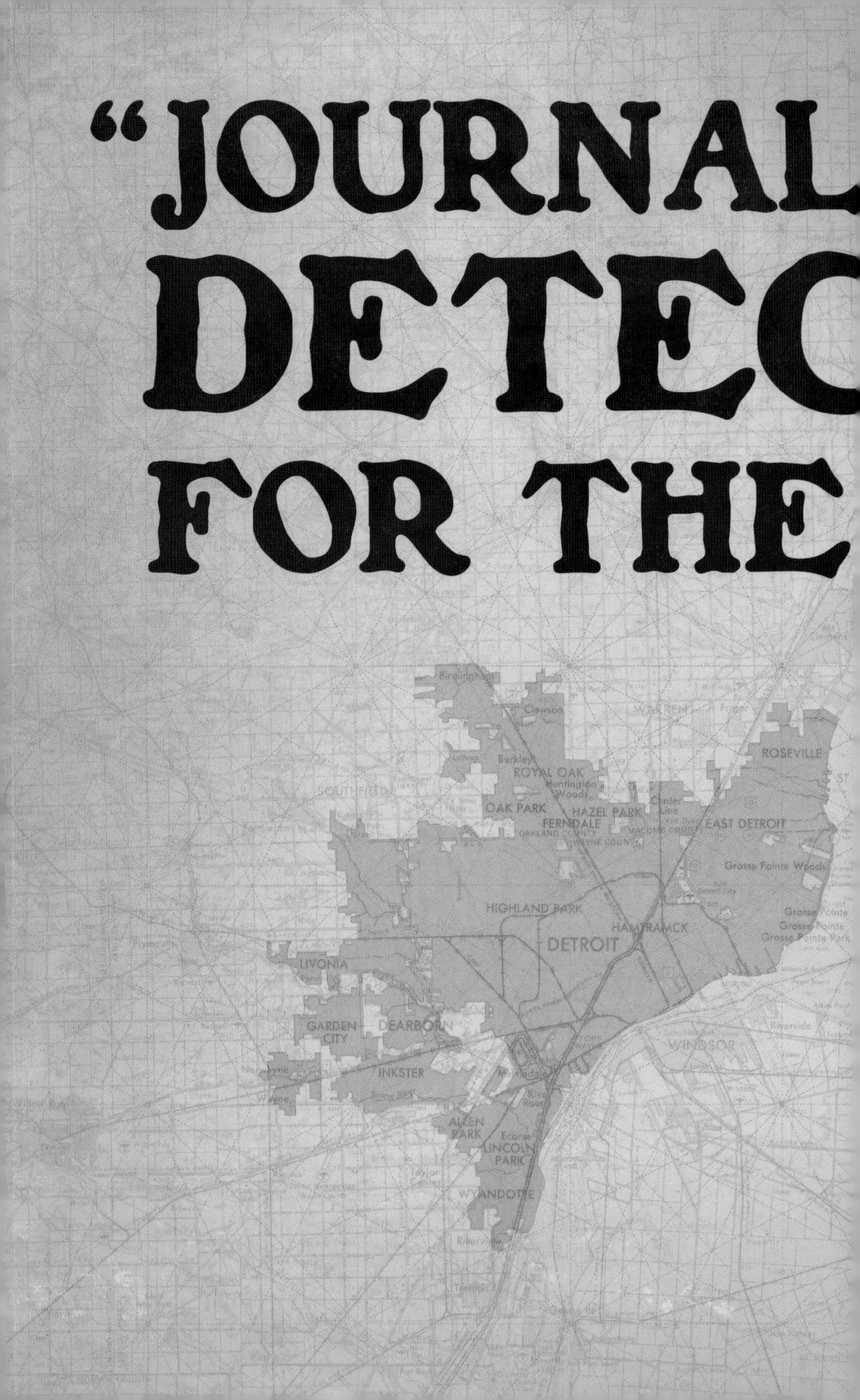

Birmingham
Clawson
WARREN
Fraser
ROSEVILLE
Berkley
ROYAL OAK
Huntington Woods
SOUTHFIELD
OAK PARK
HAZEL PARK
Center Line
FERNDALE
EAST DETROIT
OAKLAND COUNTY
WAYNE COUNTY
Grosse Pointe Woods
HIGHLAND PARK
HAMTRAMCK
DETROIT
Grosse Pointe
Grosse Pointe Park
Plymouth
LIVONIA
GARDEN CITY
DEARBORN
Riverside
WINDSOR
INKSTER
Wayne
ALLEN PARK
Ecorse
LINCOLN PARK
WYANDOTTE
Riverview

ISTS ARE TIVES PEOPLE"
-WAYNE BARRETT

Written by
Saladin Ahmed

Illustrated by
Sami Kivelä

Colored by
Jason Wordie

Lettered by
Jim Campbell

Cover by
Taj Tenfold

Series Designer
Michelle Ankley

Collection Designer
Jillian Crab

Editors
Chris Rosa
Eric Harburn

Abbott Created by
Saladin Ahmed

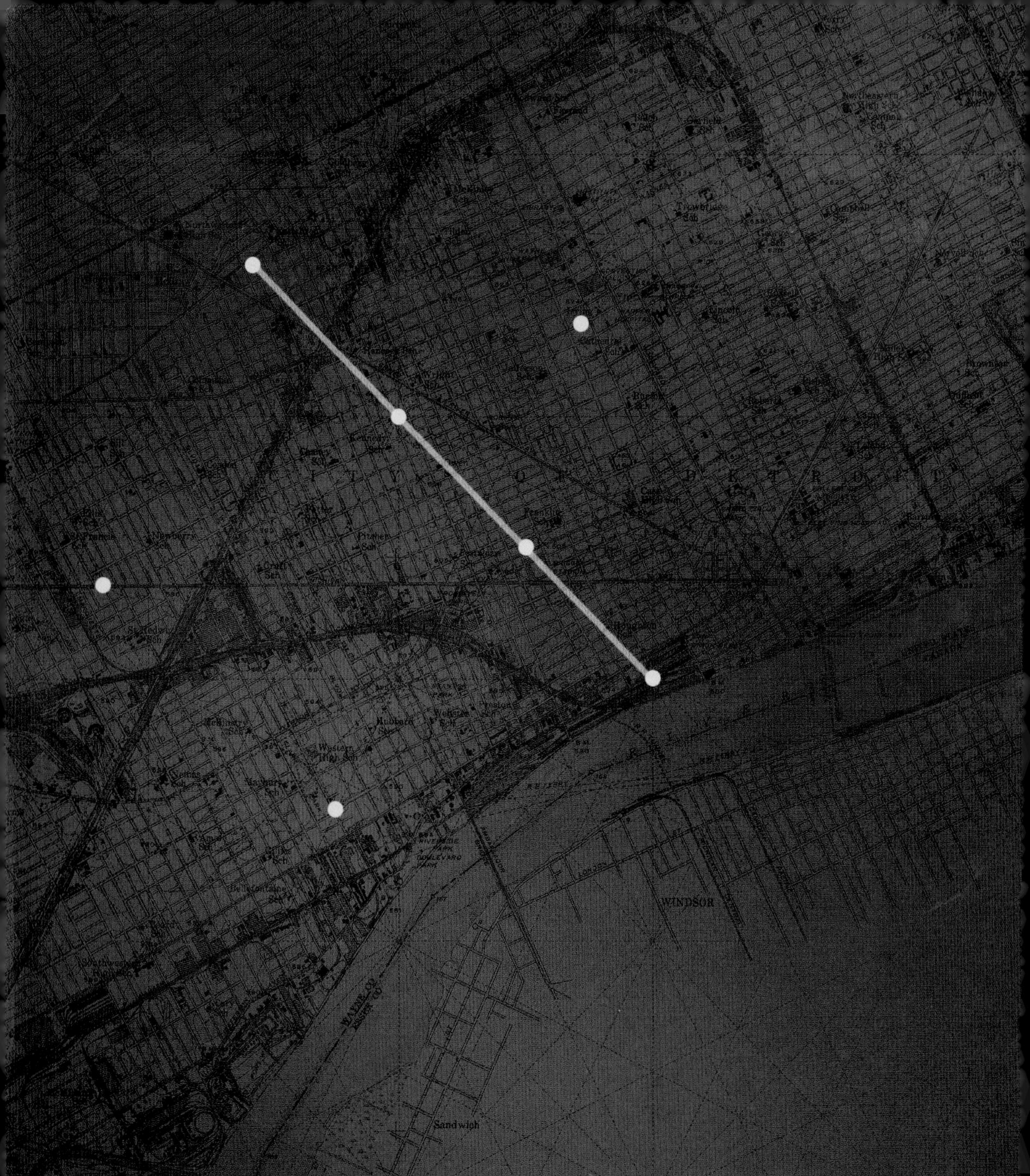
WINDSOR
Sandwich

JUST MY IMAGINATION

Chapter One

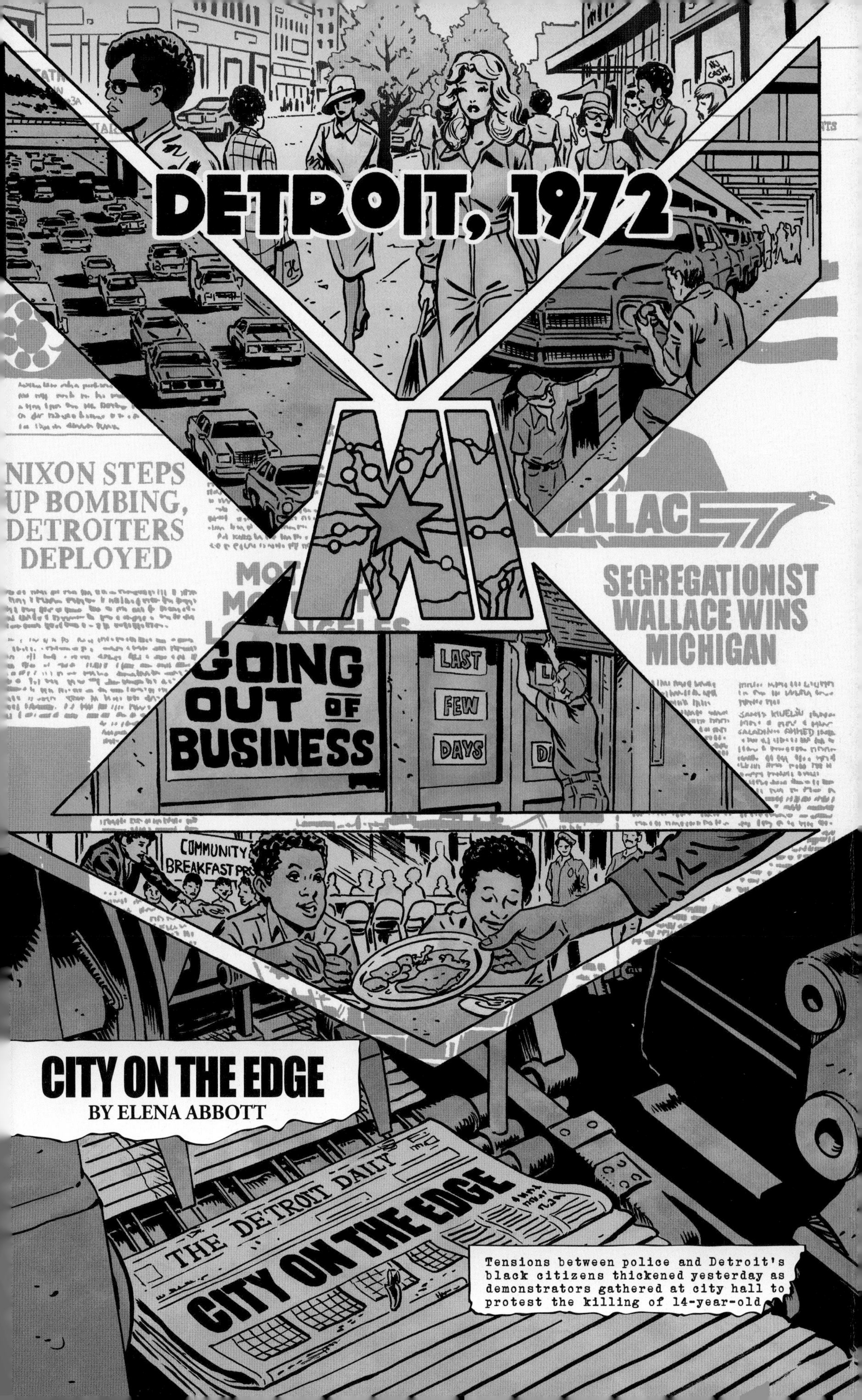
DETROIT, 1972
NIXON STEPS UP BOMBING, DETROITERS DEPLOYED
SEGREGATIONIST WALLACE WINS MICHIGAN
GOING OUT OF BUSINESS
LAST FEW DAYS
CITY ON THE EDGE
BY ELENA ABBOTT
THE DETROIT DAILY
CITY ON THE EDGE
Tensions between police and Detroit's black citizens thickened yesterday as demonstrators gathered at city hall to protest the killing of 14-year-old

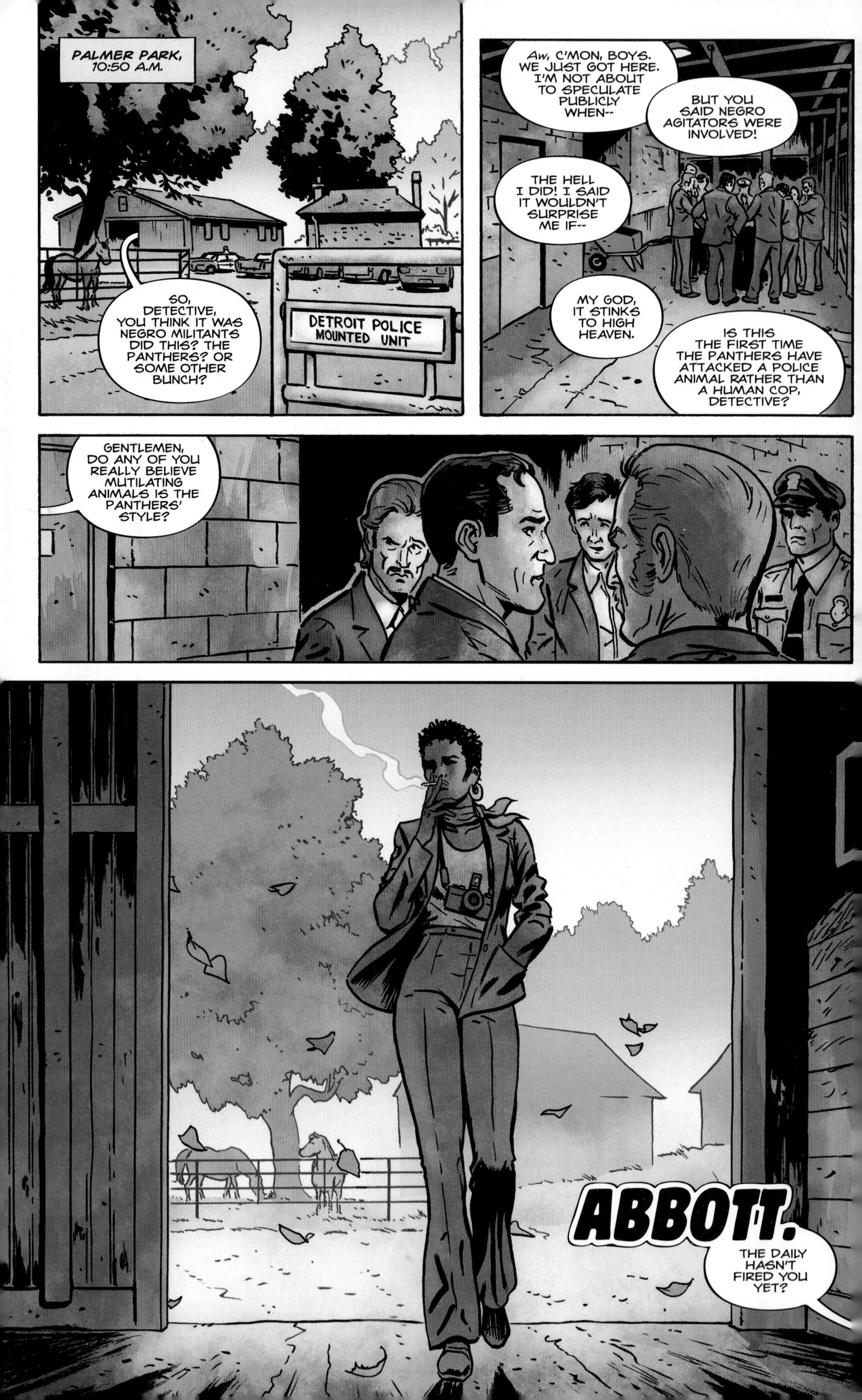
PALMER PARK, 10:50 A.M.
DETROIT POLICE MOUNTED UNIT
SO, DETECTIVE, YOU THINK IT WAS NEGRO MILITANTS DID THIS? THE PANTHERS? OR SOME OTHER BUNCH?
AW, C'MON, BOYS. WE JUST GOT HERE. I'M NOT ABOUT TO SPECULATE PUBLICLY WHEN--
BUT YOU SAID NEGRO AGITATORS WERE INVOLVED!
THE HELL I DID! I SAID IT WOULDN'T SURPRISE ME IF--
MY GOD, IT STINKS TO HIGH HEAVEN.
IS THIS THE FIRST TIME THE PANTHERS HAVE ATTACKED A POLICE ANIMAL RATHER THAN A HUMAN COP, DETECTIVE?
GENTLEMEN, DO ANY OF YOU REALLY BELIEVE MUTILATING ANIMALS IS THE PANTHERS' STYLE?
ABBOTT.
THE DAILY HASN'T FIRED YOU YET?

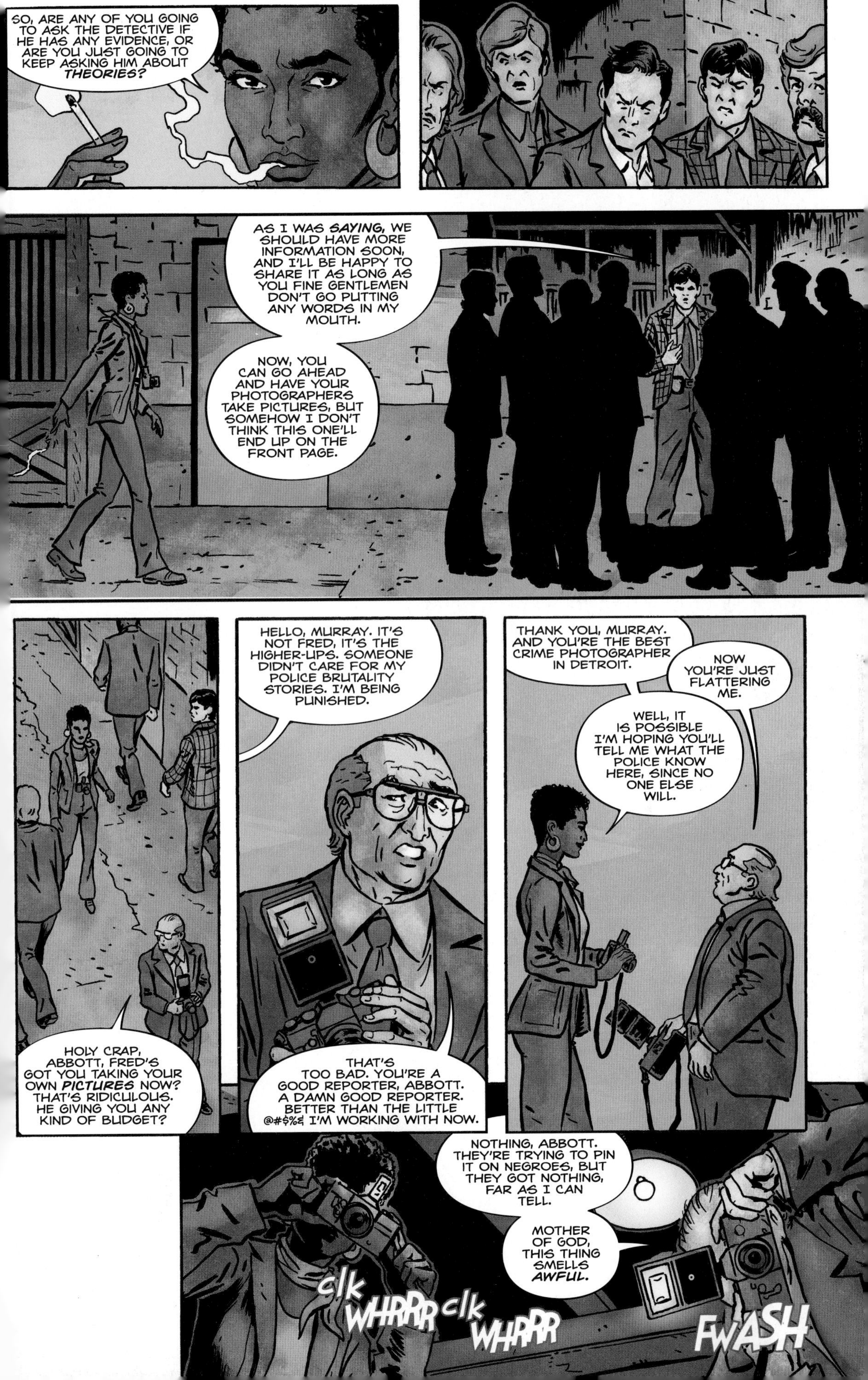
SO, ARE ANY OF YOU GOING TO ASK THE DETECTIVE IF HE HAS ANY EVIDENCE, OR ARE YOU JUST GOING TO KEEP ASKING HIM ABOUT THEORIES?
AS I WAS SAYING, WE SHOULD HAVE MORE INFORMATION SOON, AND I'LL BE HAPPY TO SHARE IT AS LONG AS YOU FINE GENTLEMEN DON'T GO PUTTING ANY WORDS IN MY MOUTH.
NOW, YOU CAN GO AHEAD AND HAVE YOUR PHOTOGRAPHERS TAKE PICTURES, BUT SOMEHOW I DON'T THINK THIS ONE'LL END UP ON THE FRONT PAGE.
HOLY CRAP, ABBOTT, FRED'S GOT YOU TAKING YOUR OWN PICTURES NOW? THAT'S RIDICULOUS. HE GIVING YOU ANY KIND OF BUDGET?
HELLO, MURRAY. IT'S NOT FRED, IT'S THE HIGHER-UPS. SOMEONE DIDN'T CARE FOR MY POLICE BRUTALITY STORIES. I'M BEING PUNISHED.
THAT'S TOO BAD. YOU'RE A GOOD REPORTER, ABBOTT. A DAMN GOOD REPORTER. BETTER THAN THE LITTLE @#$%& I'M WORKING WITH NOW.
THANK YOU, MURRAY. AND YOU'RE THE BEST CRIME PHOTOGRAPHER IN DETROIT.
NOW YOU'RE JUST FLATTERING ME.
WELL, IT IS POSSIBLE I'M HOPING YOU'LL TELL ME WHAT THE POLICE KNOW HERE, SINCE NO ONE ELSE WILL.
NOTHING, ABBOTT. THEY'RE TRYING TO PIN IT ON NEGROES, BUT THEY GOT NOTHING, FAR AS I CAN TELL.
MOTHER OF GOD, THIS THING SMELLS AWFUL.
CLK WHRRR CLK WHRRR
FWASH

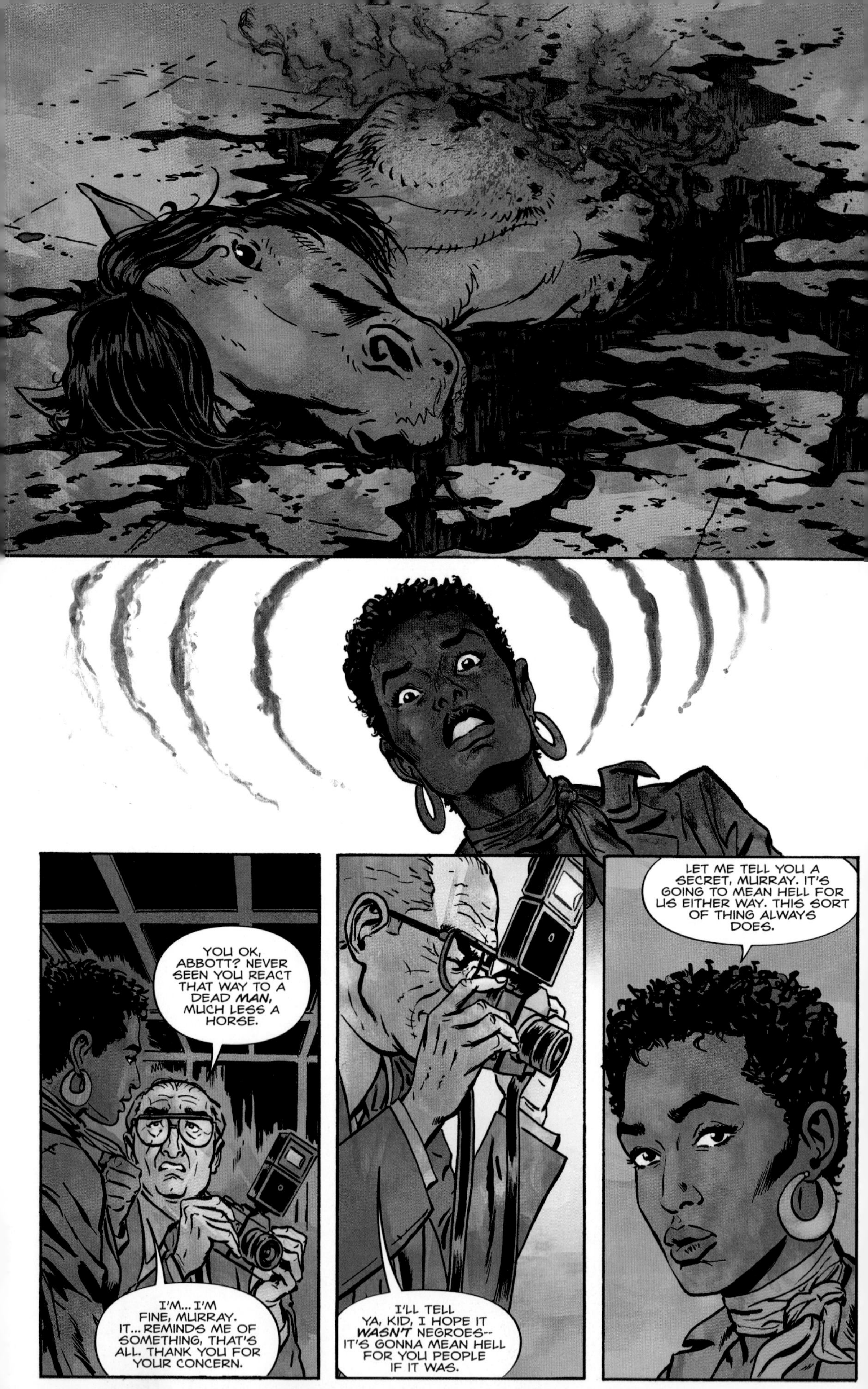
YOU OK, ABBOTT? NEVER SEEN YOU REACT THAT WAY TO A DEAD *MAN*, MUCH LESS A HORSE.
I'M... I'M FINE, MURRAY. IT... REMINDS ME OF SOMETHING, THAT'S ALL. THANK YOU FOR YOUR CONCERN.
I'LL TELL YA, KID, I HOPE IT *WASN'T* NEGROES-- IT'S GONNA MEAN HELL FOR YOU PEOPLE IF IT WAS.
LET ME TELL YOU A SECRET, MURRAY. IT'S GOING TO MEAN HELL FOR US EITHER WAY. THIS SORT OF THING ALWAYS DOES.

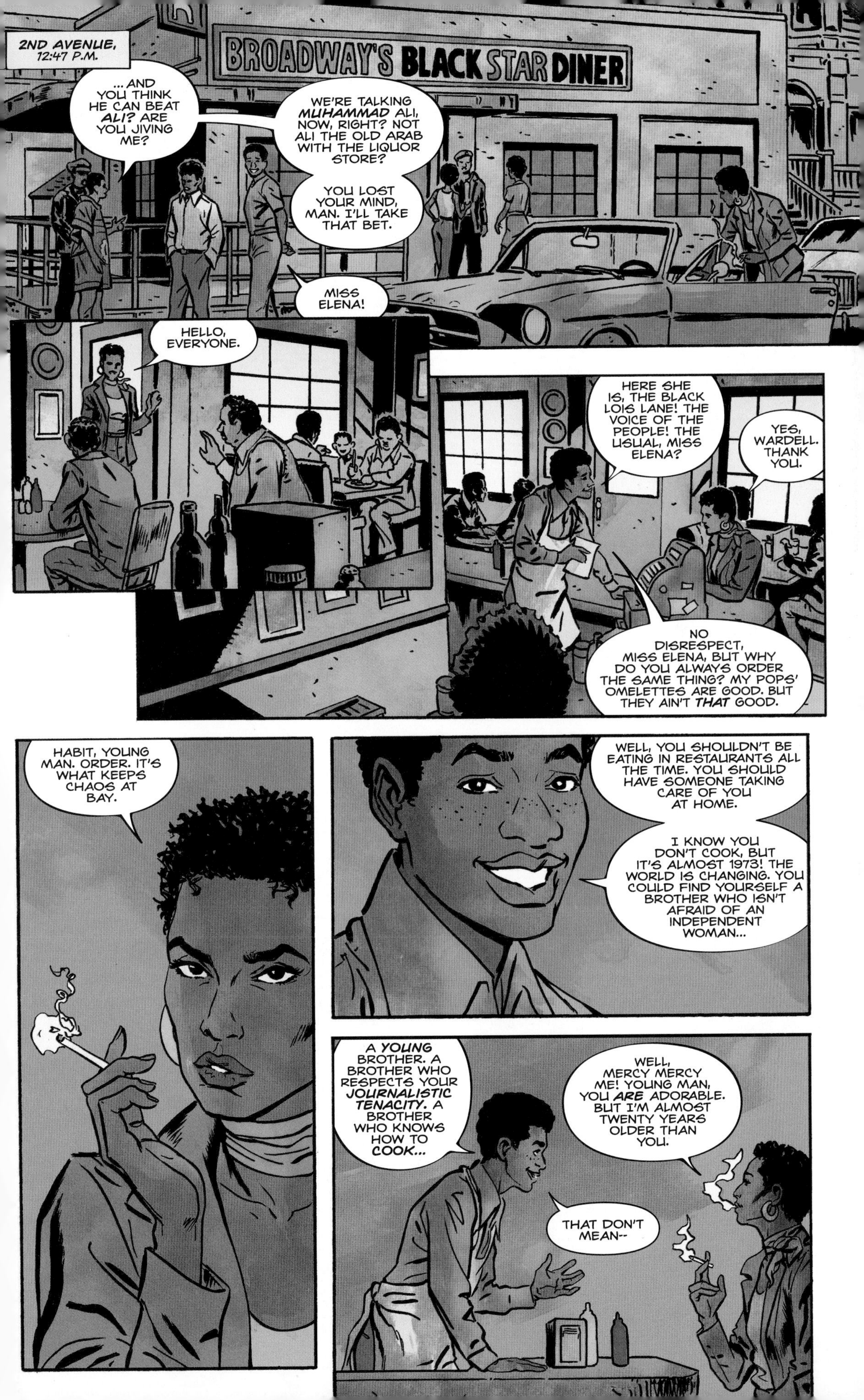
2ND AVENUE, 12:47 P.M.
BROADWAY'S BLACK STAR DINER
...AND YOU THINK HE CAN BEAT ALI? ARE YOU JIVING ME?
WE'RE TALKING MUHAMMAD ALI, NOW, RIGHT? NOT ALI THE OLD ARAB WITH THE LIQUOR STORE?
YOU LOST YOUR MIND, MAN. I'LL TAKE THAT BET.
MISS ELENA!
HELLO, EVERYONE.
HERE SHE IS, THE BLACK LOIS LANE! THE VOICE OF THE PEOPLE! THE USUAL, MISS ELENA?
YES, WARDELL. THANK YOU.
NO DISRESPECT, MISS ELENA, BUT WHY DO YOU ALWAYS ORDER THE SAME THING? MY POPS' OMELETTES ARE GOOD. BUT THEY AIN'T THAT GOOD.
HABIT, YOUNG MAN. ORDER. IT'S WHAT KEEPS CHAOS AT BAY.
WELL, YOU SHOULDN'T BE EATING IN RESTAURANTS ALL THE TIME. YOU SHOULD HAVE SOMEONE TAKING CARE OF YOU AT HOME.
I KNOW YOU DON'T COOK, BUT IT'S ALMOST 1973! THE WORLD IS CHANGING. YOU COULD FIND YOURSELF A BROTHER WHO ISN'T AFRAID OF AN INDEPENDENT WOMAN...
A YOUNG BROTHER. A BROTHER WHO RESPECTS YOUR JOURNALISTIC TENACITY. A BROTHER WHO KNOWS HOW TO COOK...
WELL, MERCY MERCY ME! YOUNG MAN, YOU ARE ADORABLE. BUT I'M ALMOST TWENTY YEARS OLDER THAN YOU.
THAT DON'T MEAN--

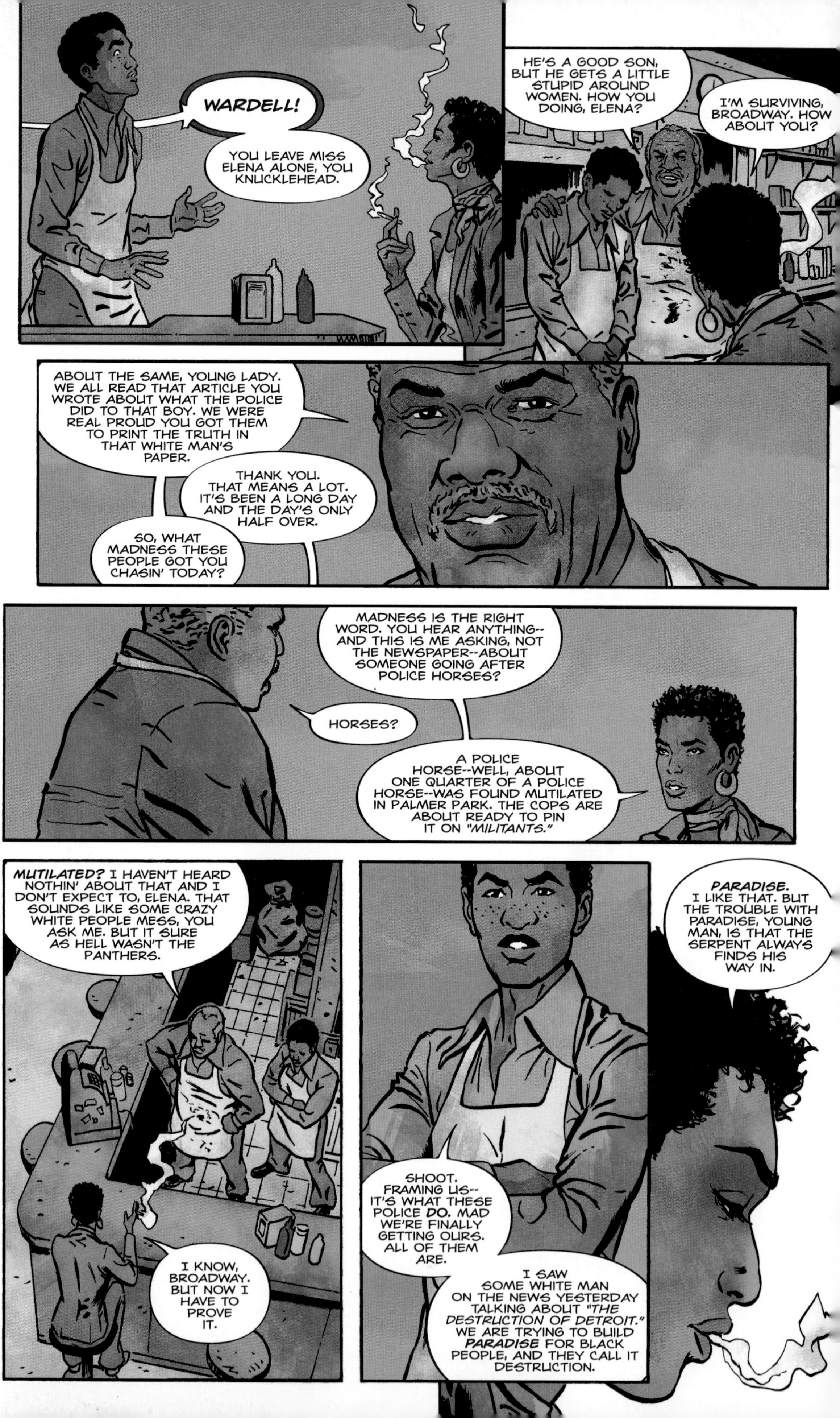
WARDELL!
YOU LEAVE MISS ELENA ALONE, YOU KNUCKLEHEAD.
HE'S A GOOD SON, BUT HE GETS A LITTLE STUPID AROUND WOMEN. HOW YOU DOING, ELENA?
I'M SURVIVING, BROADWAY. HOW ABOUT YOU?
ABOUT THE SAME, YOUNG LADY. WE ALL READ THAT ARTICLE YOU WROTE ABOUT WHAT THE POLICE DID TO THAT BOY. WE WERE REAL PROUD YOU GOT THEM TO PRINT THE TRUTH IN THAT WHITE MAN'S PAPER.
THANK YOU. THAT MEANS A LOT. IT'S BEEN A LONG DAY AND THE DAY'S ONLY HALF OVER.
SO, WHAT MADNESS THESE PEOPLE GOT YOU CHASIN' TODAY?
MADNESS IS THE RIGHT WORD. YOU HEAR ANYTHING-- AND THIS IS ME ASKING, NOT THE NEWSPAPER--ABOUT SOMEONE GOING AFTER POLICE HORSES?
HORSES?
A POLICE HORSE--WELL, ABOUT ONE QUARTER OF A POLICE HORSE--WAS FOUND MUTILATED IN PALMER PARK. THE COPS ARE ABOUT READY TO PIN IT ON "MILITANTS."
MUTILATED? I HAVEN'T HEARD NOTHIN' ABOUT THAT AND I DON'T EXPECT TO, ELENA. THAT SOUNDS LIKE SOME CRAZY WHITE PEOPLE MESS, YOU ASK ME. BUT IT SURE AS HELL WASN'T THE PANTHERS.
I KNOW, BROADWAY. BUT NOW I HAVE TO PROVE IT.
SHOOT. FRAMING US-- IT'S WHAT THESE POLICE DO. MAD WE'RE FINALLY GETTING OURS. ALL OF THEM ARE.
I SAW SOME WHITE MAN ON THE NEWS YESTERDAY TALKING ABOUT "THE DESTRUCTION OF DETROIT." WE ARE TRYING TO BUILD PARADISE FOR BLACK PEOPLE, AND THEY CALL IT DESTRUCTION.
PARADISE. I LIKE THAT. BUT THE TROUBLE WITH PARADISE, YOUNG MAN, IS THAT THE SERPENT ALWAYS FINDS HIS WAY IN.

DOWNTOWN,
2:53 P.M.

that there are, as one longtime resident put it, two Detroits: one white, one black

INTERNATIONAL VISITORS INFORMATION →

THE IMAGE OF DETROIT STARTS WITH YOU.

and that the former would rather leave the city than truly share it with the latter.

FOR SALE

FOR SALE

FOR SALE

Free Press

The Detroit New

DETROIT DAILY

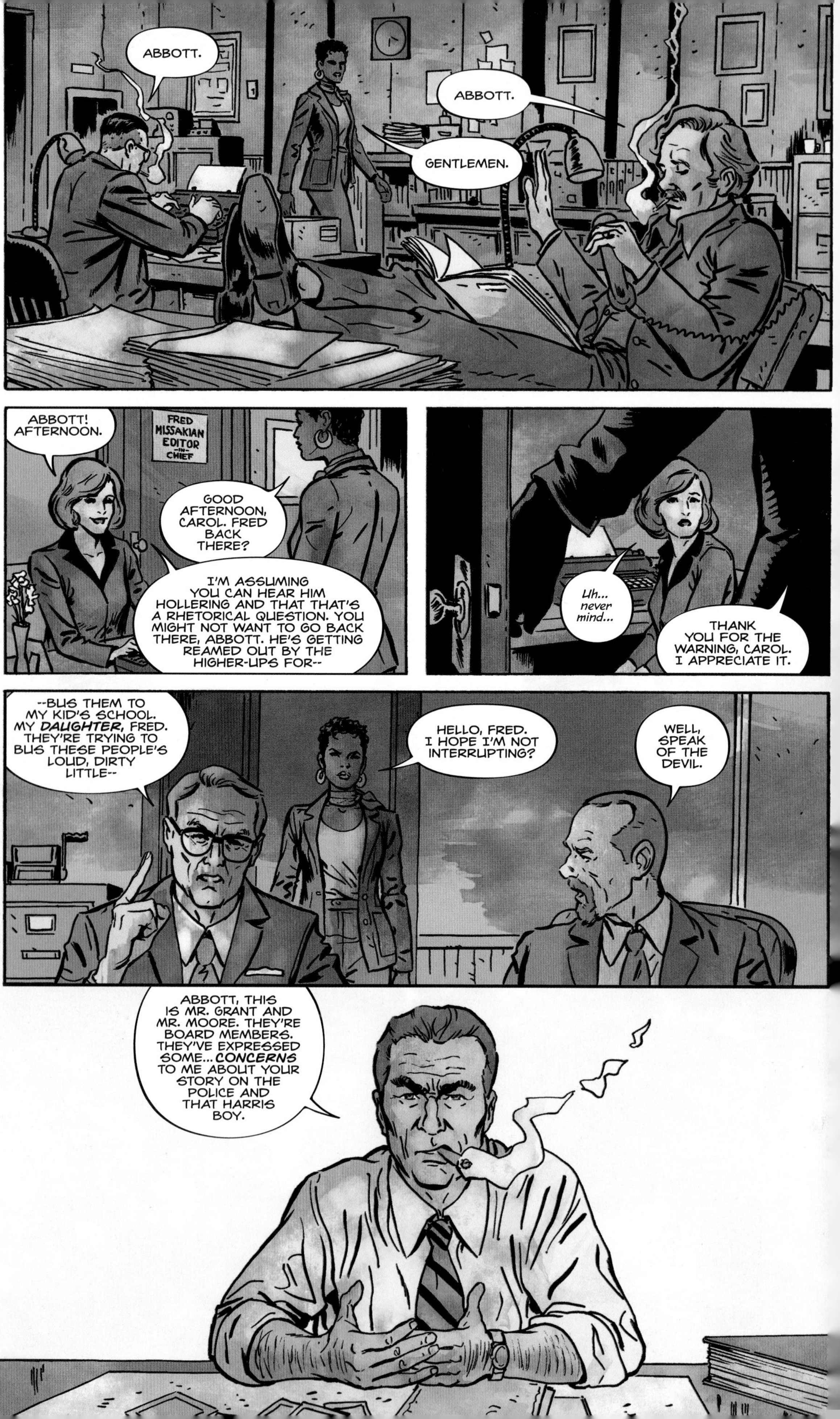
ABBOTT.
ABBOTT.
GENTLEMEN.
ABBOTT! AFTERNOON.
FRED MISSAKIAN EDITOR -IN- CHIEF
GOOD AFTERNOON, CAROL. FRED BACK THERE?
I'M ASSUMING YOU CAN HEAR HIM HOLLERING AND THAT THAT'S A RHETORICAL QUESTION. YOU MIGHT NOT WANT TO GO BACK THERE, ABBOTT. HE'S GETTING REAMED OUT BY THE HIGHER-UPS FOR--
Uh... never mind...
THANK YOU FOR THE WARNING, CAROL. I APPRECIATE IT.
--BUS THEM TO MY KID'S SCHOOL. MY DAUGHTER, FRED. THEY'RE TRYING TO BUS THESE PEOPLE'S LOUD, DIRTY LITTLE--
HELLO, FRED. I HOPE I'M NOT INTERRUPTING?
WELL, SPEAK OF THE DEVIL.
ABBOTT, THIS IS MR. GRANT AND MR. MOORE. THEY'RE BOARD MEMBERS. THEY'VE EXPRESSED SOME... CONCERNS TO ME ABOUT YOUR STORY ON THE POLICE AND THAT HARRIS BOY.

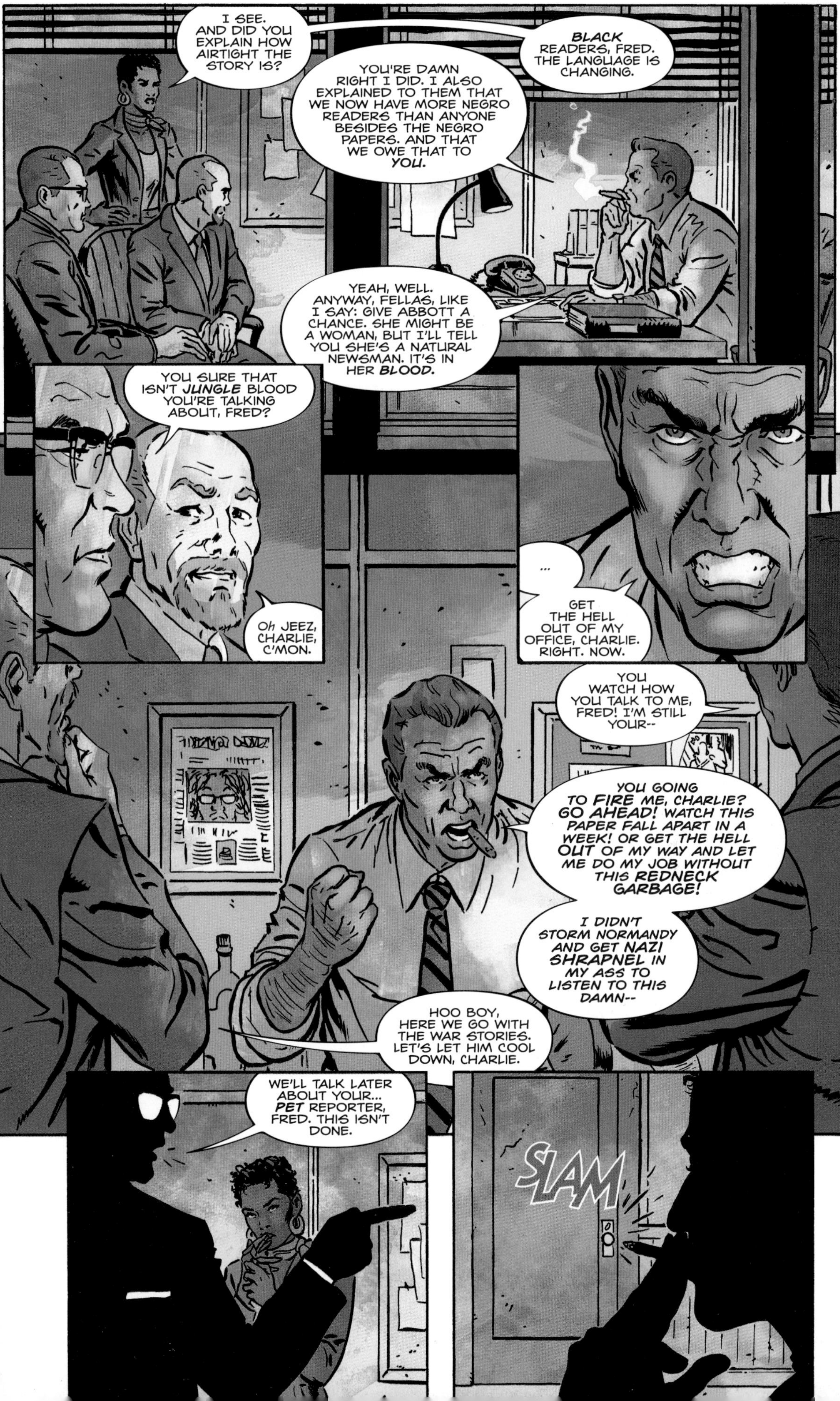
I SEE. AND DID YOU EXPLAIN HOW AIRTIGHT THE STORY IS?
YOU'RE DAMN RIGHT I DID. I ALSO EXPLAINED TO THEM THAT WE NOW HAVE MORE NEGRO READERS THAN ANYONE BESIDES THE NEGRO PAPERS. AND THAT WE OWE THAT TO YOU.
BLACK READERS, FRED. THE LANGUAGE IS CHANGING.
YEAH, WELL. ANYWAY, FELLAS, LIKE I SAY: GIVE ABBOTT A CHANCE. SHE MIGHT BE A WOMAN, BUT I'LL TELL YOU SHE'S A NATURAL NEWSMAN. IT'S IN HER BLOOD.
YOU SURE THAT ISN'T JUNGLE BLOOD YOU'RE TALKING ABOUT, FRED?
Oh JEEZ, CHARLIE, C'MON.
...
GET THE HELL OUT OF MY OFFICE, CHARLIE. RIGHT. NOW.
YOU WATCH HOW YOU TALK TO ME, FRED! I'M STILL YOUR--
YOU GOING TO FIRE ME, CHARLIE? GO AHEAD! WATCH THIS PAPER FALL APART IN A WEEK! OR GET THE HELL OUT OF MY WAY AND LET ME DO MY JOB WITHOUT THIS REDNECK GARBAGE!
I DIDN'T STORM NORMANDY AND GET NAZI SHRAPNEL IN MY ASS TO LISTEN TO THIS DAMN--
HOO BOY, HERE WE GO WITH THE WAR STORIES. LET'S LET HIM COOL DOWN, CHARLIE.
WE'LL TALK LATER ABOUT YOUR... PET REPORTER, FRED. THIS ISN'T DONE.
SLAM

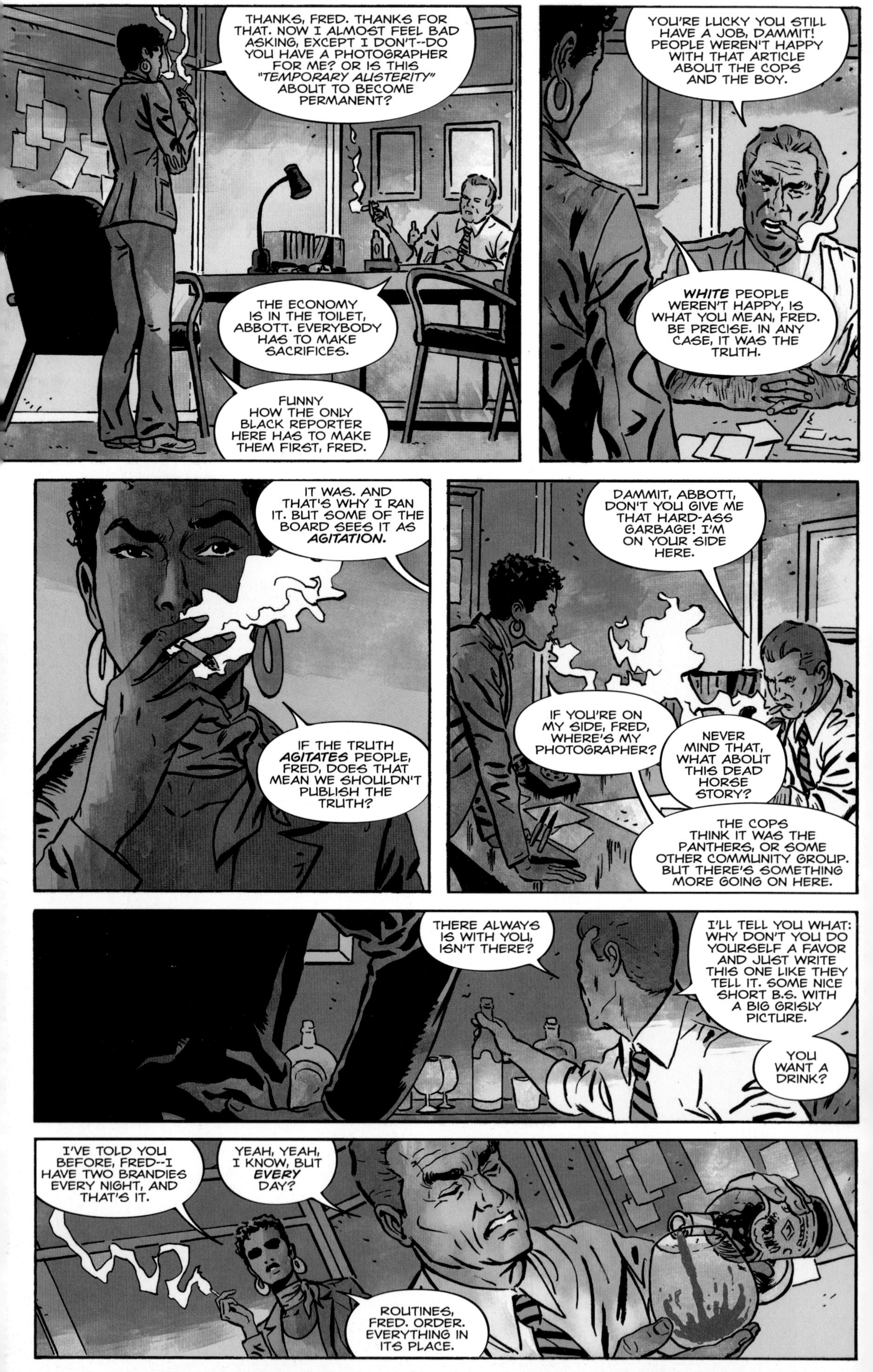
THANKS, FRED. THANKS FOR THAT. NOW I ALMOST FEEL BAD ASKING, EXCEPT I DON'T--DO YOU HAVE A PHOTOGRAPHER FOR ME? OR IS THIS "TEMPORARY AUSTERITY" ABOUT TO BECOME PERMANENT?
THE ECONOMY IS IN THE TOILET, ABBOTT. EVERYBODY HAS TO MAKE SACRIFICES.
FUNNY HOW THE ONLY BLACK REPORTER HERE HAS TO MAKE THEM FIRST, FRED.
YOU'RE LUCKY YOU STILL HAVE A JOB, DAMMIT! PEOPLE WEREN'T HAPPY WITH THAT ARTICLE ABOUT THE COPS AND THE BOY.
WHITE PEOPLE WEREN'T HAPPY, IS WHAT YOU MEAN, FRED. BE PRECISE. IN ANY CASE, IT WAS THE TRUTH.
IT WAS. AND THAT'S WHY I RAN IT. BUT SOME OF THE BOARD SEES IT AS AGITATION.
IF THE TRUTH AGITATES PEOPLE, FRED, DOES THAT MEAN WE SHOULDN'T PUBLISH THE TRUTH?
DAMMIT, ABBOTT, DON'T YOU GIVE ME THAT HARD-ASS GARBAGE! I'M ON YOUR SIDE HERE.
IF YOU'RE ON MY SIDE, FRED, WHERE'S MY PHOTOGRAPHER?
NEVER MIND THAT, WHAT ABOUT THIS DEAD HORSE STORY?
THE COPS THINK IT WAS THE PANTHERS, OR SOME OTHER COMMUNITY GROUP. BUT THERE'S SOMETHING MORE GOING ON HERE.
THERE ALWAYS IS WITH YOU, ISN'T THERE?
I'LL TELL YOU WHAT: WHY DON'T YOU DO YOURSELF A FAVOR AND JUST WRITE THIS ONE LIKE THEY TELL IT. SOME NICE SHORT B.S. WITH A BIG GRISLY PICTURE.
YOU WANT A DRINK?
I'VE TOLD YOU BEFORE, FRED--I HAVE TWO BRANDIES EVERY NIGHT, AND THAT'S IT.
YEAH, YEAH, I KNOW, BUT EVERY DAY?
ROUTINES, FRED. ORDER. EVERYTHING IN ITS PLACE.

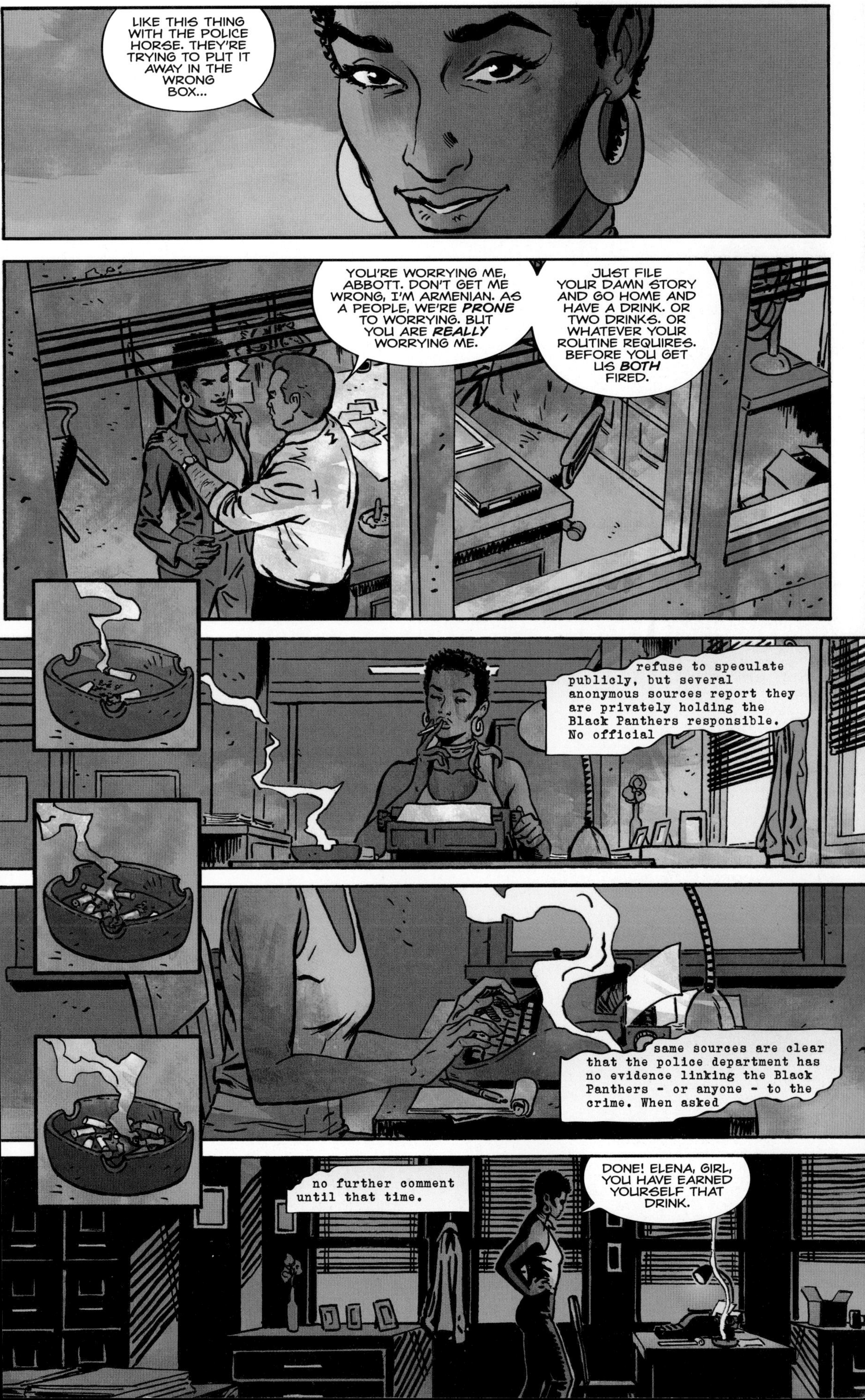
LIKE THIS THING WITH THE POLICE HORSE. THEY'RE TRYING TO PUT IT AWAY IN THE WRONG BOX...
YOU'RE WORRYING ME, ABBOTT. DON'T GET ME WRONG, I'M ARMENIAN. AS A PEOPLE, WE'RE PRONE TO WORRYING. BUT YOU ARE REALLY WORRYING ME.
JUST FILE YOUR DAMN STORY AND GO HOME AND HAVE A DRINK. OR TWO DRINKS. OR WHATEVER YOUR ROUTINE REQUIRES. BEFORE YOU GET US BOTH FIRED.
refuse to speculate publicly, but several anonymous sources report they are privately holding the Black Panthers responsible. No official
same sources are clear that the police department has no evidence linking the Black Panthers - or anyone - to the crime. When asked
no further comment until that time.
DONE! ELENA, GIRL, YOU HAVE EARNED YOURSELF THAT DRINK.

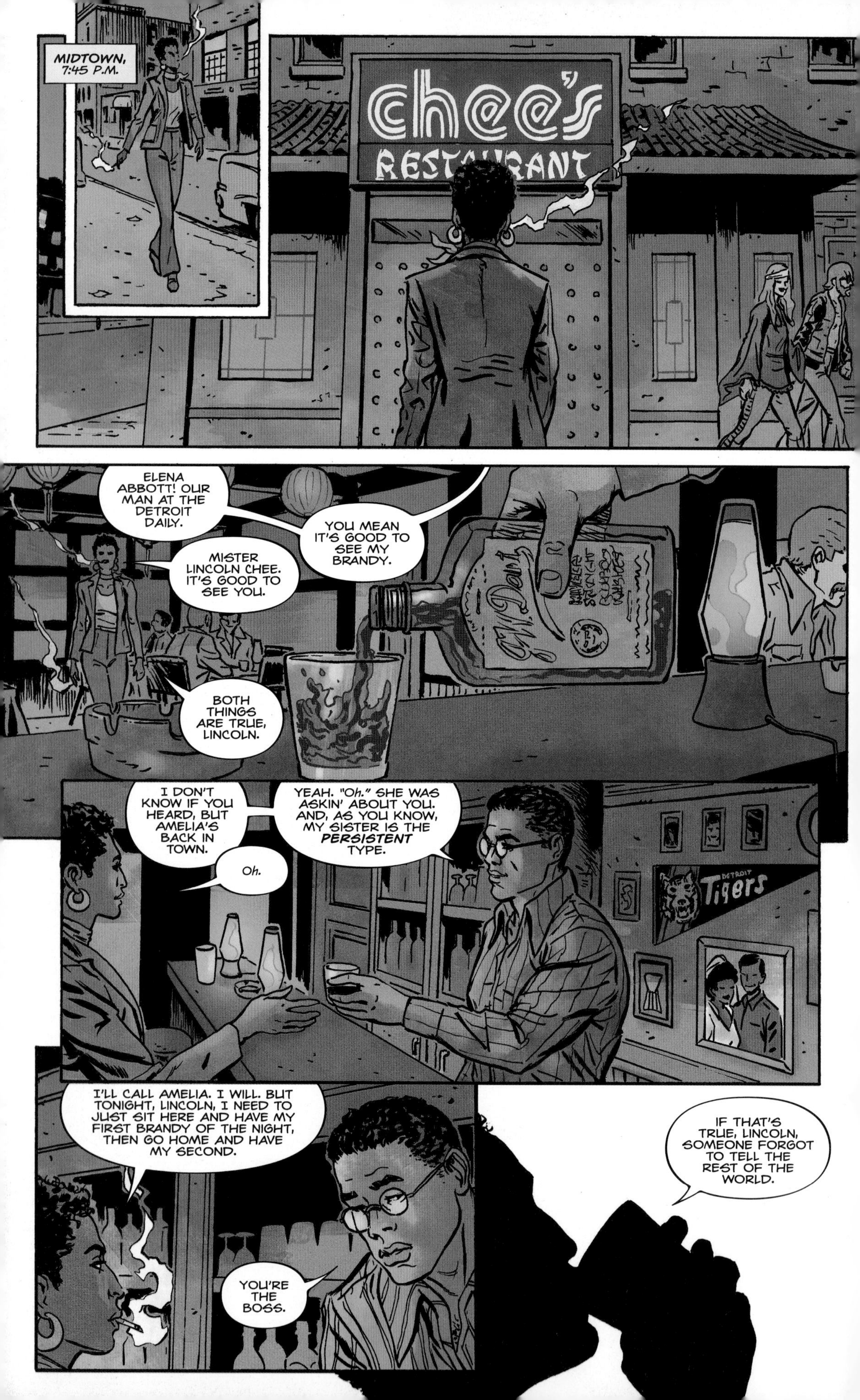
MIDTOWN, 7:45 P.M.
chee's
RESTAURANT
ELENA ABBOTT! OUR MAN AT THE DETROIT DAILY.
MISTER LINCOLN CHEE. IT'S GOOD TO SEE YOU.
YOU MEAN IT'S GOOD TO SEE MY BRANDY.
BOTH THINGS ARE TRUE, LINCOLN.
I DON'T KNOW IF YOU HEARD, BUT AMELIA'S BACK IN TOWN.
Oh.
YEAH. "Oh." SHE WAS ASKIN' ABOUT YOU. AND, AS YOU KNOW, MY SISTER IS THE PERSISTENT TYPE.
DETROIT Tigers
I'LL CALL AMELIA. I WILL. BUT TONIGHT, LINCOLN, I NEED TO JUST SIT HERE AND HAVE MY FIRST BRANDY OF THE NIGHT, THEN GO HOME AND HAVE MY SECOND.
YOU'RE THE BOSS.
IF THAT'S TRUE, LINCOLN, SOMEONE FORGOT TO TELL THE REST OF THE WORLD.

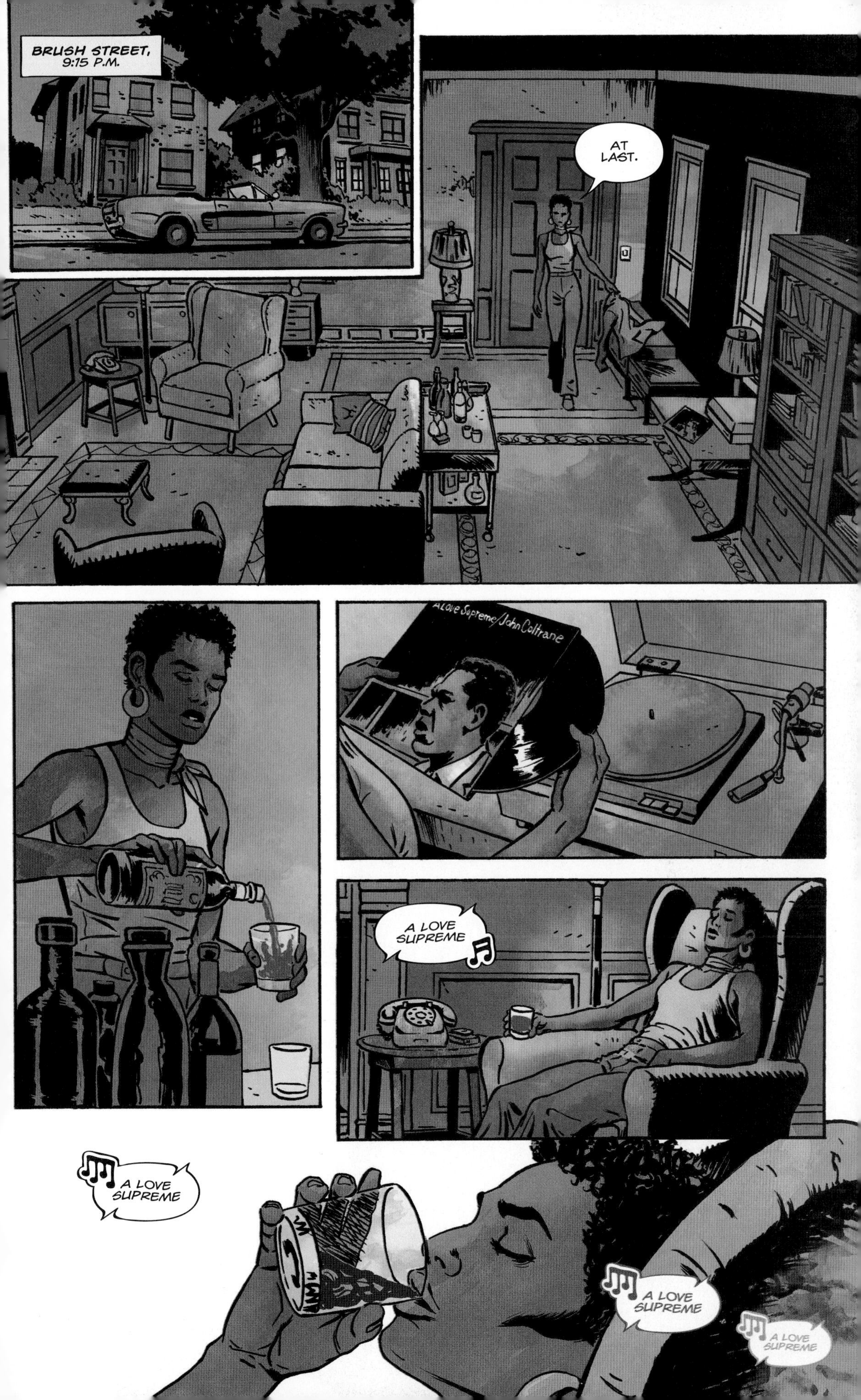
BRUSH STREET, 9:15 P.M.
AT LAST.
A Love Supreme/John Coltrane
A LOVE SUPREME
A LOVE SUPREME
A LOVE SUPREME
A LOVE SUPREME

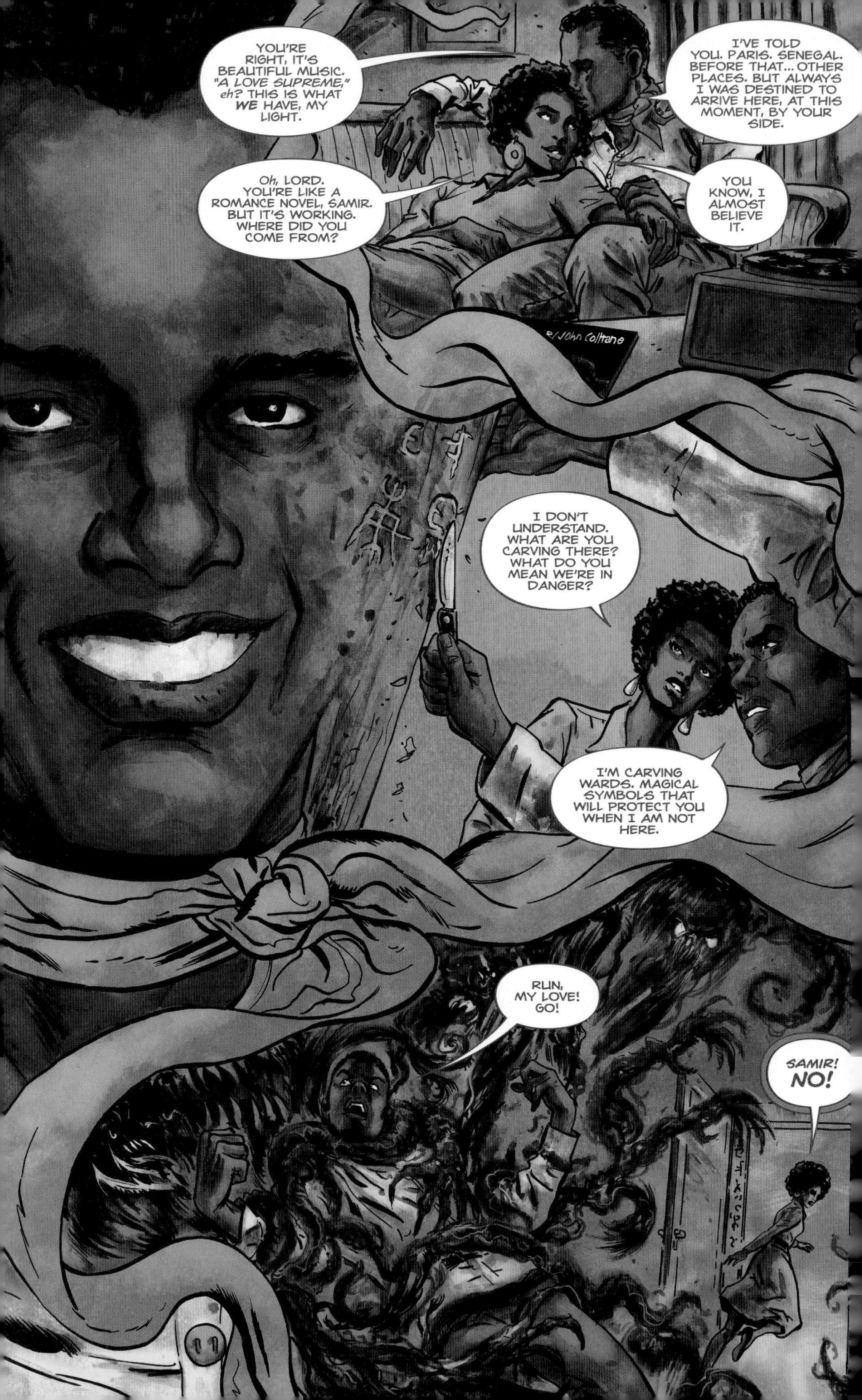
YOU'RE RIGHT, IT'S BEAUTIFUL MUSIC. "A LOVE SUPREME," eh? THIS IS WHAT WE HAVE, MY LIGHT.
I'VE TOLD YOU. PARIS. SENEGAL. BEFORE THAT... OTHER PLACES. BUT ALWAYS I WAS DESTINED TO ARRIVE HERE, AT THIS MOMENT, BY YOUR SIDE.
Oh, LORD. YOU'RE LIKE A ROMANCE NOVEL, SAMIR. BUT IT'S WORKING. WHERE DID YOU COME FROM?
YOU KNOW, I ALMOST BELIEVE IT.
e/John Coltrane
I DON'T UNDERSTAND. WHAT ARE YOU CARVING THERE? WHAT DO YOU MEAN WE'RE IN DANGER?
I'M CARVING WARDS. MAGICAL SYMBOLS THAT WILL PROTECT YOU WHEN I AM NOT HERE.
RUN, MY LOVE! GO!
SAMIR! NO!

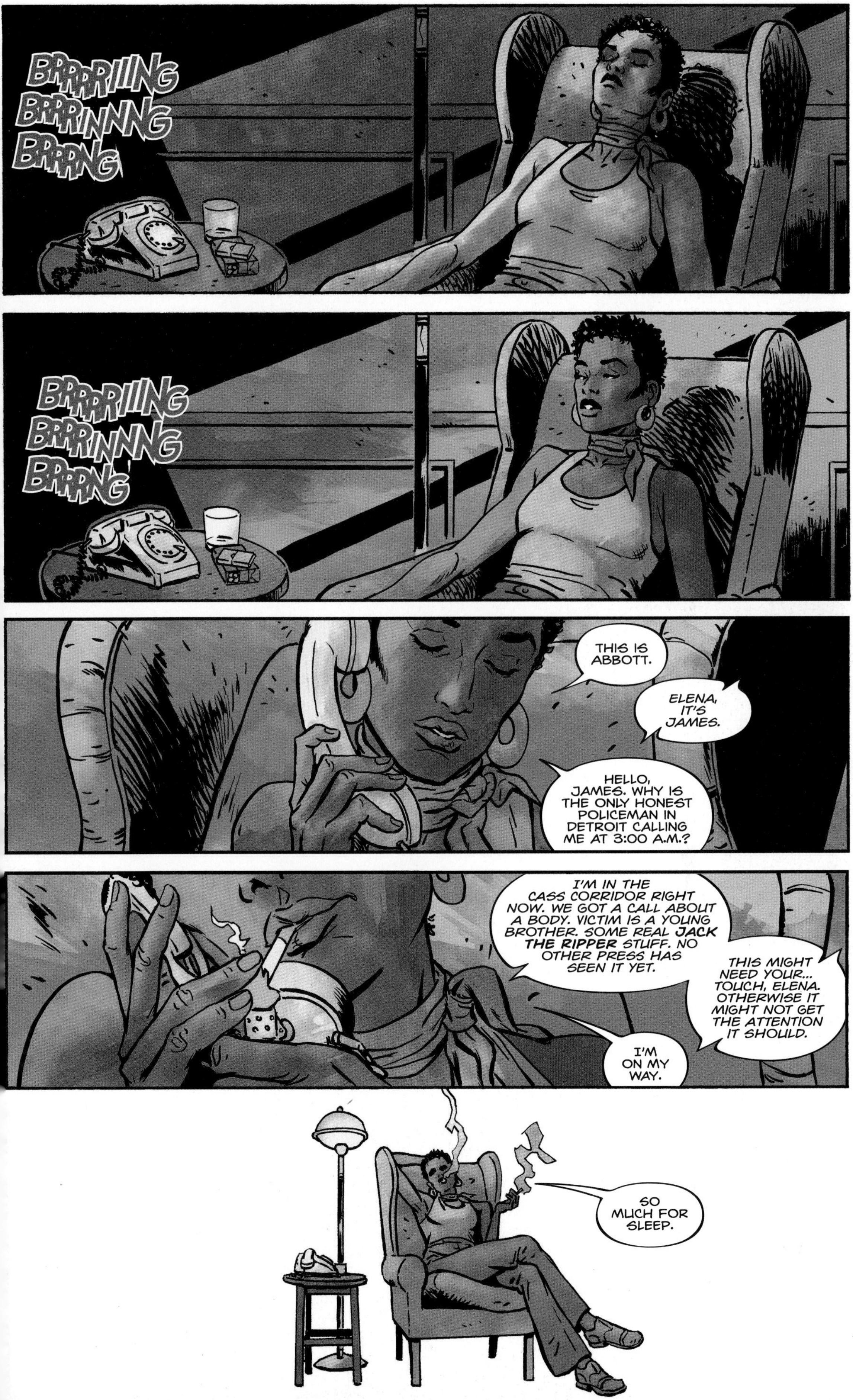

BRRRRRIIING
BRRRRINNNG
BRRRRNG
BRRRRRIIING
BRRRRINNNG
BRRRRNG
THIS IS ABBOTT.
ELENA, IT'S JAMES.
HELLO, JAMES. WHY IS THE ONLY HONEST POLICEMAN IN DETROIT CALLING ME AT 3:00 A.M.?
I'M IN THE CASS CORRIDOR RIGHT NOW. WE GOT A CALL ABOUT A BODY. VICTIM IS A YOUNG BROTHER. SOME REAL JACK THE RIPPER STUFF. NO OTHER PRESS HAS SEEN IT YET.
THIS MIGHT NEED YOUR... TOUCH, ELENA. OTHERWISE IT MIGHT NOT GET THE ATTENTION IT SHOULD.
I'M ON MY WAY.
SO MUCH FOR SLEEP.

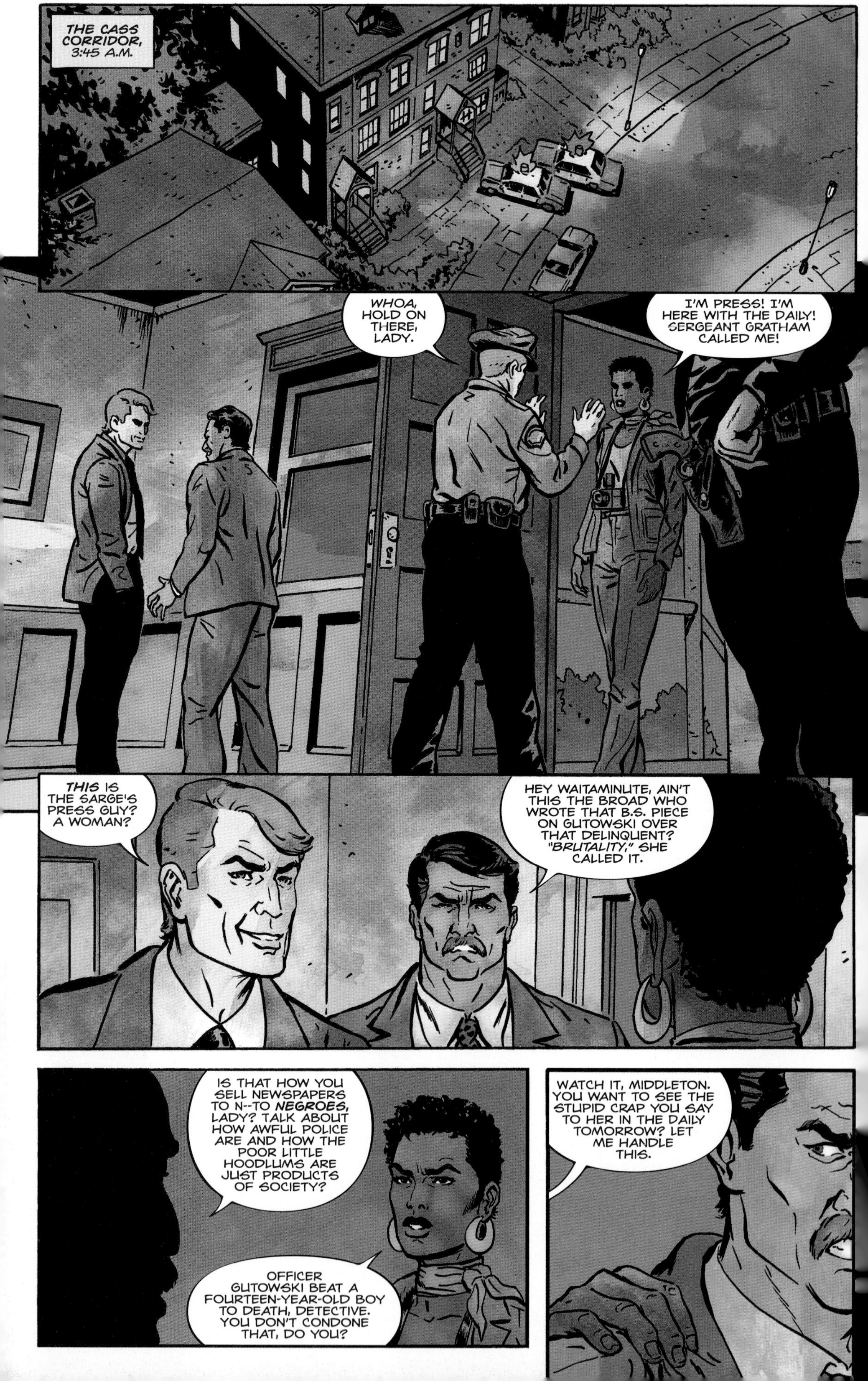
THE CASS CORRIDOR, 3:45 A.M.
WHOA, HOLD ON THERE, LADY.
I'M PRESS! I'M HERE WITH THE DAILY! SERGEANT GRATHAM CALLED ME!
THIS IS THE SARGE'S PRESS GUY? A WOMAN?
HEY WAITAMINUTE, AIN'T THIS THE BROAD WHO WROTE THAT B.S. PIECE ON GUTOWSKI OVER THAT DELINQUENT? "BRUTALITY," SHE CALLED IT.
IS THAT HOW YOU SELL NEWSPAPERS TO N--TO NEGROES, LADY? TALK ABOUT HOW AWFUL POLICE ARE AND HOW THE POOR LITTLE HOODLUMS ARE JUST PRODUCTS OF SOCIETY?
OFFICER GUTOWSKI BEAT A FOURTEEN-YEAR-OLD BOY TO DEATH, DETECTIVE. YOU DON'T CONDONE THAT, DO YOU?
WATCH IT, MIDDLETON. YOU WANT TO SEE THE STUPID CRAP YOU SAY TO HER IN THE DAILY TOMORROW? LET ME HANDLE THIS.

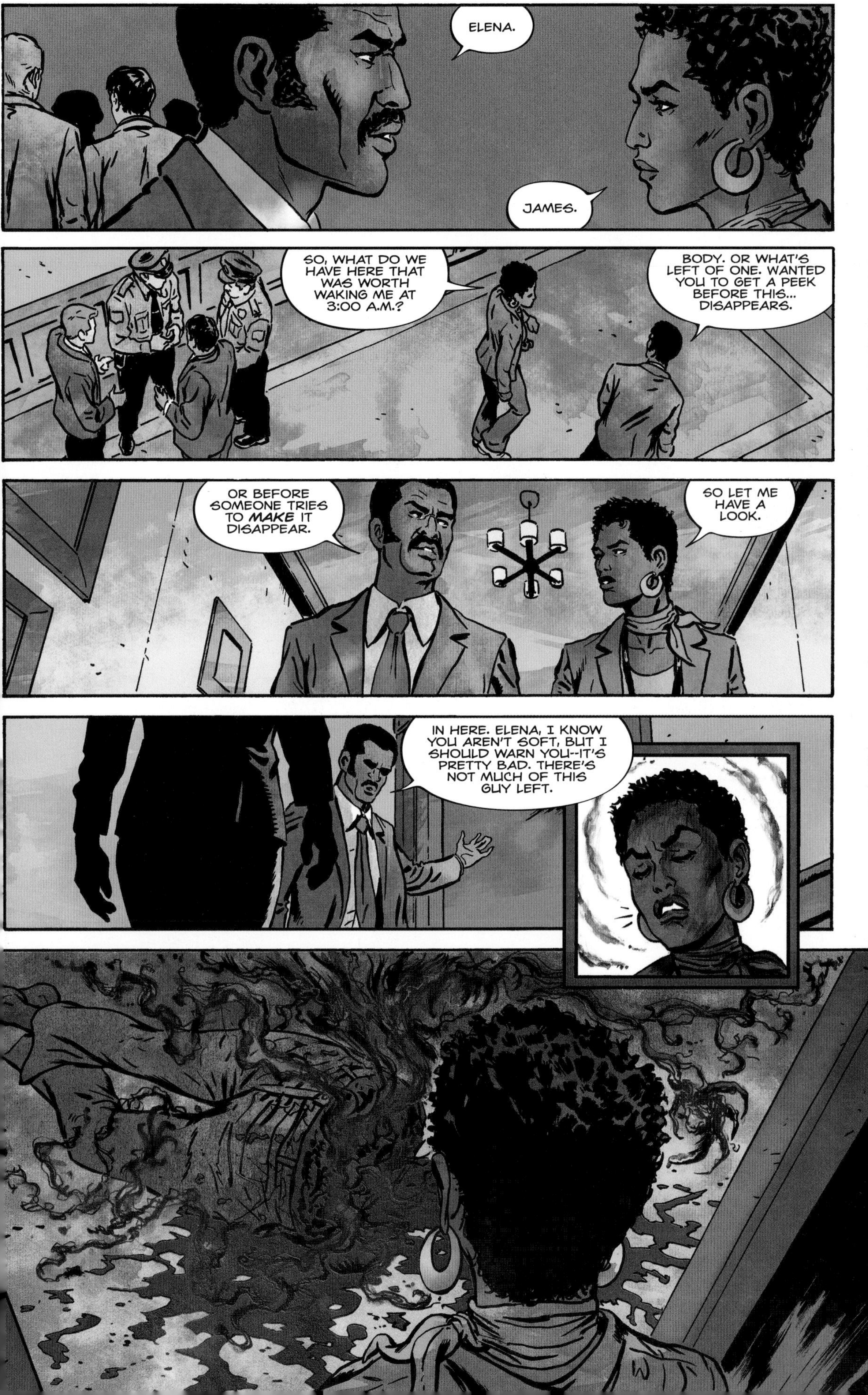
ELENA.
JAMES.
SO, WHAT DO WE HAVE HERE THAT WAS WORTH WAKING ME AT 3:00 A.M.?
BODY. OR WHAT'S LEFT OF ONE. WANTED YOU TO GET A PEEK BEFORE THIS... DISAPPEARS.
OR BEFORE SOMEONE TRIES TO MAKE IT DISAPPEAR.
SO LET ME HAVE A LOOK.
IN HERE. ELENA, I KNOW YOU AREN'T SOFT, BUT I SHOULD WARN YOU--IT'S PRETTY BAD. THERE'S NOT MUCH OF THIS GUY LEFT.

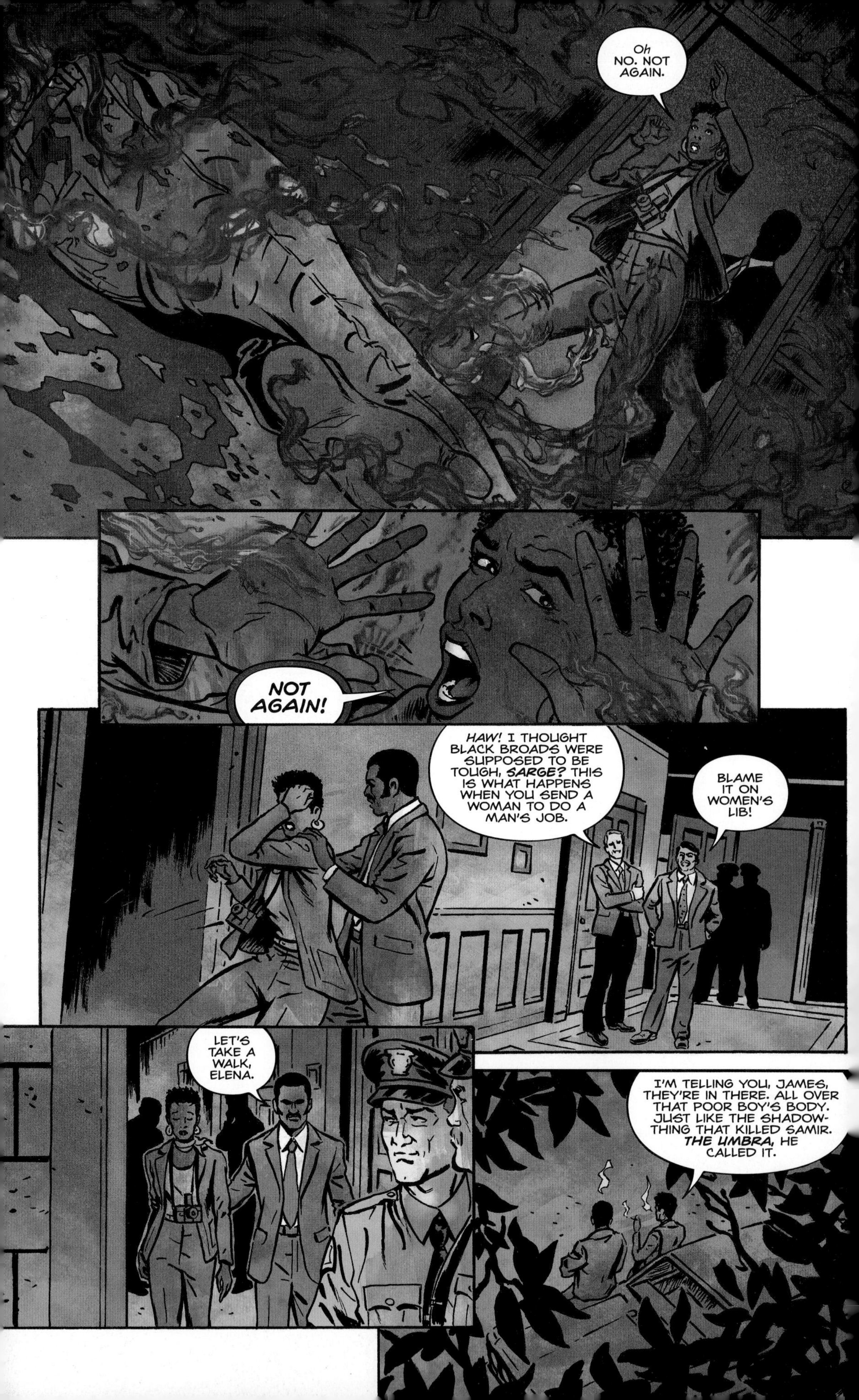
Oh NO. NOT AGAIN.
NOT AGAIN!
HAW! I THOUGHT BLACK BROADS WERE SUPPOSED TO BE TOUGH, SARGE? THIS IS WHAT HAPPENS WHEN YOU SEND A WOMAN TO DO A MAN'S JOB.
BLAME IT ON WOMEN'S LIB!
LET'S TAKE A WALK, ELENA.
I'M TELLING YOU, JAMES, THEY'RE IN THERE. ALL OVER THAT POOR BOY'S BODY. JUST LIKE THE SHADOW-THING THAT KILLED SAMIR. THE UMBRA, HE CALLED IT.

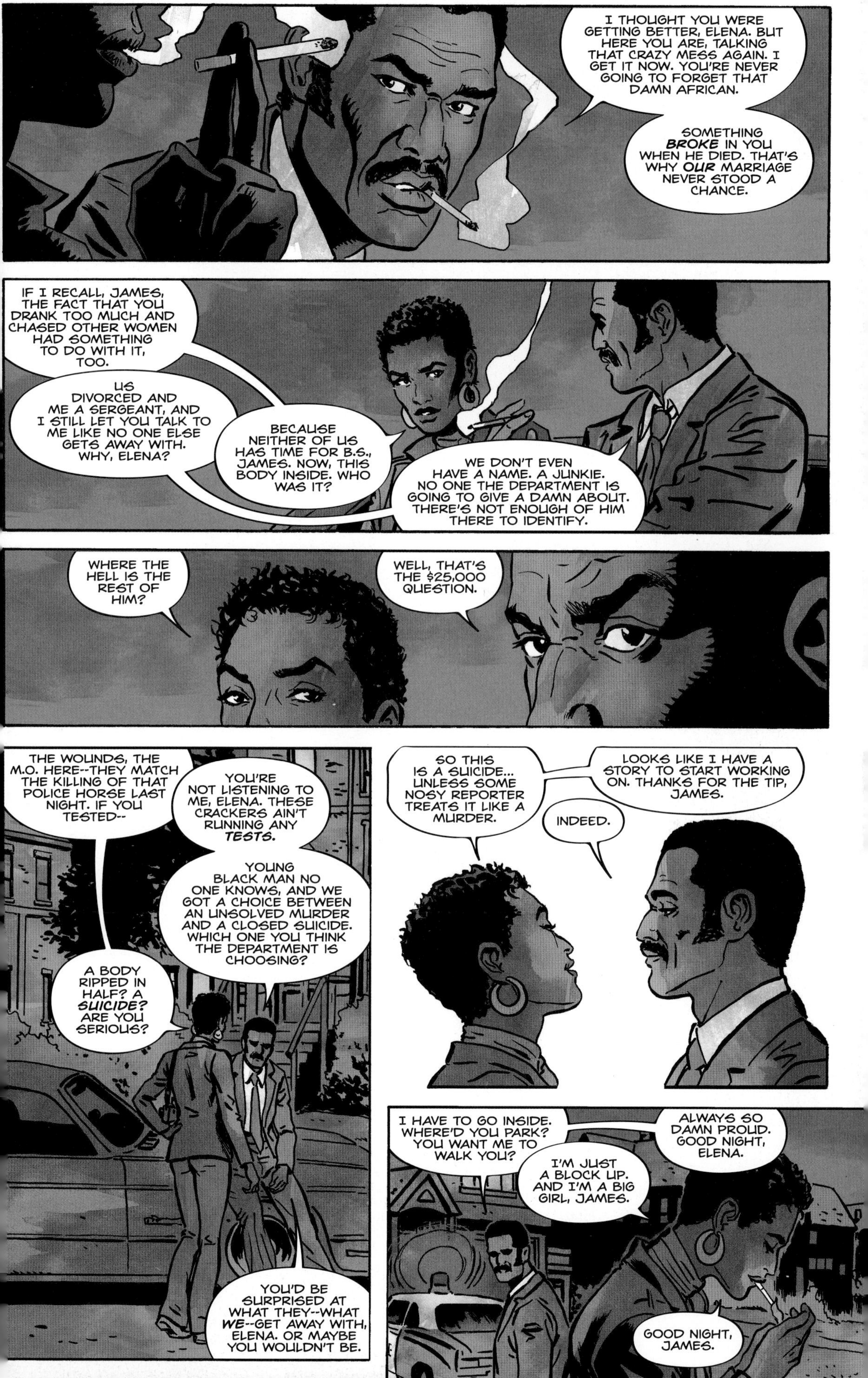
I THOUGHT YOU WERE GETTING BETTER, ELENA. BUT HERE YOU ARE, TALKING THAT CRAZY MESS AGAIN. I GET IT NOW. YOU'RE NEVER GOING TO FORGET THAT DAMN AFRICAN.
SOMETHING BROKE IN YOU WHEN HE DIED. THAT'S WHY OUR MARRIAGE NEVER STOOD A CHANCE.
IF I RECALL, JAMES, THE FACT THAT YOU DRANK TOO MUCH AND CHASED OTHER WOMEN HAD SOMETHING TO DO WITH IT, TOO.
US DIVORCED AND ME A SERGEANT, AND I STILL LET YOU TALK TO ME LIKE NO ONE ELSE GETS AWAY WITH. WHY, ELENA?
BECAUSE NEITHER OF US HAS TIME FOR B.S., JAMES. NOW, THIS BODY INSIDE. WHO WAS IT?
WE DON'T EVEN HAVE A NAME. A JUNKIE. NO ONE THE DEPARTMENT IS GOING TO GIVE A DAMN ABOUT. THERE'S NOT ENOUGH OF HIM THERE TO IDENTIFY.
WHERE THE HELL IS THE REST OF HIM?
WELL, THAT'S THE $25,000 QUESTION.
THE WOUNDS, THE M.O. HERE--THEY MATCH THE KILLING OF THAT POLICE HORSE LAST NIGHT. IF YOU TESTED--
YOU'RE NOT LISTENING TO ME, ELENA. THESE CRACKERS AIN'T RUNNING ANY TESTS.
YOUNG BLACK MAN NO ONE KNOWS, AND WE GOT A CHOICE BETWEEN AN UNSOLVED MURDER AND A CLOSED SUICIDE. WHICH ONE YOU THINK THE DEPARTMENT IS CHOOSING?
A BODY RIPPED IN HALF? A SUICIDE? ARE YOU SERIOUS?
YOU'D BE SURPRISED AT WHAT THEY--WHAT WE--GET AWAY WITH, ELENA. OR MAYBE YOU WOULDN'T BE.
SO THIS IS A SUICIDE... UNLESS SOME NOSY REPORTER TREATS IT LIKE A MURDER.
INDEED.
LOOKS LIKE I HAVE A STORY TO START WORKING ON. THANKS FOR THE TIP, JAMES.
I HAVE TO GO INSIDE. WHERE'D YOU PARK? YOU WANT ME TO WALK YOU?
I'M JUST A BLOCK UP. AND I'M A BIG GIRL, JAMES.
ALWAYS SO DAMN PROUD. GOOD NIGHT, ELENA.
GOOD NIGHT, JAMES.

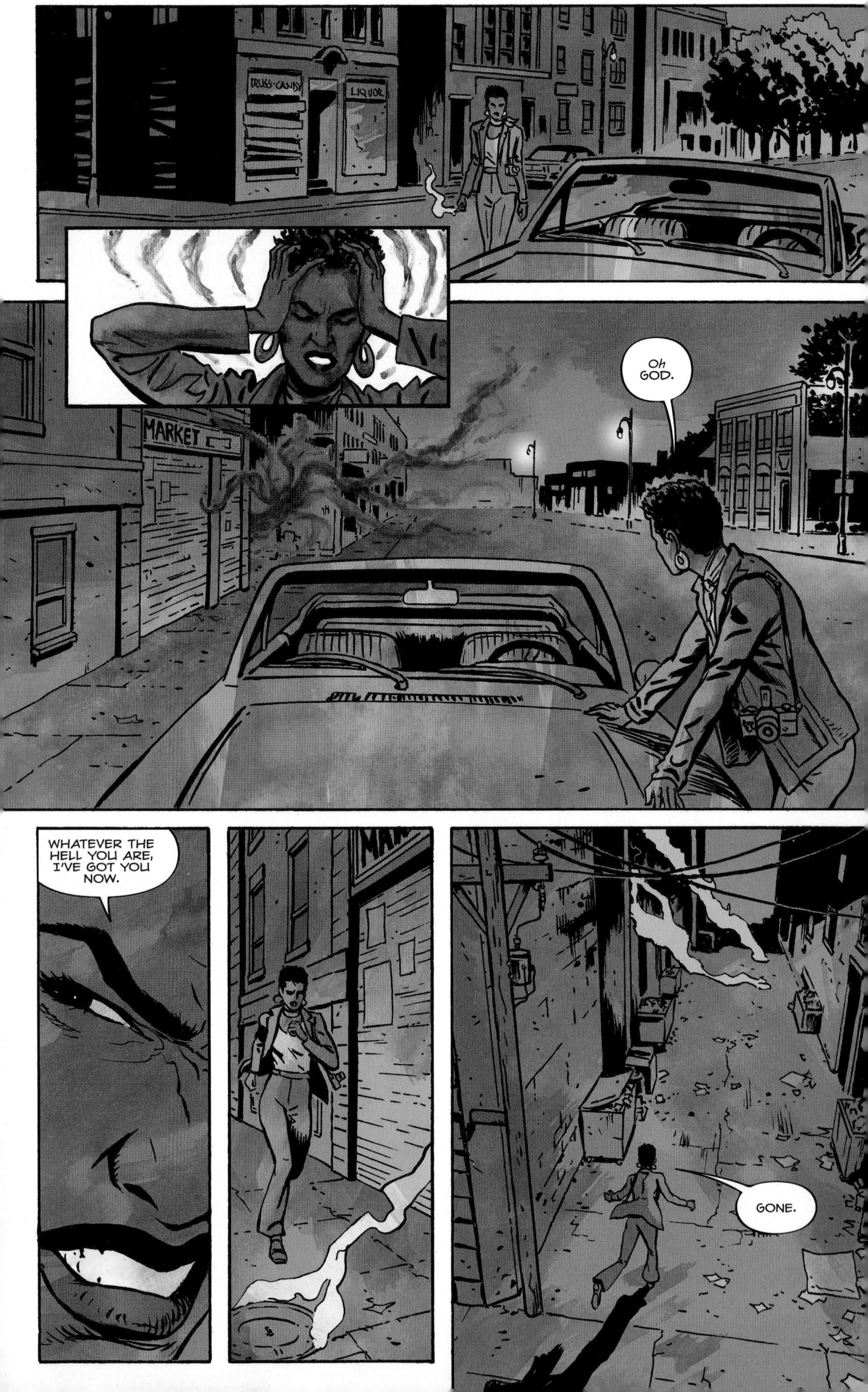
DRUGS·CANDY
LIQUOR
MARKET
Oh GOD.
WHATEVER THE HELL YOU ARE, I'VE GOT YOU NOW.
GONE.

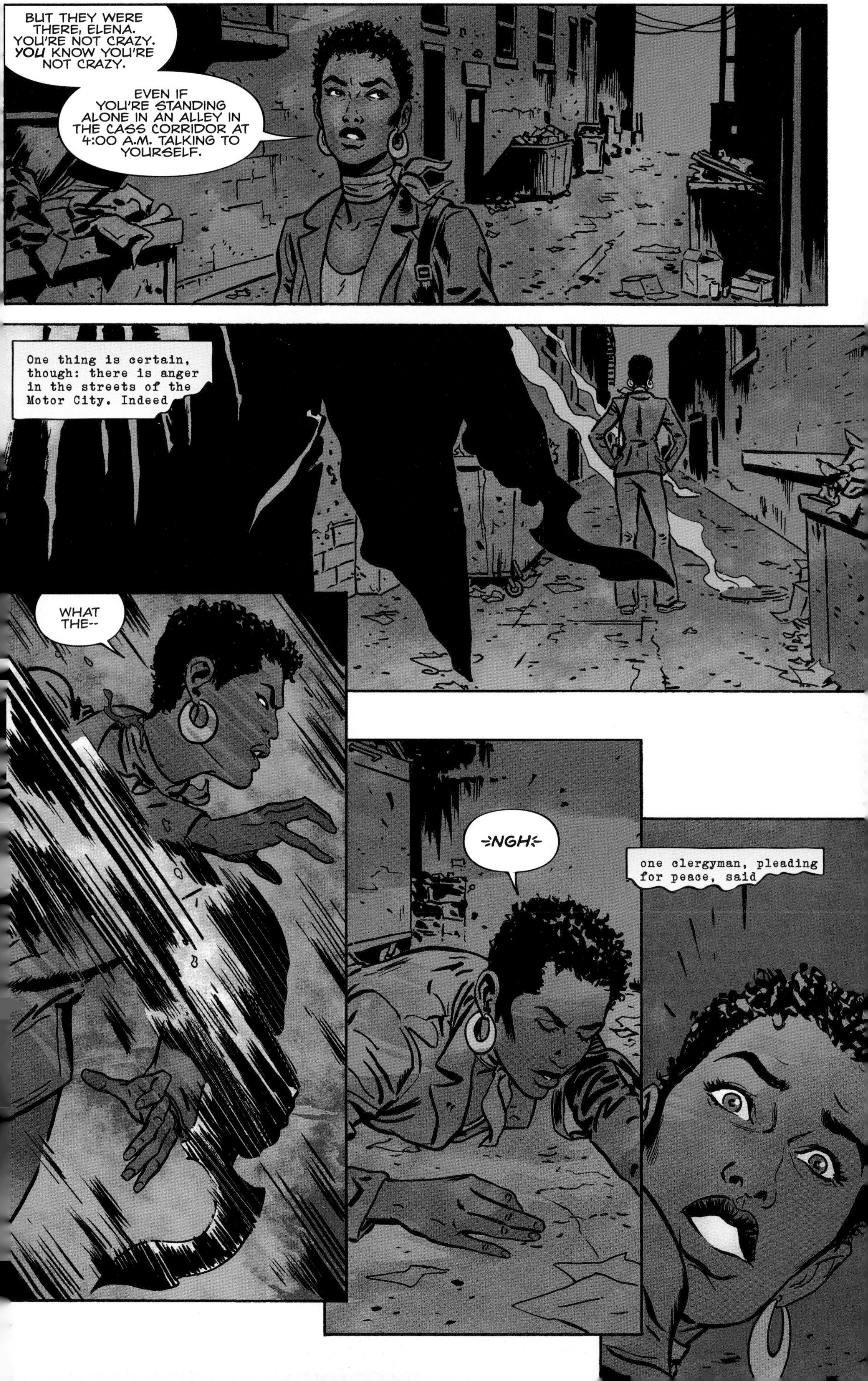
BUT THEY WERE THERE, ELENA. YOU'RE NOT CRAZY. YOU KNOW YOU'RE NOT CRAZY.
EVEN IF YOU'RE STANDING ALONE IN AN ALLEY IN THE CASS CORRIDOR AT 4:00 A.M. TALKING TO YOURSELF.
One thing is certain, though: there is anger in the streets of the Motor City. Indeed
WHAT THE--
NGH
one clergyman, pleading for peace, said

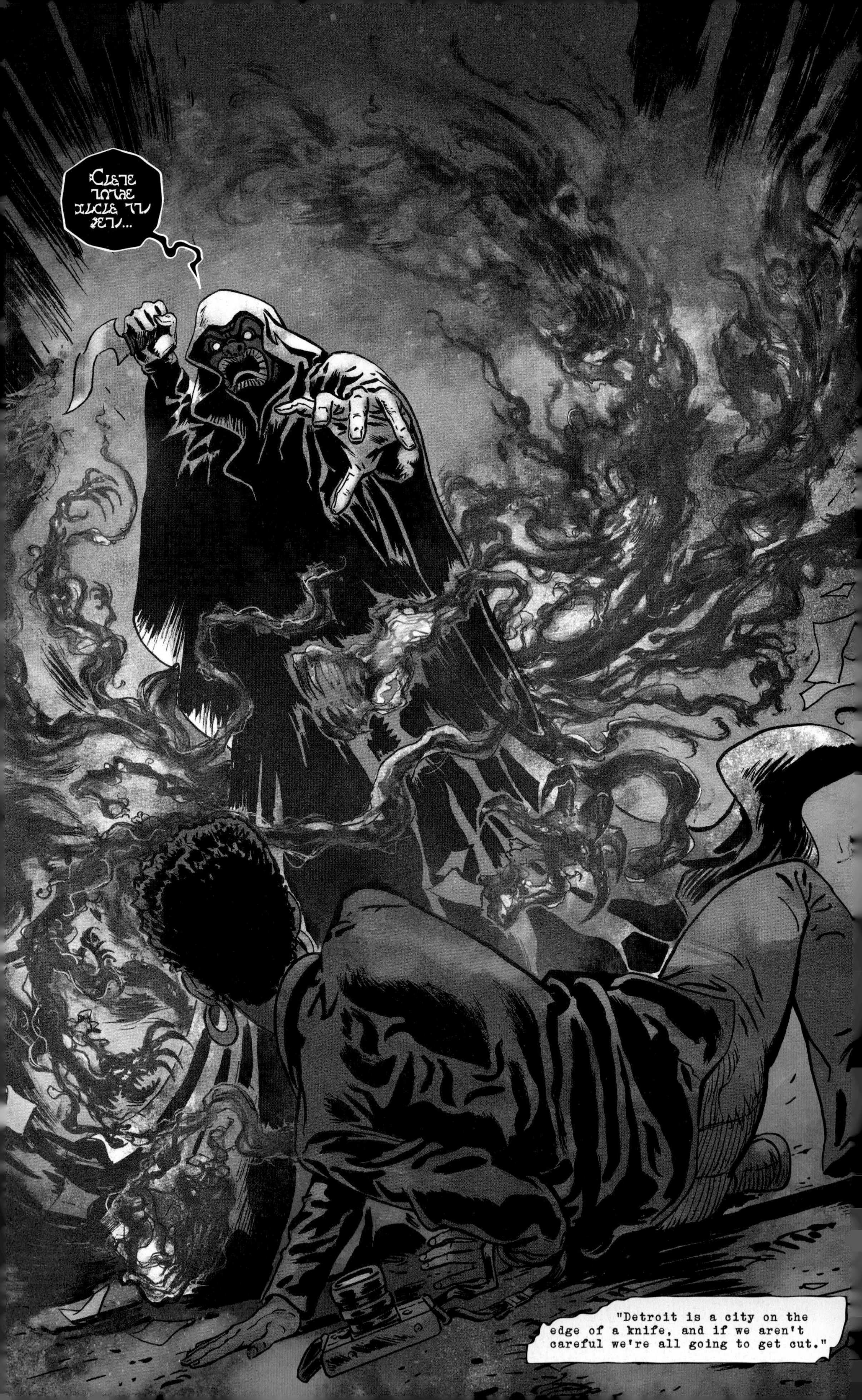
"Detroit is a city on the edge of a knife, and if we aren't careful we're all going to get cut."

Issue One 2nd Print Cover by
Taj Tenfold

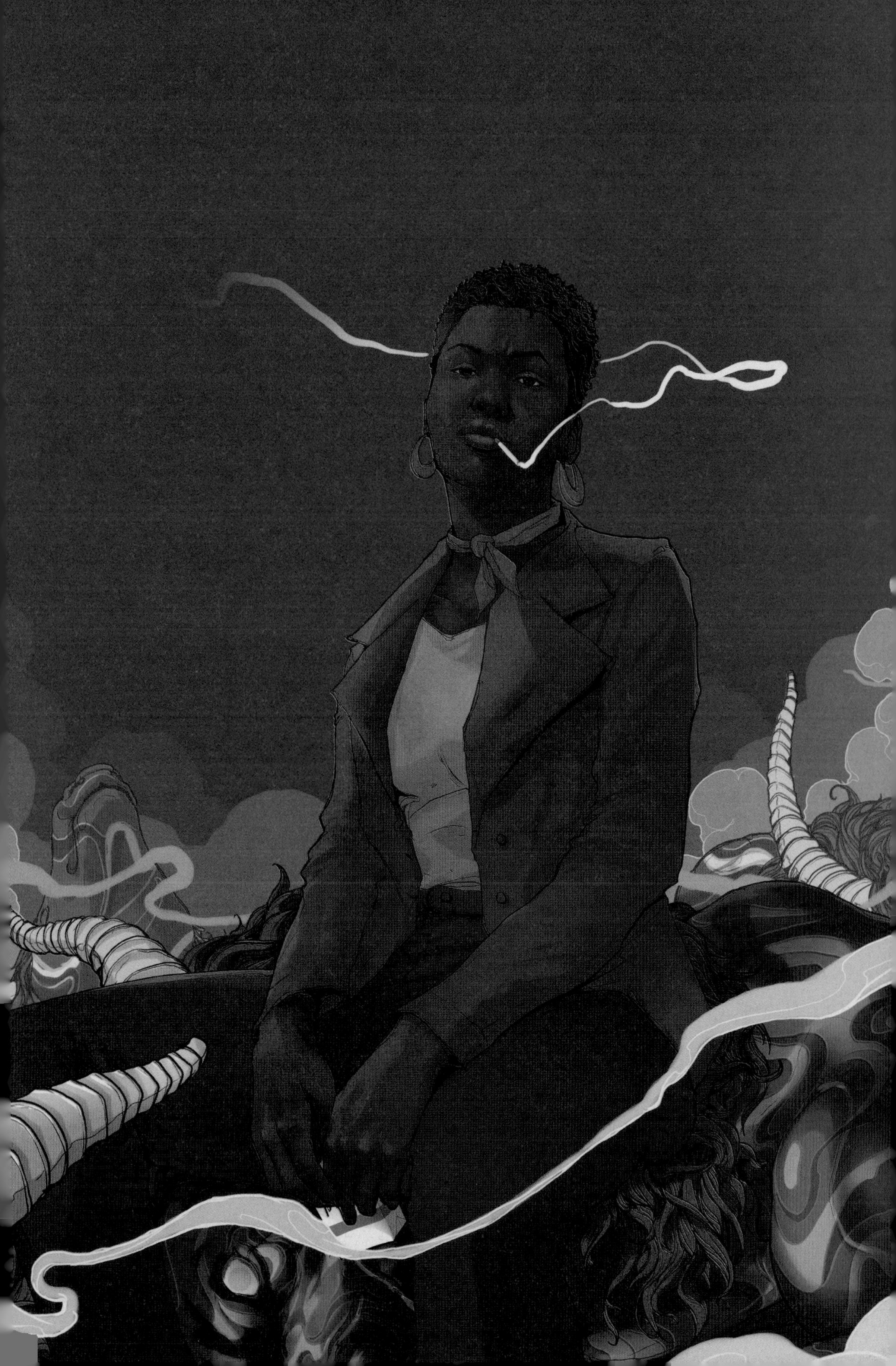

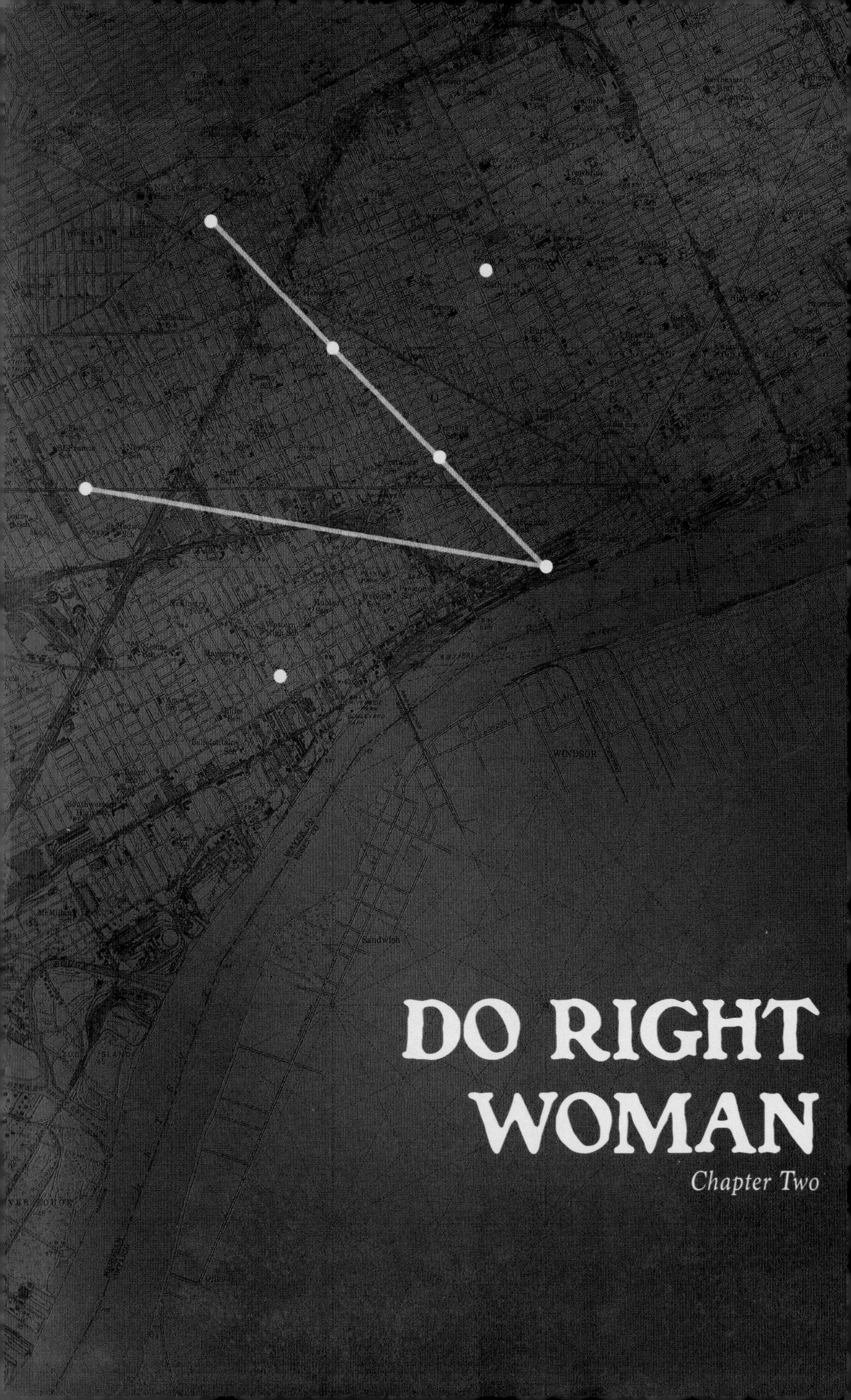
WINDSOR
Sandwich

DO RIGHT WOMAN

Chapter Two

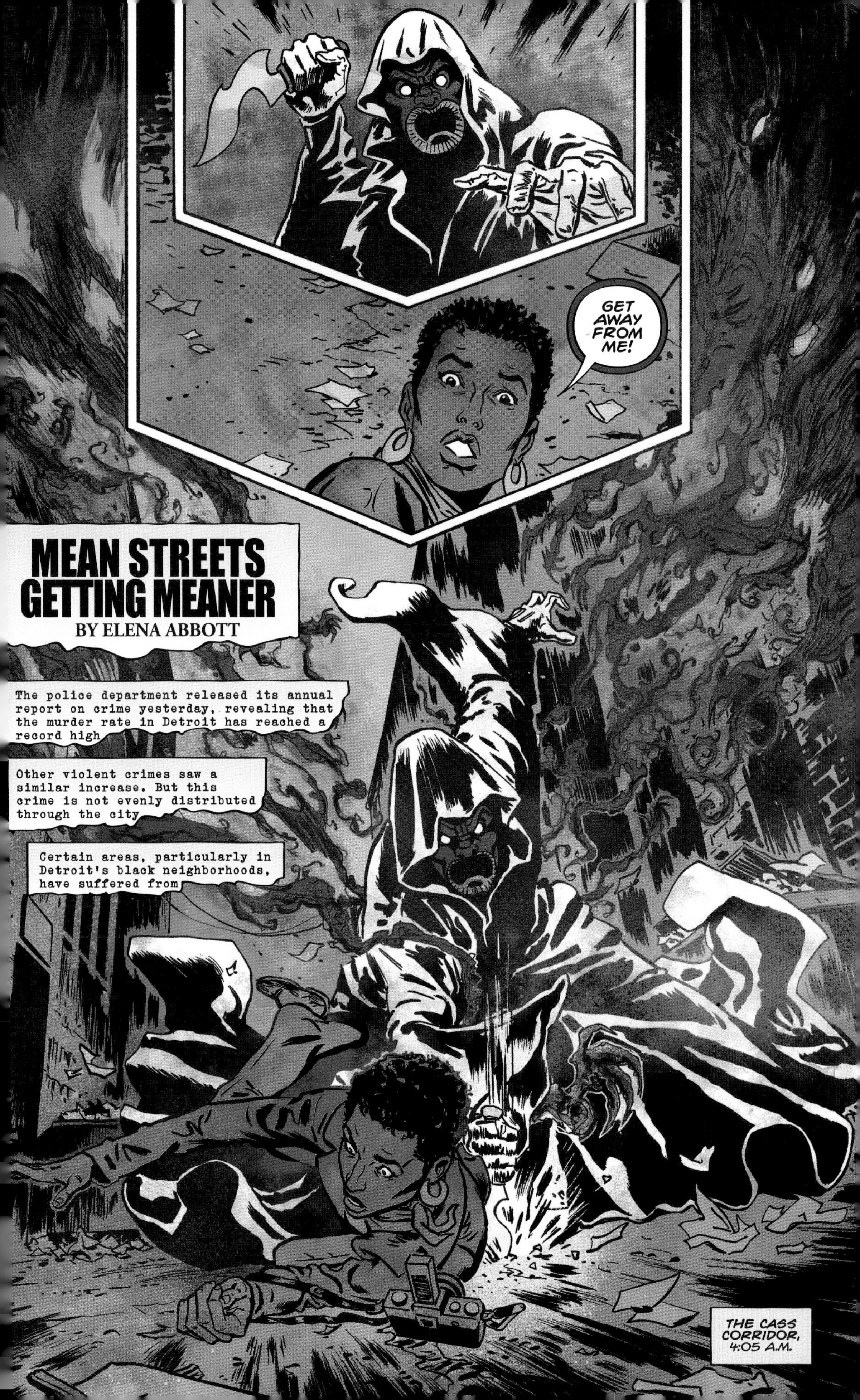
GET AWAY FROM ME!
MEAN STREETS GETTING MEANER
BY ELENA ABBOTT
The police department released its annual report on crime yesterday, revealing that the murder rate in Detroit has reached a record high
Other violent crimes saw a similar increase. But this crime is not evenly distributed through the city
Certain areas, particularly in Detroit's black neighborhoods, have suffered from
THE CASS CORRIDOR, 4:05 A.M.

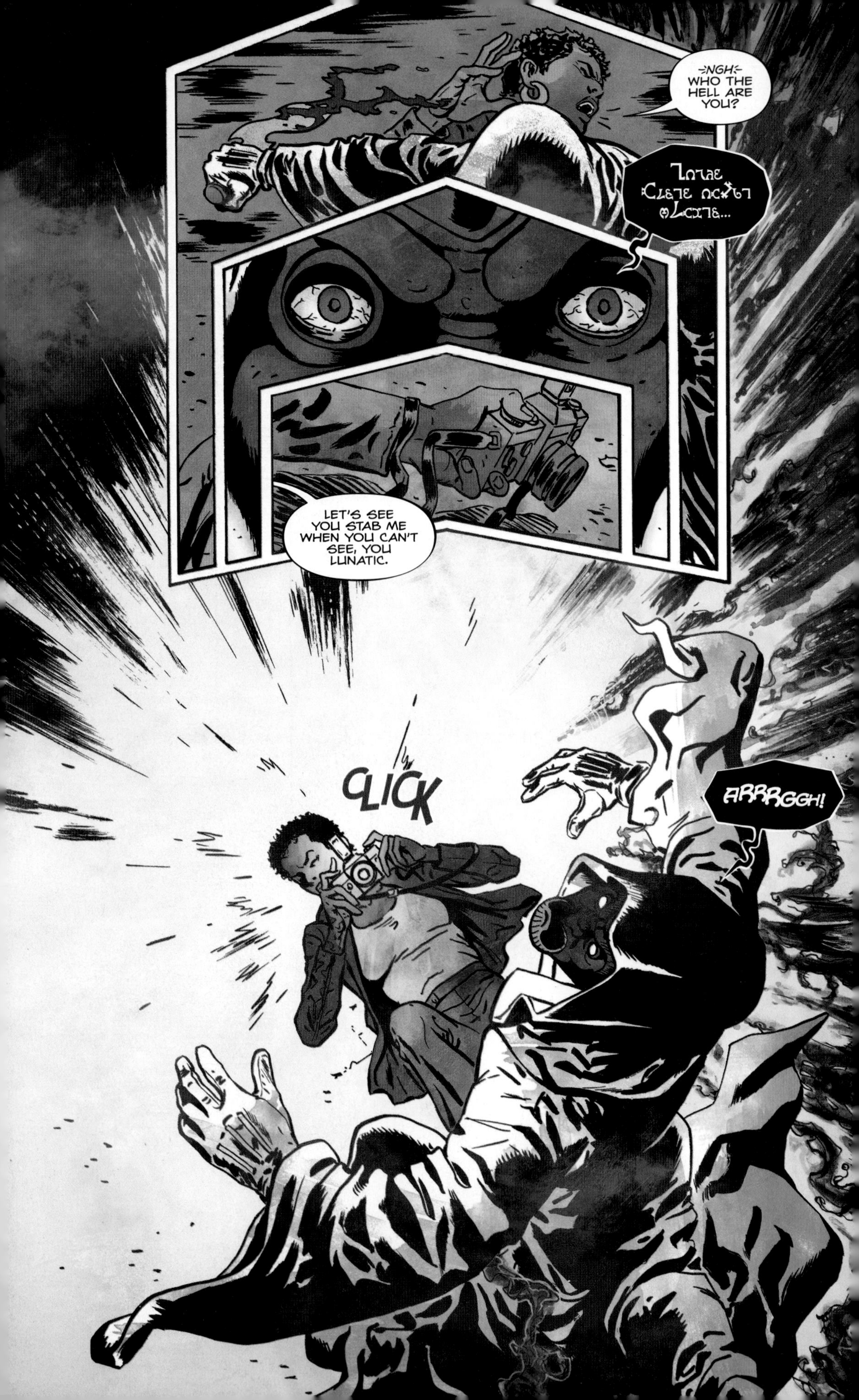
-NGH- WHO THE HELL ARE YOU?
LET'S SEE YOU STAB ME WHEN YOU CAN'T SEE, YOU LUNATIC.
CLICK
ARRRGGH!

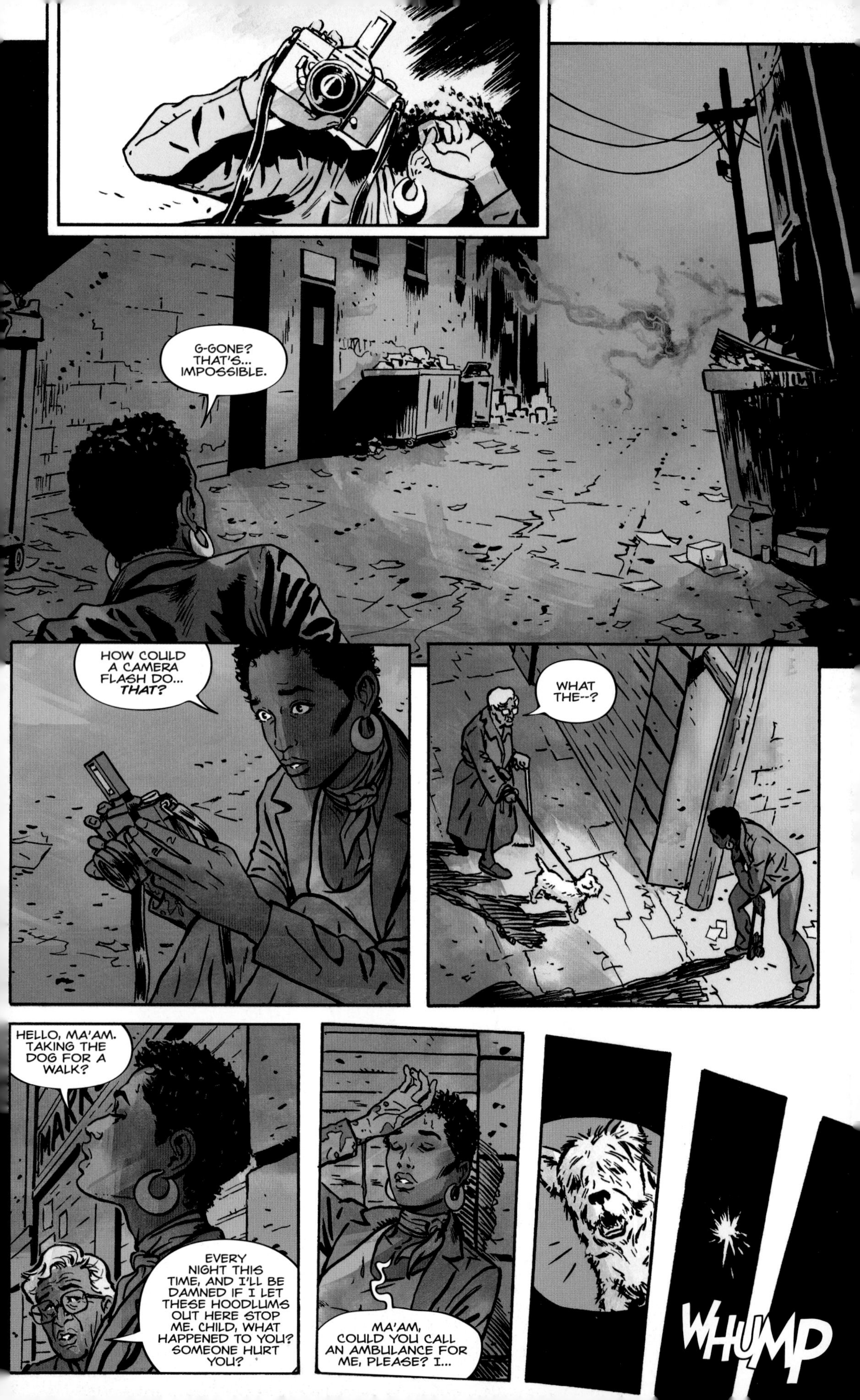
G-GONE? THAT'S... IMPOSSIBLE.
HOW COULD A CAMERA FLASH DO... *THAT?*
WHAT THE--?
HELLO, MA'AM. TAKING THE DOG FOR A WALK?
EVERY NIGHT THIS TIME, AND I'LL BE DAMNED IF I LET THESE HOODLUMS OUT HERE STOP ME. CHILD, WHAT HAPPENED TO YOU? SOMEONE HURT YOU?
MA'AM, COULD YOU CALL AN AMBULANCE FOR ME, PLEASE? I...
WHUMP

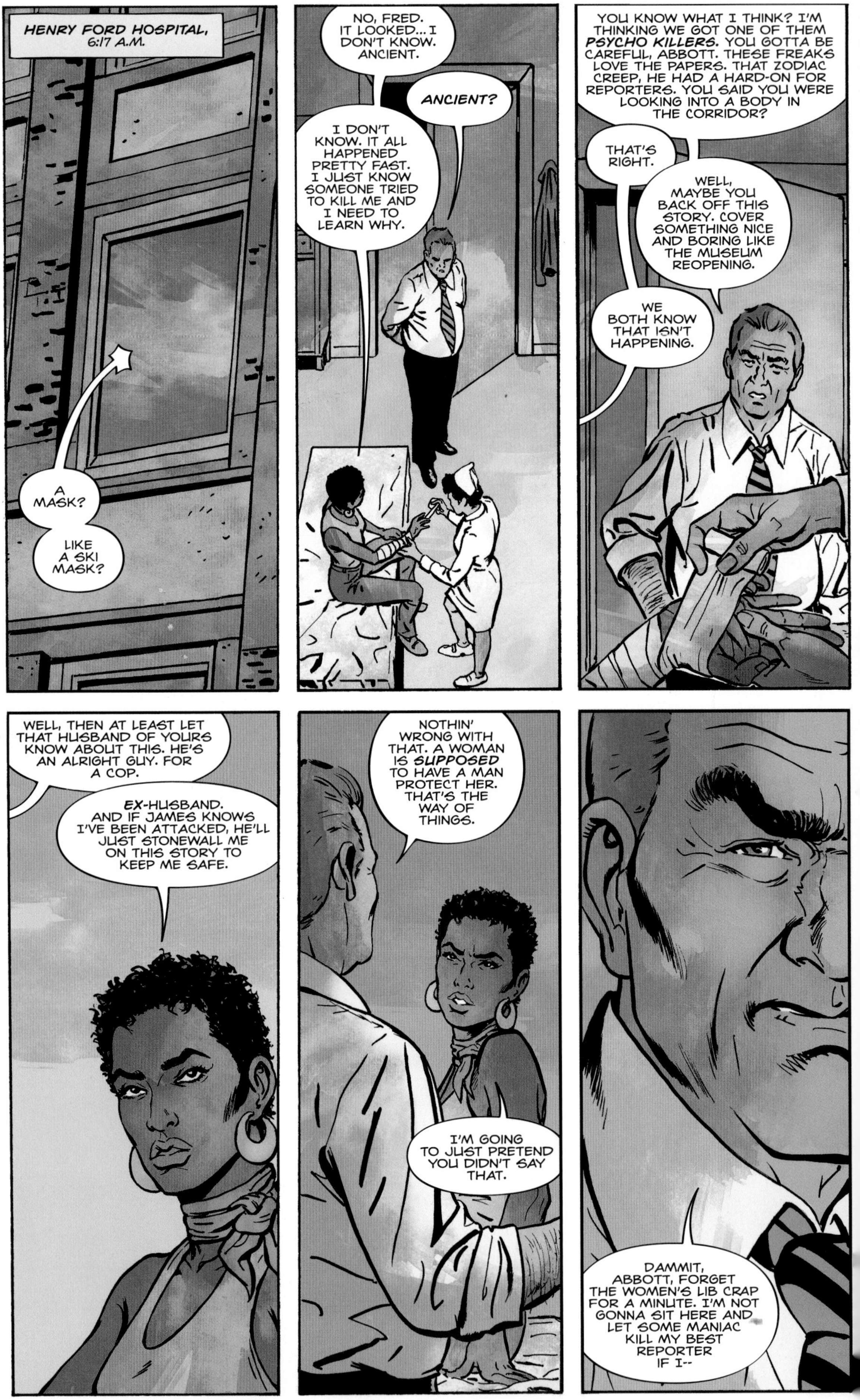
HENRY FORD HOSPITAL, 6:17 A.M.
A MASK?
LIKE A SKI MASK?
NO, FRED. IT LOOKED... I DON'T KNOW. ANCIENT.
ANCIENT?
I DON'T KNOW. IT ALL HAPPENED PRETTY FAST. I JUST KNOW SOMEONE TRIED TO KILL ME AND I NEED TO LEARN WHY.
YOU KNOW WHAT I THINK? I'M THINKING WE GOT ONE OF THEM PSYCHO KILLERS. YOU GOTTA BE CAREFUL, ABBOTT. THESE FREAKS LOVE THE PAPERS. THAT ZODIAC CREEP, HE HAD A HARD-ON FOR REPORTERS. YOU SAID YOU WERE LOOKING INTO A BODY IN THE CORRIDOR?
THAT'S RIGHT.
WELL, MAYBE YOU BACK OFF THIS STORY. COVER SOMETHING NICE AND BORING LIKE THE MUSEUM REOPENING.
WE BOTH KNOW THAT ISN'T HAPPENING.
WELL, THEN AT LEAST LET THAT HUSBAND OF YOURS KNOW ABOUT THIS. HE'S AN ALRIGHT GUY. FOR A COP.
EX-HUSBAND. AND IF JAMES KNOWS I'VE BEEN ATTACKED, HE'LL JUST STONEWALL ME ON THIS STORY TO KEEP ME SAFE.
NOTHIN' WRONG WITH THAT. A WOMAN IS SUPPOSED TO HAVE A MAN PROTECT HER. THAT'S THE WAY OF THINGS.
I'M GOING TO JUST PRETEND YOU DIDN'T SAY THAT.
DAMMIT, ABBOTT, FORGET THE WOMEN'S LIB CRAP FOR A MINUTE. I'M NOT GONNA SIT HERE AND LET SOME MANIAC KILL MY BEST REPORTER IF I--

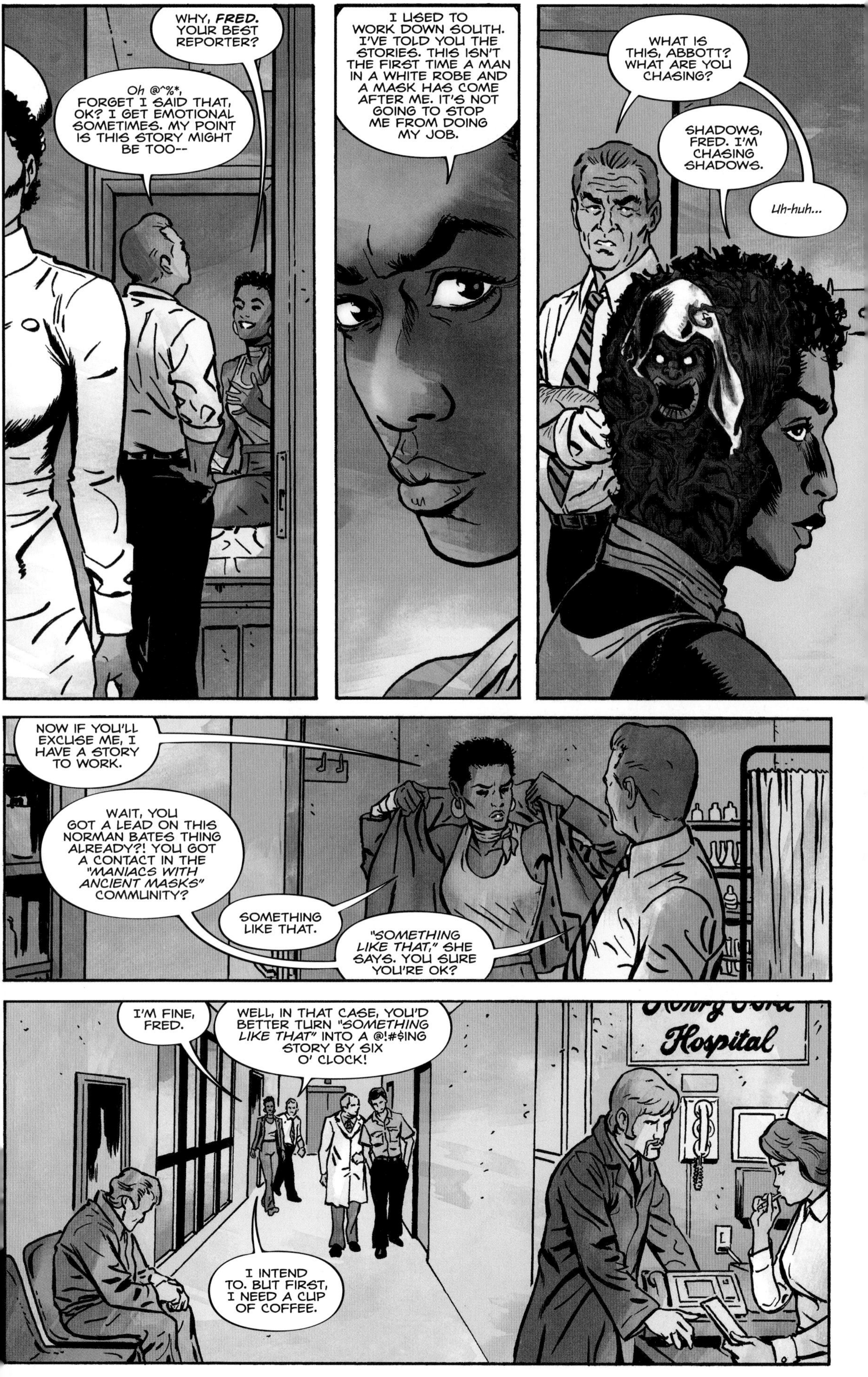
WHY, FRED. YOUR BEST REPORTER?
Oh @^%*, FORGET I SAID THAT, OK? I GET EMOTIONAL SOMETIMES. MY POINT IS THIS STORY MIGHT BE TOO--
I USED TO WORK DOWN SOUTH. I'VE TOLD YOU THE STORIES. THIS ISN'T THE FIRST TIME A MAN IN A WHITE ROBE AND A MASK HAS COME AFTER ME. IT'S NOT GOING TO STOP ME FROM DOING MY JOB.
WHAT IS THIS, ABBOTT? WHAT ARE YOU CHASING?
SHADOWS, FRED. I'M CHASING SHADOWS.
Uh-huh...
NOW IF YOU'LL EXCUSE ME, I HAVE A STORY TO WORK.
WAIT, YOU GOT A LEAD ON THIS NORMAN BATES THING ALREADY?! YOU GOT A CONTACT IN THE "MANIACS WITH ANCIENT MASKS" COMMUNITY?
SOMETHING LIKE THAT.
"SOMETHING LIKE THAT," SHE SAYS. YOU SURE YOU'RE OK?
I'M FINE, FRED.
WELL, IN THAT CASE, YOU'D BETTER TURN "SOMETHING LIKE THAT" INTO A @!#$ING STORY BY SIX O' CLOCK!
Hospital
I INTEND TO. BUT FIRST, I NEED A CUP OF COFFEE.

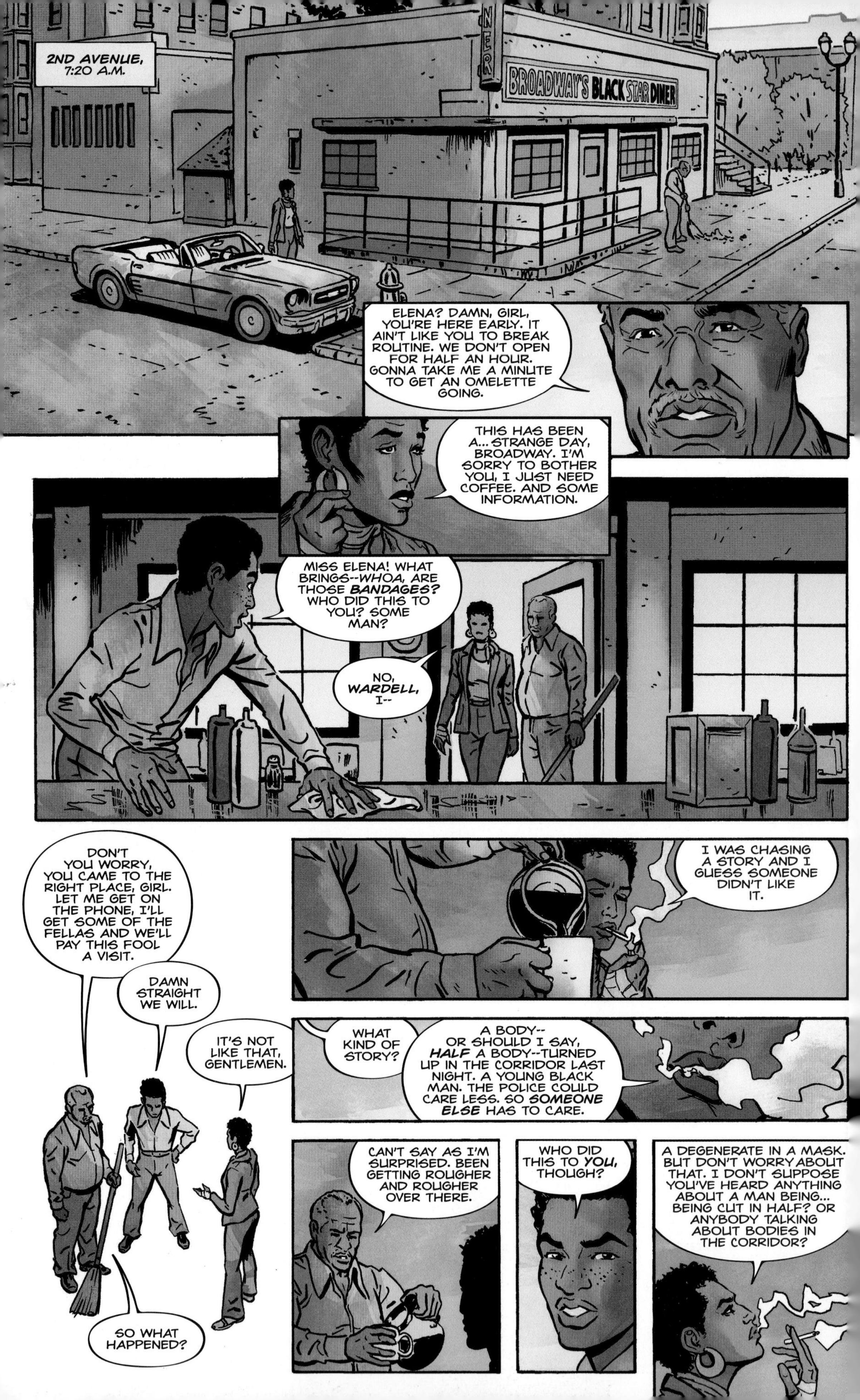
2ND AVENUE, 7:20 A.M.
BROADWAY'S BLACK STAR DINER
ELENA? DAMN, GIRL, YOU'RE HERE EARLY. IT AIN'T LIKE YOU TO BREAK ROUTINE. WE DON'T OPEN FOR HALF AN HOUR. GONNA TAKE ME A MINUTE TO GET AN OMELETTE GOING.
THIS HAS BEEN A... STRANGE DAY, BROADWAY. I'M SORRY TO BOTHER YOU, I JUST NEED COFFEE. AND SOME INFORMATION.
MISS ELENA! WHAT BRINGS--WHOA, ARE THOSE BANDAGES? WHO DID THIS TO YOU? SOME MAN?
NO, WARDELL, I--
I WAS CHASING A STORY AND I GUESS SOMEONE DIDN'T LIKE IT.
DON'T YOU WORRY, YOU CAME TO THE RIGHT PLACE, GIRL. LET ME GET ON THE PHONE, I'LL GET SOME OF THE FELLAS AND WE'LL PAY THIS FOOL A VISIT.
DAMN STRAIGHT WE WILL.
IT'S NOT LIKE THAT, GENTLEMEN.
SO WHAT HAPPENED?
WHAT KIND OF STORY?
A BODY--OR SHOULD I SAY, HALF A BODY--TURNED UP IN THE CORRIDOR LAST NIGHT. A YOUNG BLACK MAN. THE POLICE COULD CARE LESS. SO SOMEONE ELSE HAS TO CARE.
CAN'T SAY AS I'M SURPRISED. BEEN GETTING ROUGHER AND ROUGHER OVER THERE.
WHO DID THIS TO YOU, THOUGH?
A DEGENERATE IN A MASK. BUT DON'T WORRY ABOUT THAT. I DON'T SUPPOSE YOU'VE HEARD ANYTHING ABOUT A MAN BEING... BEING CUT IN HALF? OR ANYBODY TALKING ABOUT BODIES IN THE CORRIDOR?

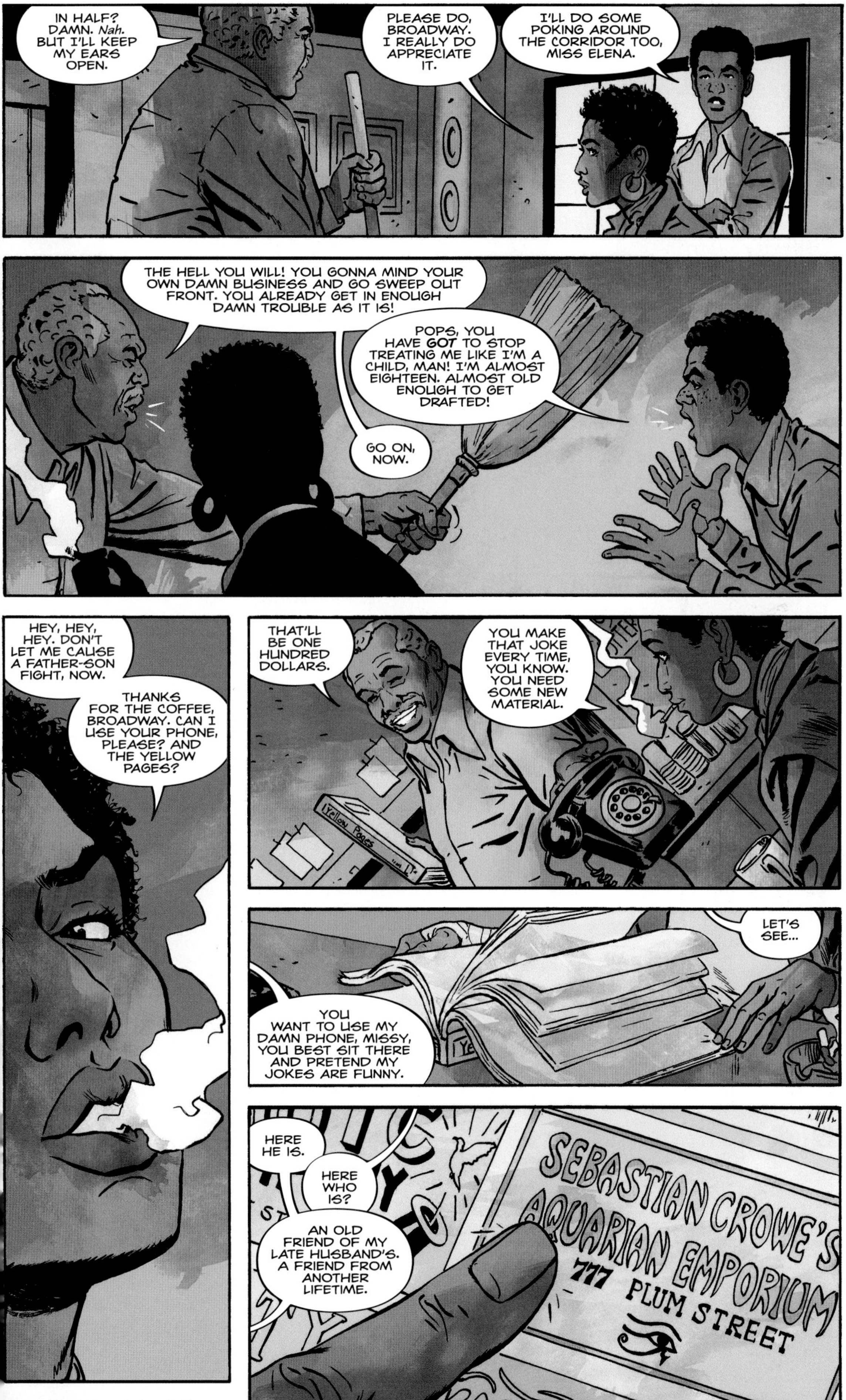
IN HALF? DAMN. *Nah.* BUT I'LL KEEP MY EARS OPEN.
PLEASE DO, BROADWAY. I REALLY DO APPRECIATE IT.
I'LL DO SOME POKING AROUND THE CORRIDOR TOO, MISS ELENA.
THE HELL YOU WILL! YOU GONNA MIND YOUR OWN DAMN BUSINESS AND GO SWEEP OUT FRONT. YOU ALREADY GET IN ENOUGH DAMN TROUBLE AS IT IS!
GO ON, NOW.
POPS, YOU HAVE **GOT** TO STOP TREATING ME LIKE I'M A CHILD, MAN! I'M ALMOST EIGHTEEN. ALMOST OLD ENOUGH TO GET DRAFTED!
HEY, HEY, HEY. DON'T LET ME CAUSE A FATHER-SON FIGHT, NOW.
THANKS FOR THE COFFEE, BROADWAY. CAN I USE YOUR PHONE, PLEASE? AND THE YELLOW PAGES?
THAT'LL BE ONE HUNDRED DOLLARS.
YOU MAKE THAT JOKE EVERY TIME, YOU KNOW. YOU NEED SOME NEW MATERIAL.
Yellow Pages
LET'S SEE...
YOU WANT TO USE MY DAMN PHONE, MISSY, YOU BEST SIT THERE AND PRETEND MY JOKES ARE FUNNY.
HERE HE IS.
HERE WHO IS?
AN OLD FRIEND OF MY LATE HUSBAND'S. A FRIEND FROM ANOTHER LIFETIME.
SEBASTIAN CROWE'S AQUARIAN EMPORIUM
777 PLUM STREET

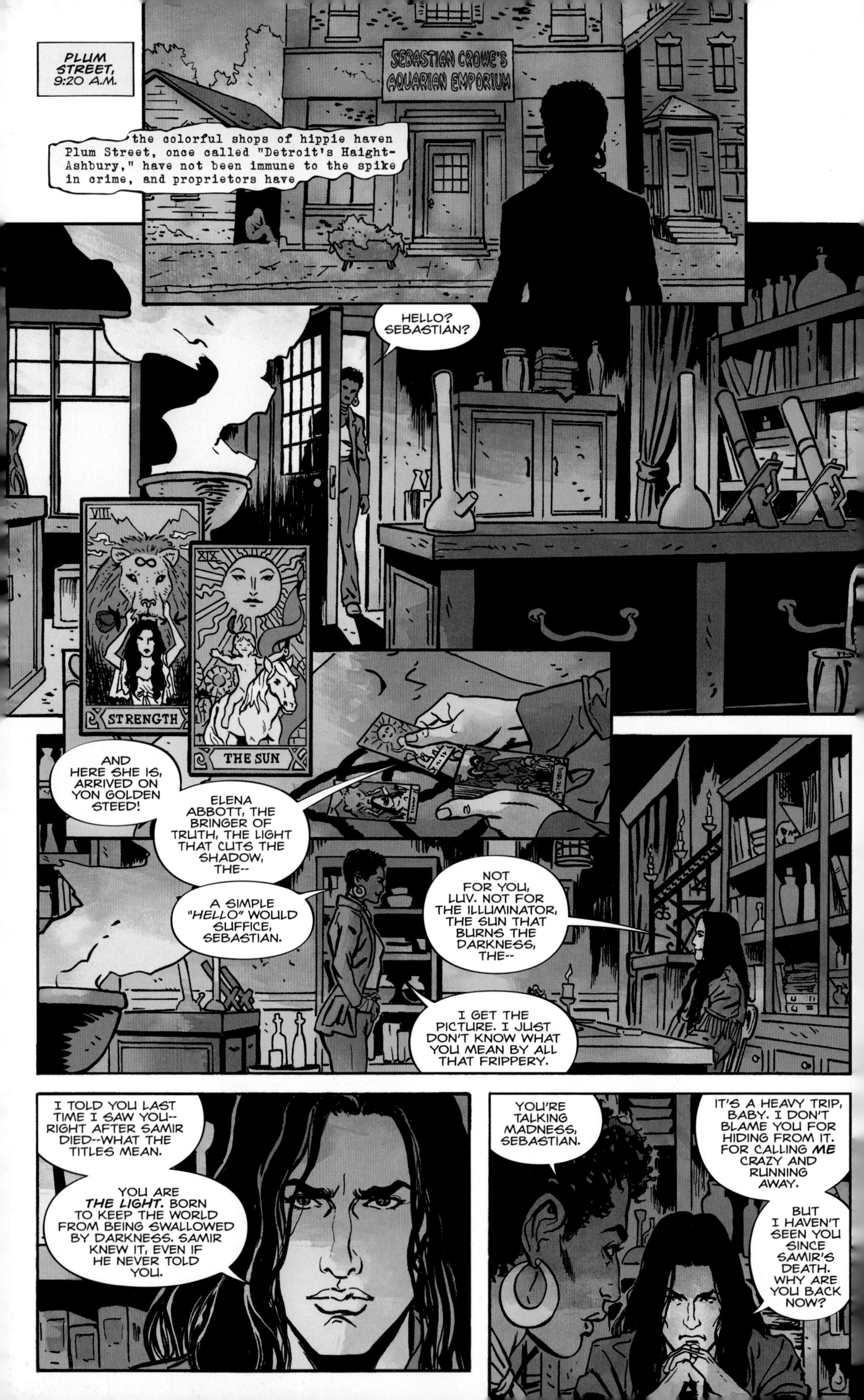
PLUM STREET, 9:20 A.M.
the colorful shops of hippie haven Plum Street, once called "Detroit's Haight-Ashbury," have not been immune to the spike in crime, and proprietors have
SEBASTIAN CROWE'S AQUARIAN EMPORIUM
HELLO? SEBASTIAN?
VIII
STRENGTH
XIX
THE SUN
AND HERE SHE IS, ARRIVED ON YON GOLDEN STEED!
ELENA ABBOTT, THE BRINGER OF TRUTH, THE LIGHT THAT CUTS THE SHADOW, THE--
A SIMPLE "HELLO" WOULD SUFFICE, SEBASTIAN.
NOT FOR YOU, LUV. NOT FOR THE ILLUMINATOR, THE SUN THAT BURNS THE DARKNESS, THE--
I GET THE PICTURE. I JUST DON'T KNOW WHAT YOU MEAN BY ALL THAT FRIPPERY.
I TOLD YOU LAST TIME I SAW YOU--RIGHT AFTER SAMIR DIED--WHAT THE TITLES MEAN.
YOU ARE THE LIGHT. BORN TO KEEP THE WORLD FROM BEING SWALLOWED BY DARKNESS. SAMIR KNEW IT, EVEN IF HE NEVER TOLD YOU.
YOU'RE TALKING MADNESS, SEBASTIAN.
IT'S A HEAVY TRIP, BABY. I DON'T BLAME YOU FOR HIDING FROM IT. FOR CALLING ME CRAZY AND RUNNING AWAY.
BUT I HAVEN'T SEEN YOU SINCE SAMIR'S DEATH. WHY ARE YOU BACK NOW?

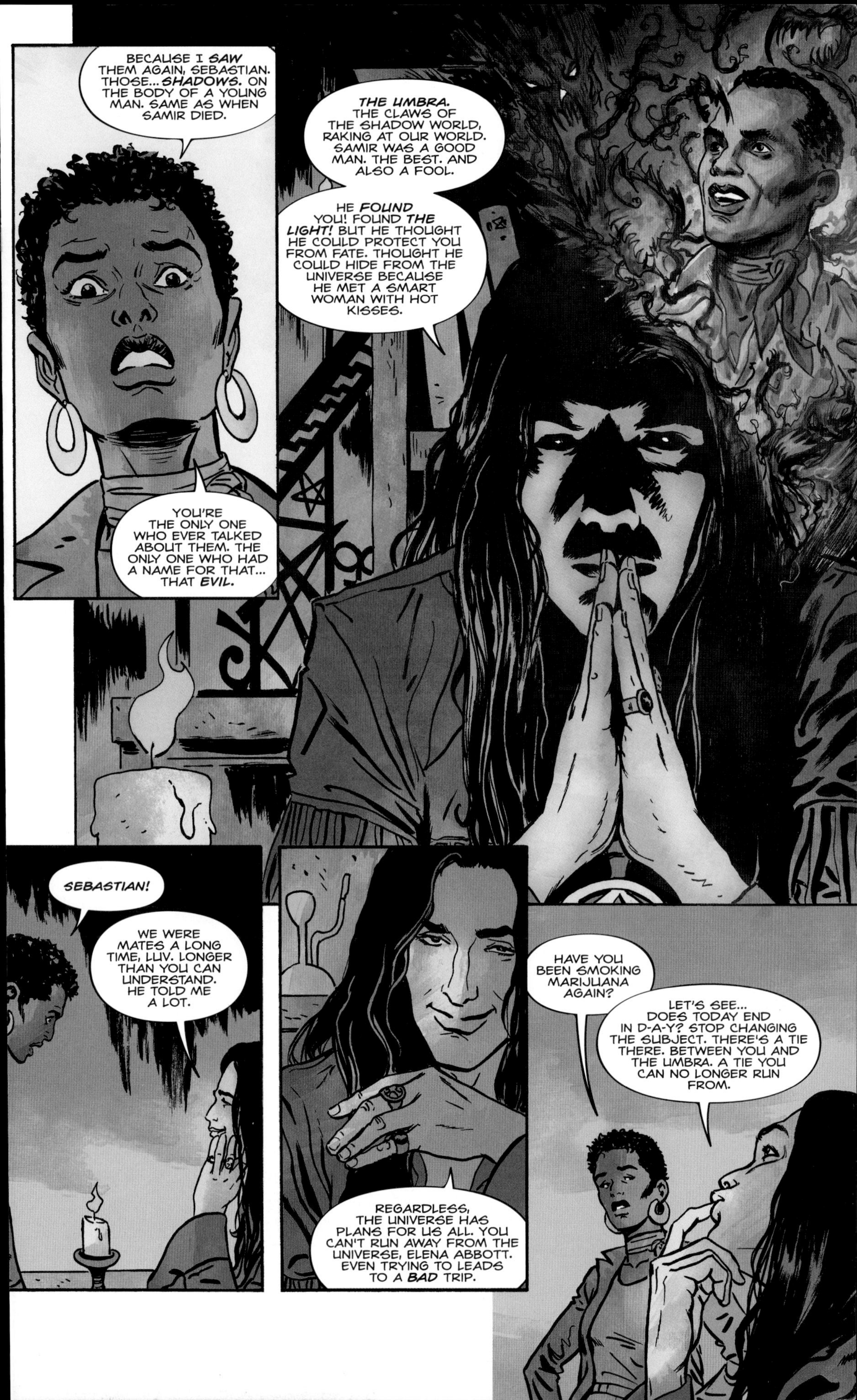
BECAUSE I SAW THEM AGAIN, SEBASTIAN. THOSE... SHADOWS. ON THE BODY OF A YOUNG MAN. SAME AS WHEN SAMIR DIED.
YOU'RE THE ONLY ONE WHO EVER TALKED ABOUT THEM. THE ONLY ONE WHO HAD A NAME FOR THAT... THAT EVIL.
THE UMBRA. THE CLAWS OF THE SHADOW WORLD, RAKING AT OUR WORLD. SAMIR WAS A GOOD MAN. THE BEST. AND ALSO A FOOL.
HE FOUND YOU! FOUND THE LIGHT! BUT HE THOUGHT HE COULD PROTECT YOU FROM FATE. THOUGHT HE COULD HIDE FROM THE UNIVERSE BECAUSE HE MET A SMART WOMAN WITH HOT KISSES.
SEBASTIAN!
WE WERE MATES A LONG TIME, LUV. LONGER THAN YOU CAN UNDERSTAND. HE TOLD ME A LOT.
REGARDLESS, THE UNIVERSE HAS PLANS FOR US ALL. YOU CAN'T RUN AWAY FROM THE UNIVERSE, ELENA ABBOTT. EVEN TRYING TO LEADS TO A BAD TRIP.
HAVE YOU BEEN SMOKING MARIJUANA AGAIN?
LET'S SEE... DOES TODAY END IN D-A-Y? STOP CHANGING THE SUBJECT. THERE'S A TIE THERE. BETWEEN YOU AND THE UMBRA. A TIE YOU CAN NO LONGER RUN FROM.

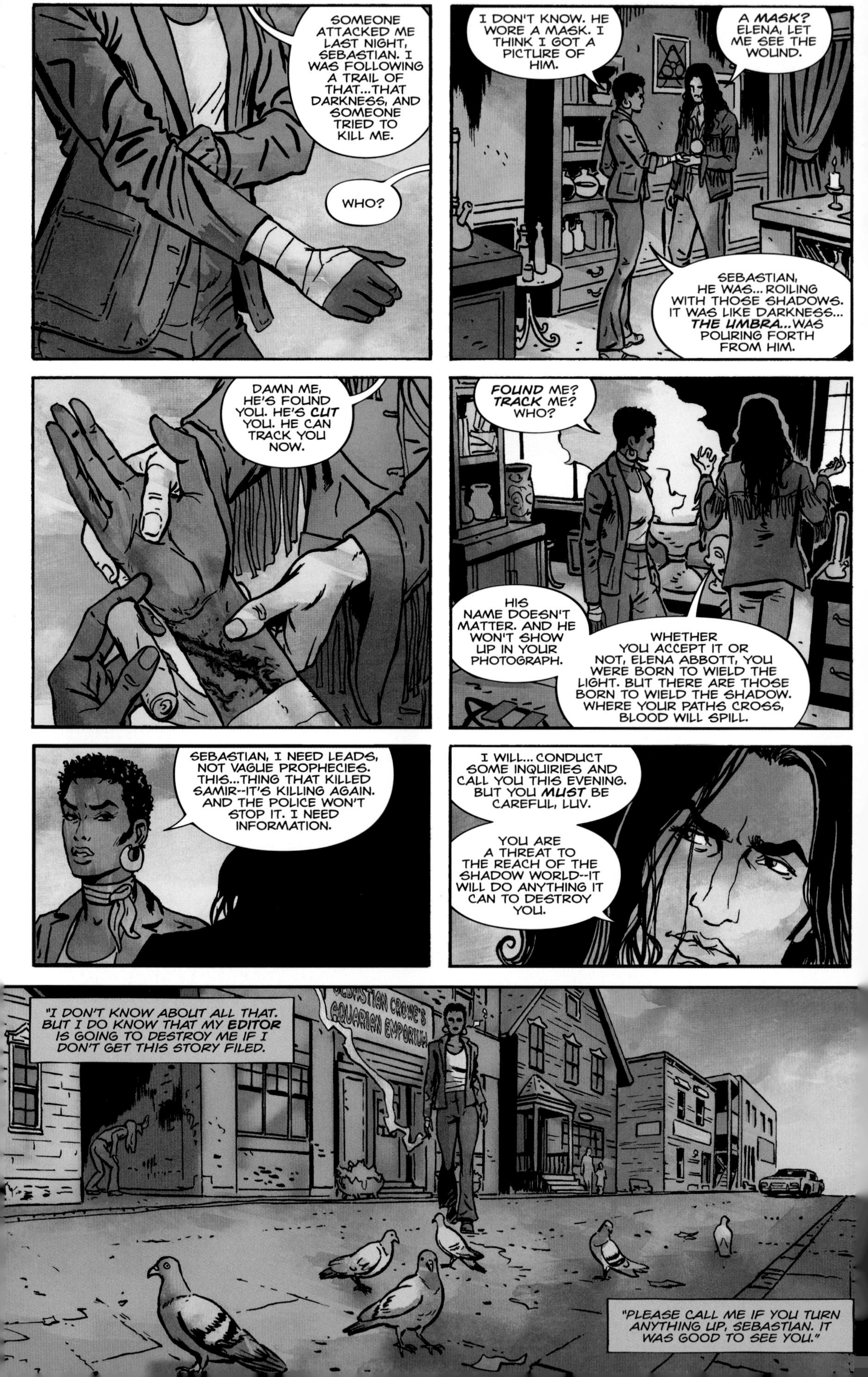
SOMEONE ATTACKED ME LAST NIGHT, SEBASTIAN. I WAS FOLLOWING A TRAIL OF THAT...THAT DARKNESS, AND SOMEONE TRIED TO KILL ME.
WHO?
I DON'T KNOW. HE WORE A MASK. I THINK I GOT A PICTURE OF HIM.
A MASK? ELENA, LET ME SEE THE WOUND.
SEBASTIAN, HE WAS... ROILING WITH THOSE SHADOWS. IT WAS LIKE DARKNESS... THE UMBRA...WAS POURING FORTH FROM HIM.
DAMN ME, HE'S FOUND YOU. HE'S CUT YOU. HE CAN TRACK YOU NOW.
FOUND ME? TRACK ME? WHO?
HIS NAME DOESN'T MATTER. AND HE WON'T SHOW UP IN YOUR PHOTOGRAPH.
WHETHER YOU ACCEPT IT OR NOT, ELENA ABBOTT, YOU WERE BORN TO WIELD THE LIGHT. BUT THERE ARE THOSE BORN TO WIELD THE SHADOW. WHERE YOUR PATHS CROSS, BLOOD WILL SPILL.
SEBASTIAN, I NEED LEADS, NOT VAGUE PROPHECIES. THIS...THING THAT KILLED SAMIR--IT'S KILLING AGAIN. AND THE POLICE WON'T STOP IT. I NEED INFORMATION.
I WILL... CONDUCT SOME INQUIRIES AND CALL YOU THIS EVENING. BUT YOU MUST BE CAREFUL, LUV.
YOU ARE A THREAT TO THE REACH OF THE SHADOW WORLD--IT WILL DO ANYTHING IT CAN TO DESTROY YOU.
"I DON'T KNOW ABOUT ALL THAT. BUT I DO KNOW THAT MY EDITOR IS GOING TO DESTROY ME IF I DON'T GET THIS STORY FILED.
SEBASTIAN CROWE'S AQUARIAN EMPORIUM
"PLEASE CALL ME IF YOU TURN ANYTHING UP, SEBASTIAN. IT WAS GOOD TO SEE YOU."

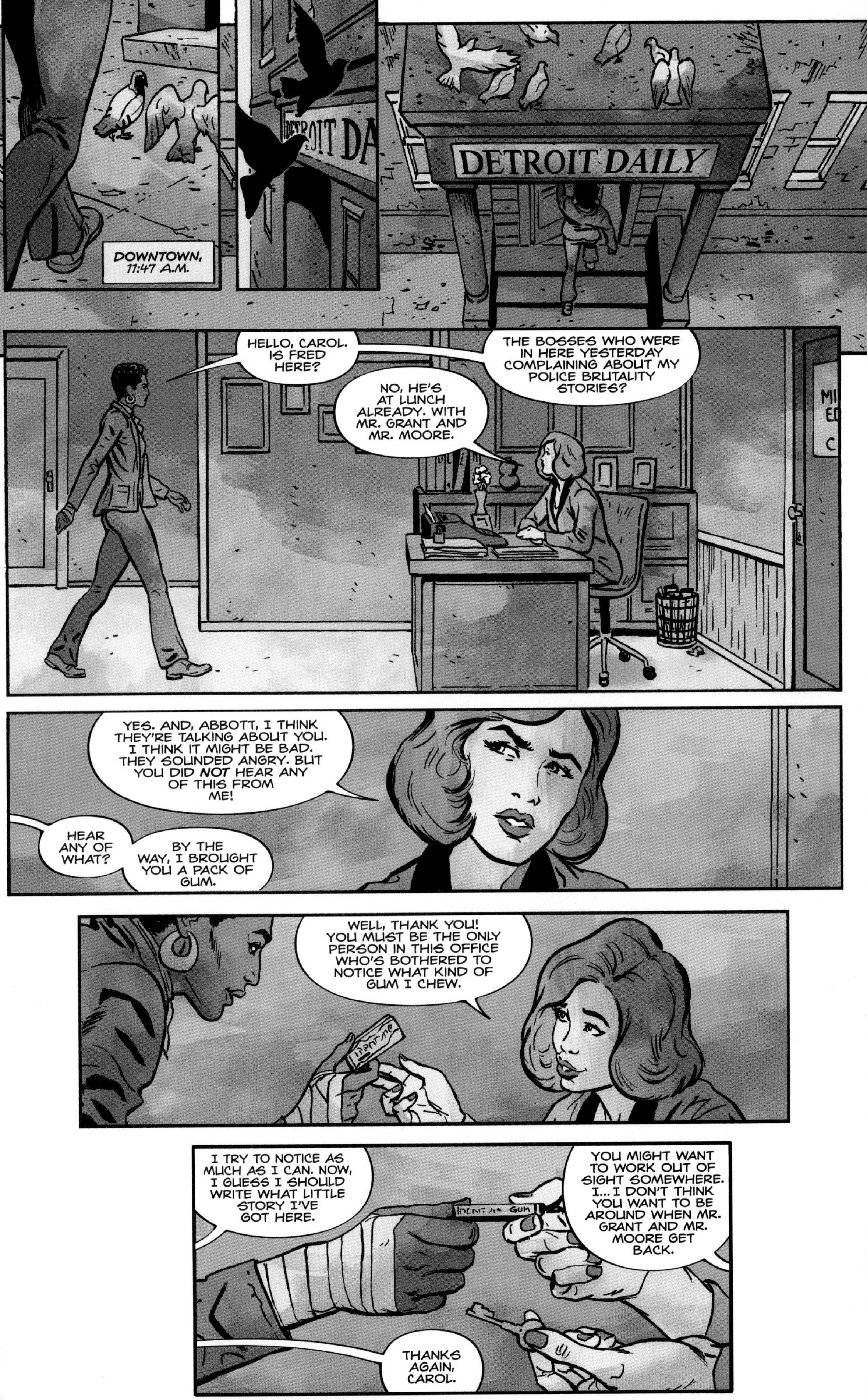
DOWNTOWN, 11:47 A.M.
DETROIT DA
DETROIT DAILY
HELLO, CAROL. IS FRED HERE?
NO, HE'S AT LUNCH ALREADY. WITH MR. GRANT AND MR. MOORE.
THE BOSSES WHO WERE IN HERE YESTERDAY COMPLAINING ABOUT MY POLICE BRUTALITY STORIES?
YES. AND, ABBOTT, I THINK THEY'RE TALKING ABOUT YOU. I THINK IT MIGHT BE BAD. THEY SOUNDED ANGRY. BUT YOU DID *NOT* HEAR ANY OF THIS FROM ME!
HEAR ANY OF WHAT?
BY THE WAY, I BROUGHT YOU A PACK OF GUM.
WELL, THANK YOU! YOU MUST BE THE ONLY PERSON IN THIS OFFICE WHO'S BOTHERED TO NOTICE WHAT KIND OF GUM I CHEW.
I TRY TO NOTICE AS MUCH AS I CAN. NOW, I GUESS I SHOULD WRITE WHAT LITTLE STORY I'VE GOT HERE.
YOU MIGHT WANT TO WORK OUT OF SIGHT SOMEWHERE. I... I DON'T THINK YOU WANT TO BE AROUND WHEN MR. GRANT AND MR. MOORE GET BACK.
THANKS AGAIN, CAROL.

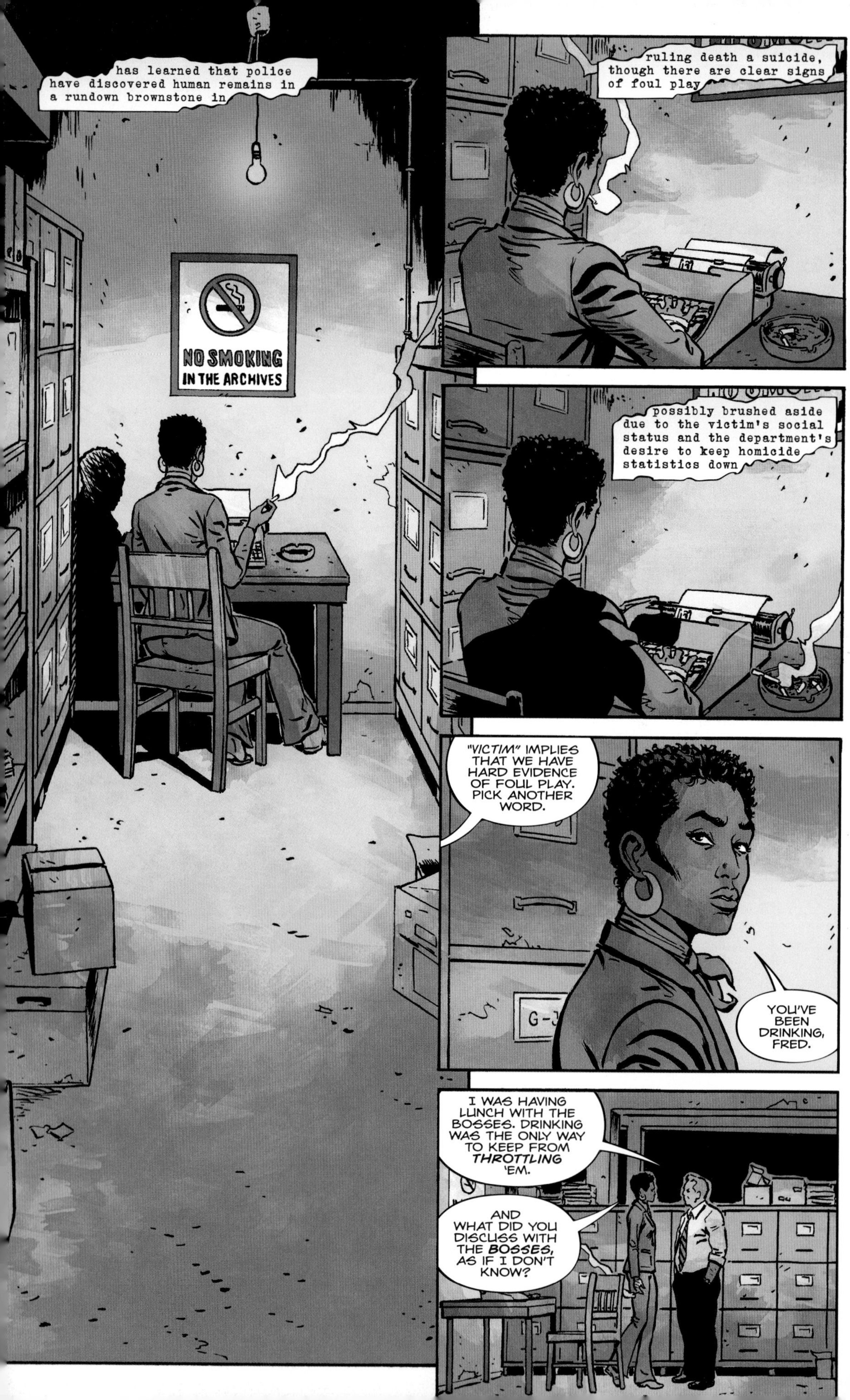

has learned that police have discovered human remains in a rundown brownstone in
NO SMOKING IN THE ARCHIVES
ruling death a suicide, though there are clear signs of foul play
possibly brushed aside due to the victim's social status and the department's desire to keep homicide statistics down
"VICTIM" IMPLIES THAT WE HAVE HARD EVIDENCE OF FOUL PLAY. PICK ANOTHER WORD.
YOU'VE BEEN DRINKING, FRED.
G-J
I WAS HAVING LUNCH WITH THE BOSSES. DRINKING WAS THE ONLY WAY TO KEEP FROM THROTTLING 'EM.
AND WHAT DID YOU DISCUSS WITH THE BOSSES, AS IF I DON'T KNOW?

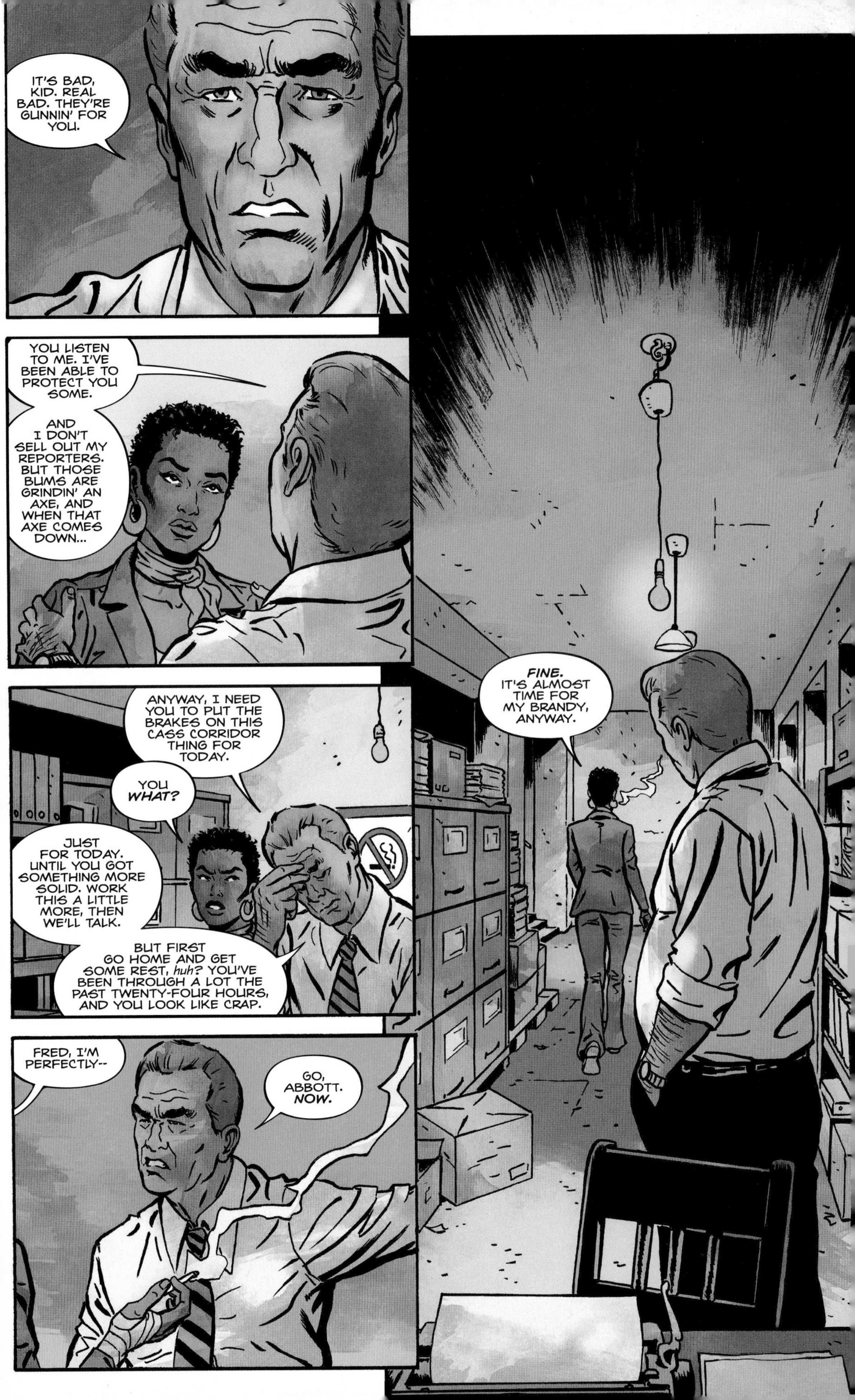
IT'S BAD, KID. REAL BAD. THEY'RE GUNNIN' FOR YOU.
YOU LISTEN TO ME. I'VE BEEN ABLE TO PROTECT YOU SOME.
AND I DON'T SELL OUT MY REPORTERS. BUT THOSE BUMS ARE GRINDIN' AN AXE, AND WHEN THAT AXE COMES DOWN...
ANYWAY, I NEED YOU TO PUT THE BRAKES ON THIS CASS CORRIDOR THING FOR TODAY.
YOU *WHAT?*
JUST FOR TODAY. UNTIL YOU GOT SOMETHING MORE SOLID. WORK THIS A LITTLE MORE, THEN WE'LL TALK.
BUT FIRST GO HOME AND GET SOME REST, *huh?* YOU'VE BEEN THROUGH A LOT THE PAST TWENTY-FOUR HOURS, AND YOU LOOK LIKE CRAP.
FRED, I'M PERFECTLY--
GO, ABBOTT. *NOW.*
FINE. IT'S ALMOST TIME FOR MY BRANDY, ANYWAY.

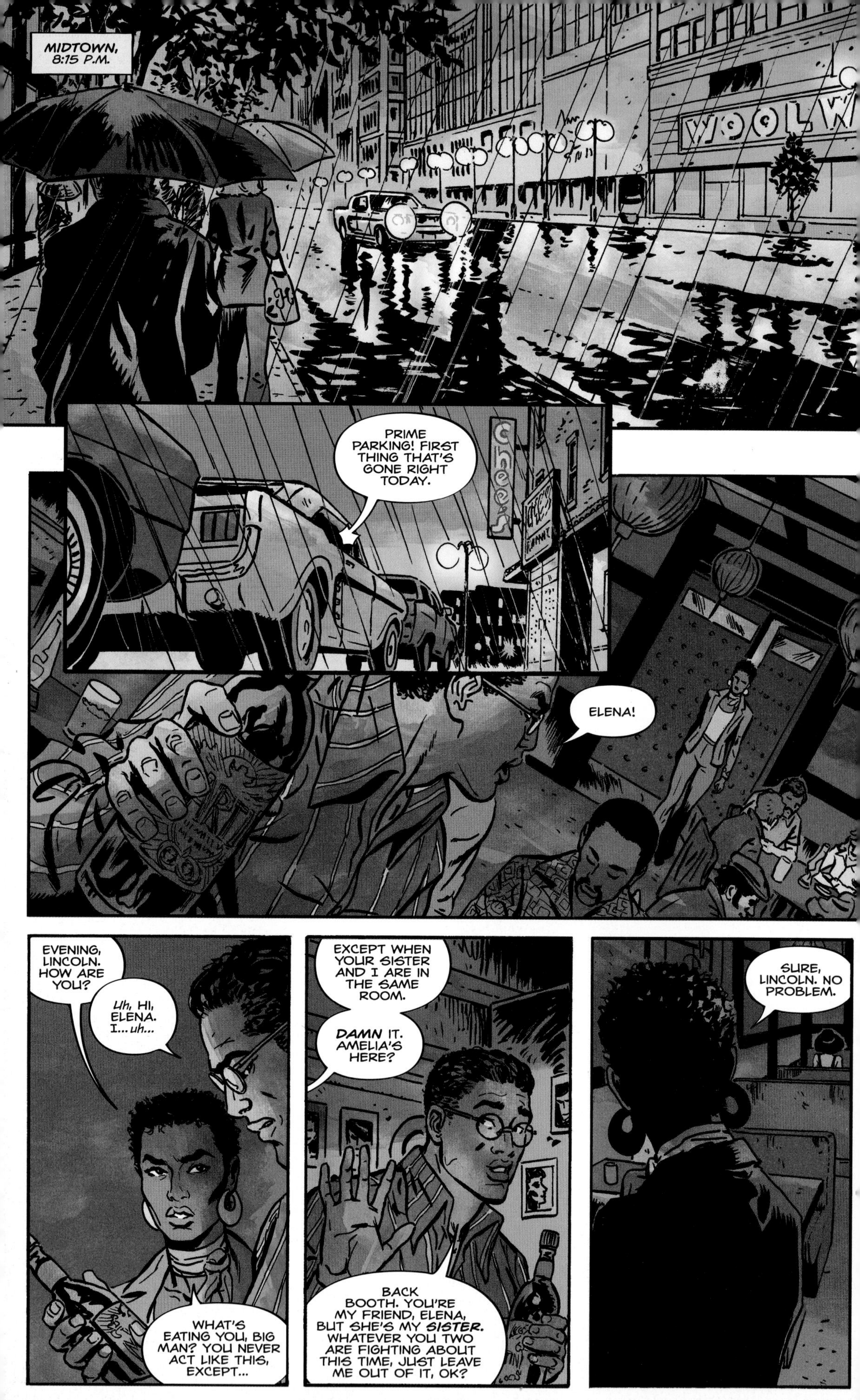
MIDTOWN, 8:15 P.M.
WOOLW
PRIME PARKING! FIRST THING THAT'S GONE RIGHT TODAY.
ELENA!
EVENING, LINCOLN. HOW ARE YOU?
UH, HI, ELENA. I...UH...
WHAT'S EATING YOU, BIG MAN? YOU NEVER ACT LIKE THIS, EXCEPT...
EXCEPT WHEN YOUR SISTER AND I ARE IN THE SAME ROOM.
DAMN IT. AMELIA'S HERE?
BACK BOOTH. YOU'RE MY FRIEND, ELENA, BUT SHE'S MY SISTER. WHATEVER YOU TWO ARE FIGHTING ABOUT THIS TIME, JUST LEAVE ME OUT OF IT, OK?
SURE, LINCOLN. NO PROBLEM.

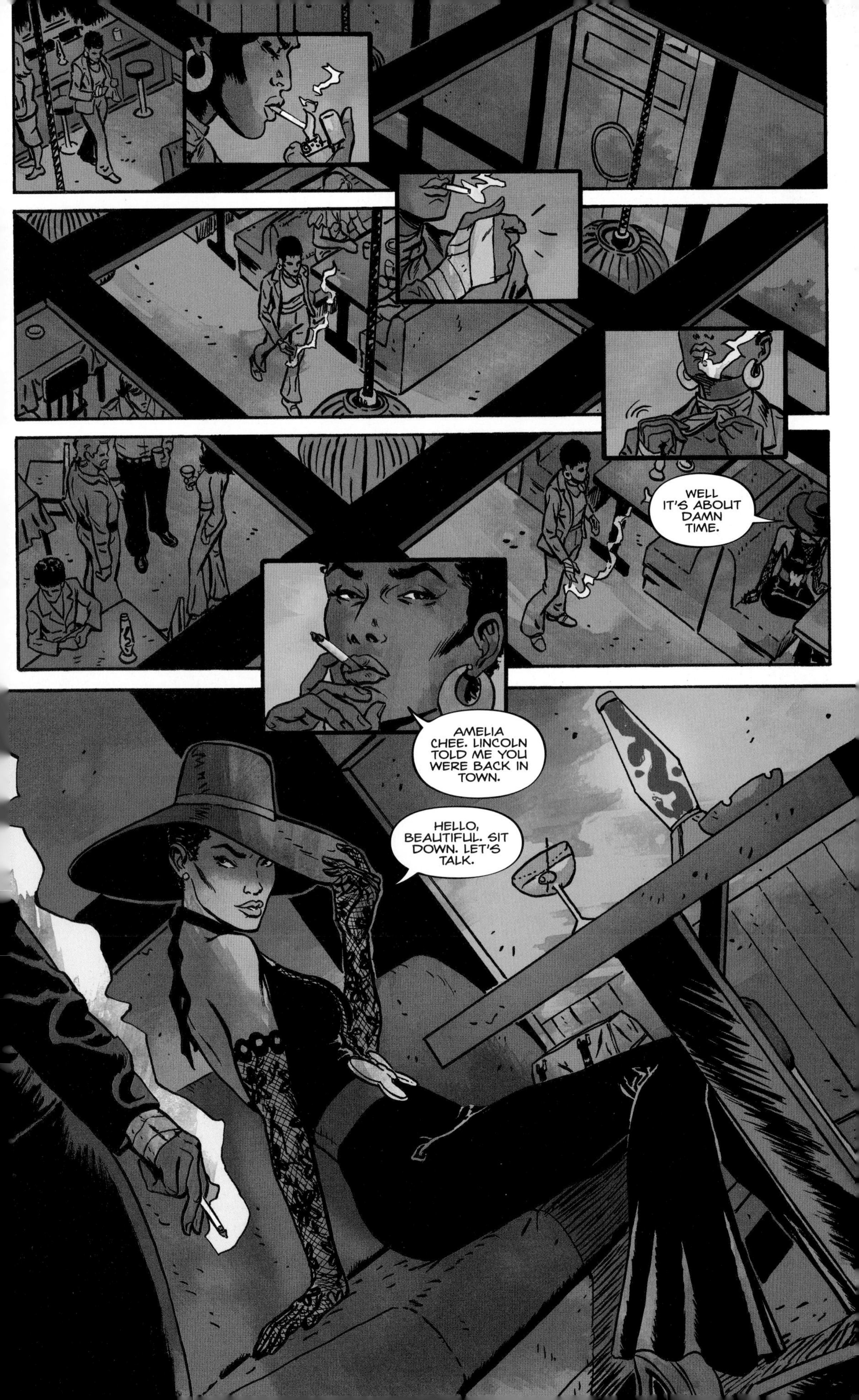
WELL IT'S ABOUT DAMN TIME.
AMELIA CHEE. LINCOLN TOLD ME YOU WERE BACK IN TOWN.
HELLO, BEAUTIFUL. SIT DOWN. LET'S TALK.

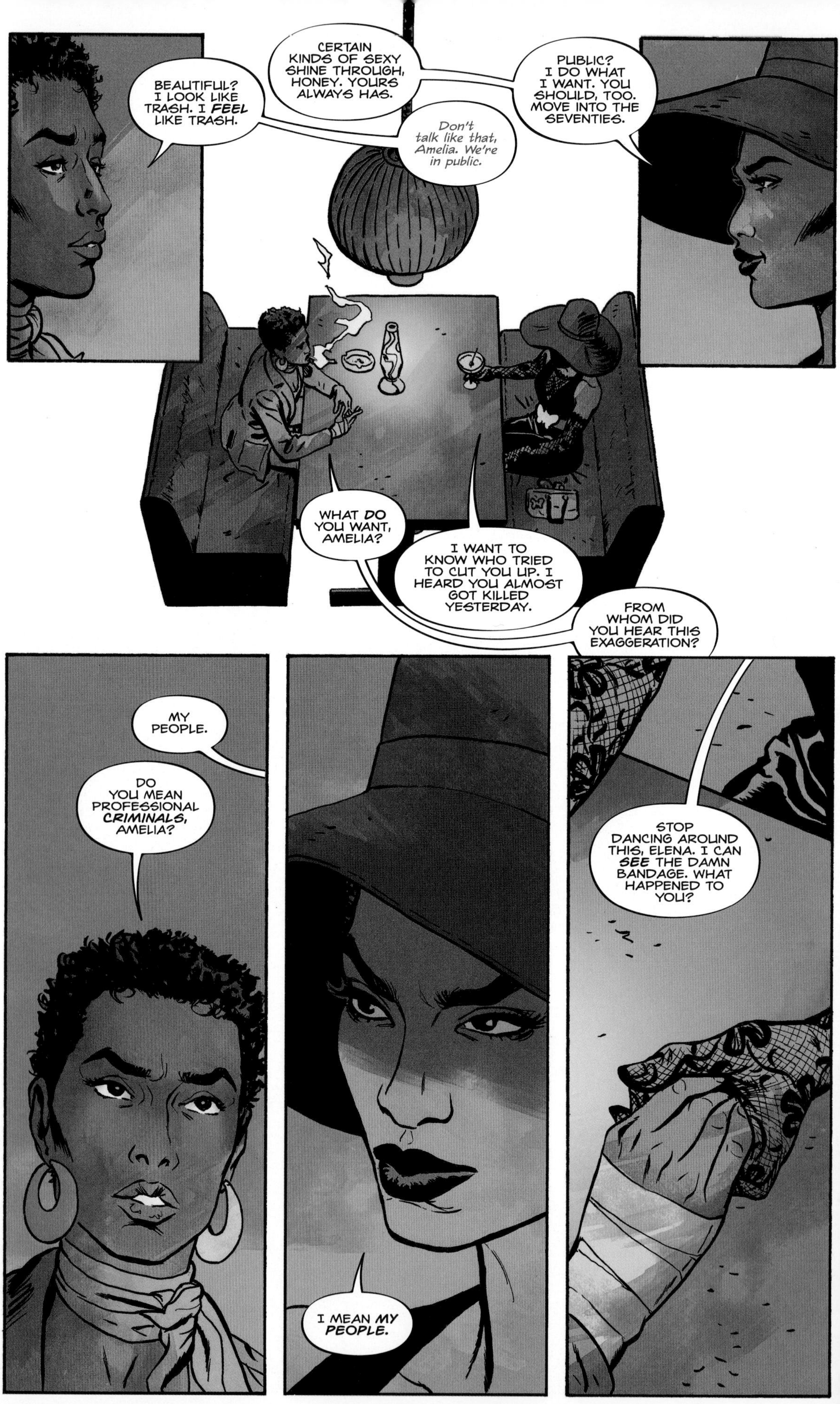
BEAUTIFUL? I LOOK LIKE TRASH. I FEEL LIKE TRASH.
CERTAIN KINDS OF SEXY SHINE THROUGH, HONEY. YOURS ALWAYS HAS.
Don't talk like that, Amelia. We're in public.
PUBLIC? I DO WHAT I WANT. YOU SHOULD, TOO. MOVE INTO THE SEVENTIES.
WHAT DO YOU WANT, AMELIA?
I WANT TO KNOW WHO TRIED TO CUT YOU UP. I HEARD YOU ALMOST GOT KILLED YESTERDAY.
FROM WHOM DID YOU HEAR THIS EXAGGERATION?
MY PEOPLE.
DO YOU MEAN PROFESSIONAL CRIMINALS, AMELIA?
I MEAN MY PEOPLE.
STOP DANCING AROUND THIS, ELENA. I CAN SEE THE DAMN BANDAGE. WHAT HAPPENED TO YOU?

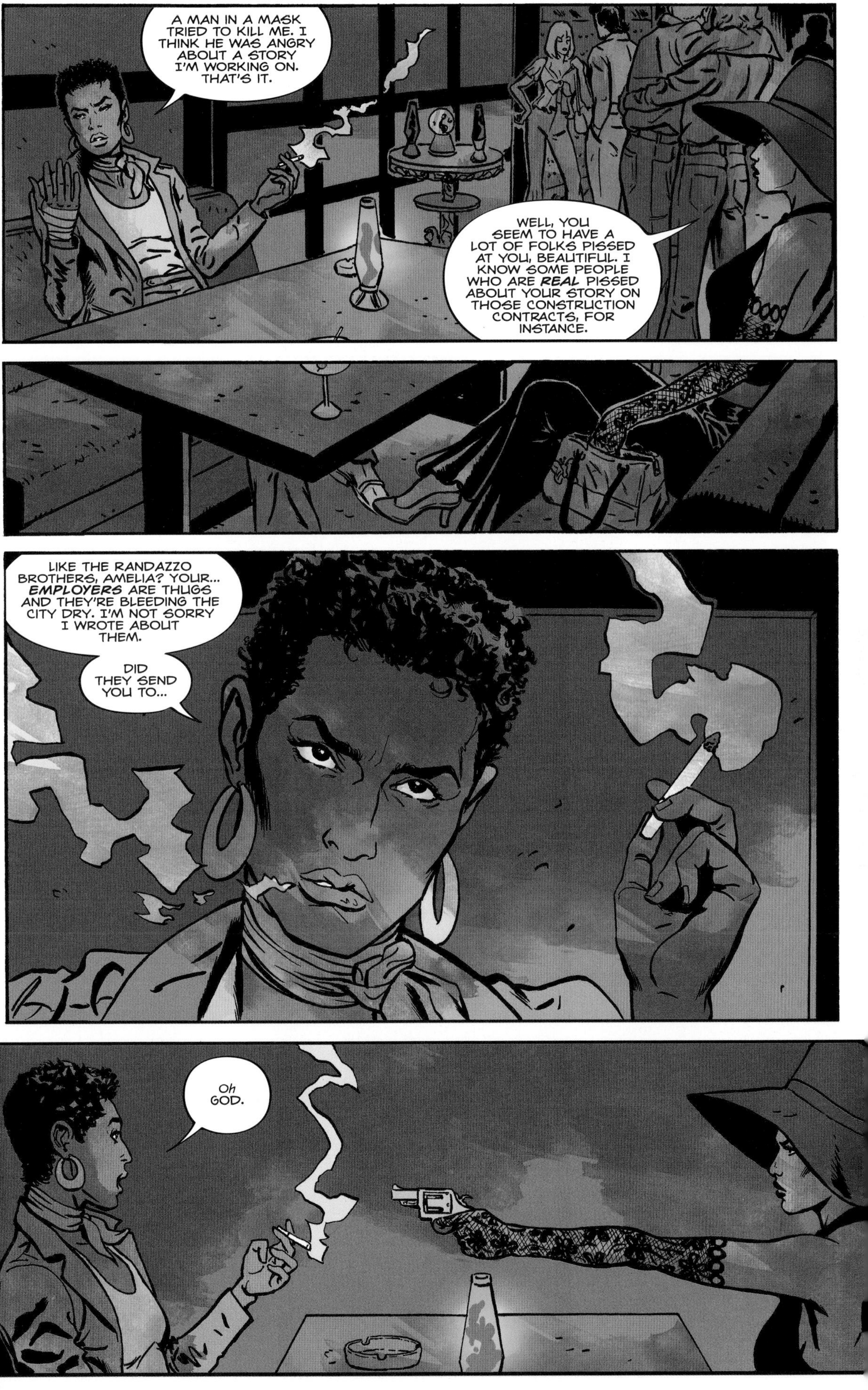
A MAN IN A MASK TRIED TO KILL ME. I THINK HE WAS ANGRY ABOUT A STORY I'M WORKING ON. THAT'S IT.
WELL, YOU SEEM TO HAVE A LOT OF FOLKS PISSED AT YOU, BEAUTIFUL. I KNOW SOME PEOPLE WHO ARE *REAL* PISSED ABOUT YOUR STORY ON THOSE CONSTRUCTION CONTRACTS, FOR INSTANCE.
LIKE THE RANDAZZO BROTHERS, AMELIA? YOUR... *EMPLOYERS* ARE THUGS AND THEY'RE BLEEDING THE CITY DRY. I'M NOT SORRY I WROTE ABOUT THEM.
DID THEY SEND YOU TO...
Oh GOD.

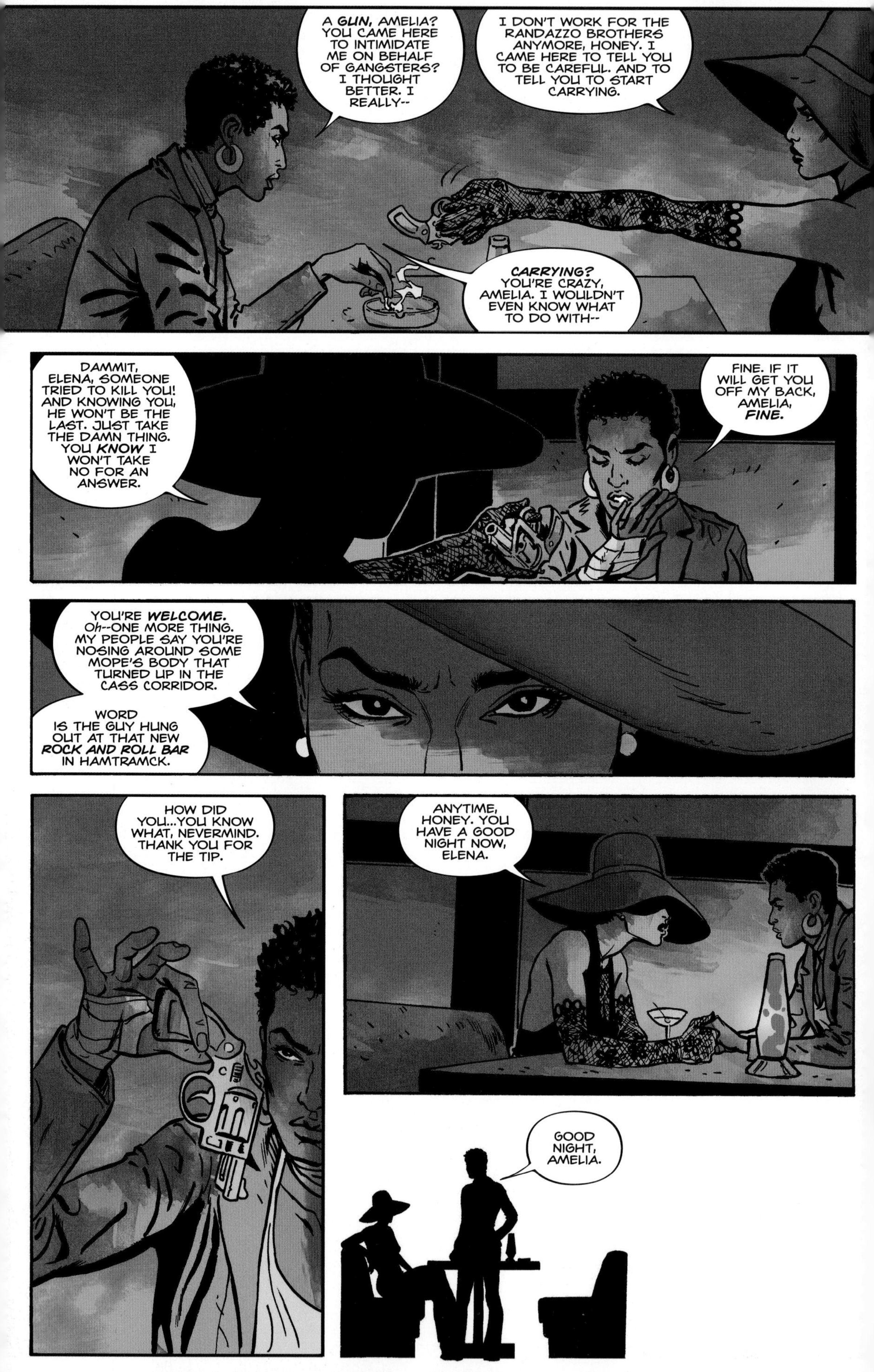
A GUN, AMELIA? YOU CAME HERE TO INTIMIDATE ME ON BEHALF OF GANGSTERS? I THOUGHT BETTER. I REALLY--
I DON'T WORK FOR THE RANDAZZO BROTHERS ANYMORE, HONEY. I CAME HERE TO TELL YOU TO BE CAREFUL. AND TO TELL YOU TO START CARRYING.
CARRYING? YOU'RE CRAZY, AMELIA. I WOULDN'T EVEN KNOW WHAT TO DO WITH--
DAMMIT, ELENA, SOMEONE TRIED TO KILL YOU! AND KNOWING YOU, HE WON'T BE THE LAST. JUST TAKE THE DAMN THING. YOU KNOW I WON'T TAKE NO FOR AN ANSWER.
FINE. IF IT WILL GET YOU OFF MY BACK, AMELIA, FINE.
YOU'RE WELCOME. Oh--ONE MORE THING. MY PEOPLE SAY YOU'RE NOSING AROUND SOME MOPE'S BODY THAT TURNED UP IN THE CASS CORRIDOR.
WORD IS THE GUY HUNG OUT AT THAT NEW ROCK AND ROLL BAR IN HAMTRAMCK.
HOW DID YOU...YOU KNOW WHAT, NEVERMIND. THANK YOU FOR THE TIP.
ANYTIME, HONEY. YOU HAVE A GOOD NIGHT NOW, ELENA.
GOOD NIGHT, AMELIA.

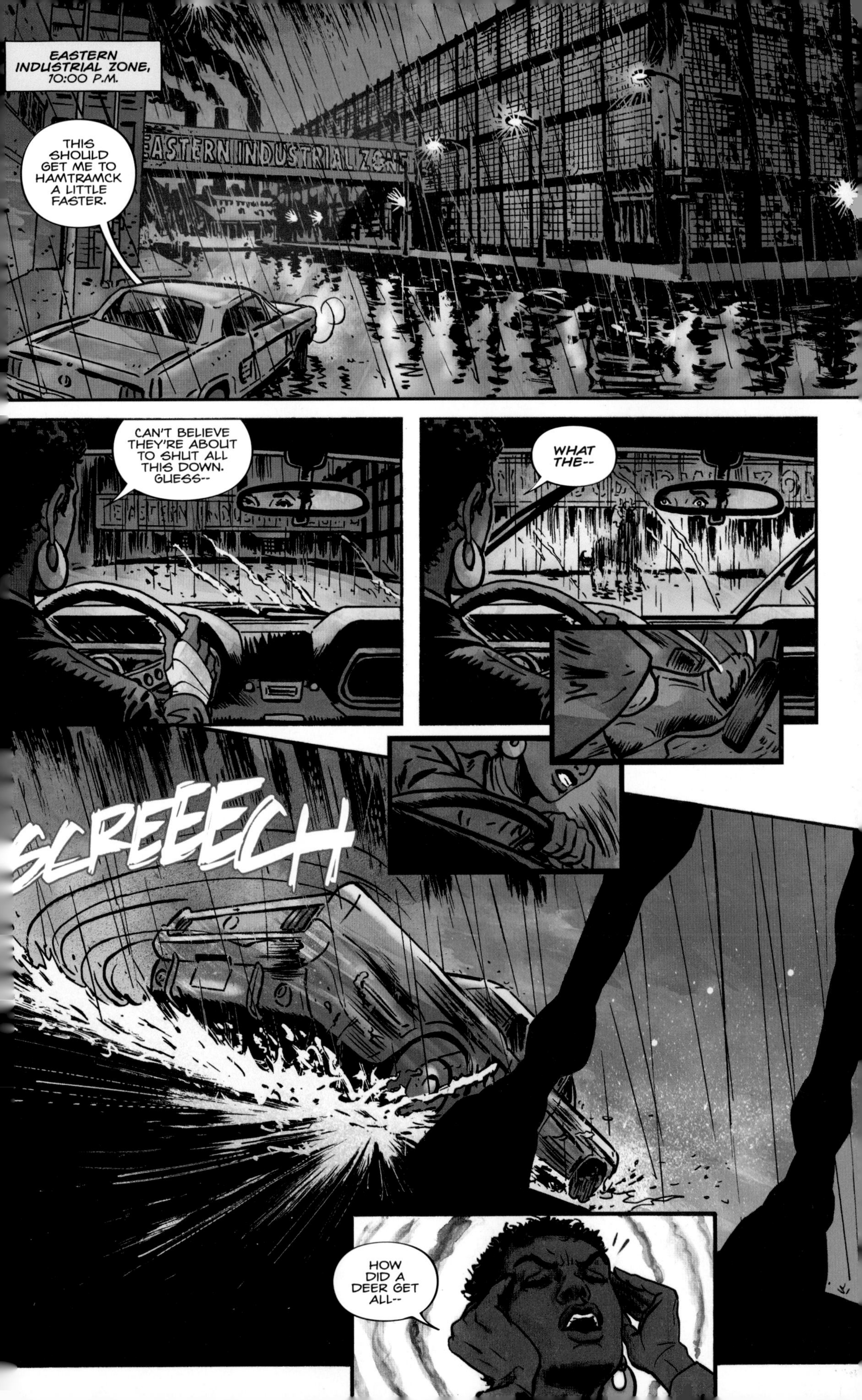
EASTERN INDUSTRIAL ZONE, 10:00 P.M.
EASTERN INDUSTRIAL ZONE
THIS SHOULD GET ME TO HAMTRAMCK A LITTLE FASTER.
CAN'T BELIEVE THEY'RE ABOUT TO SHUT ALL THIS DOWN. GUESS--
WHAT THE--
SCREEECH
HOW DID A DEER GET ALL--

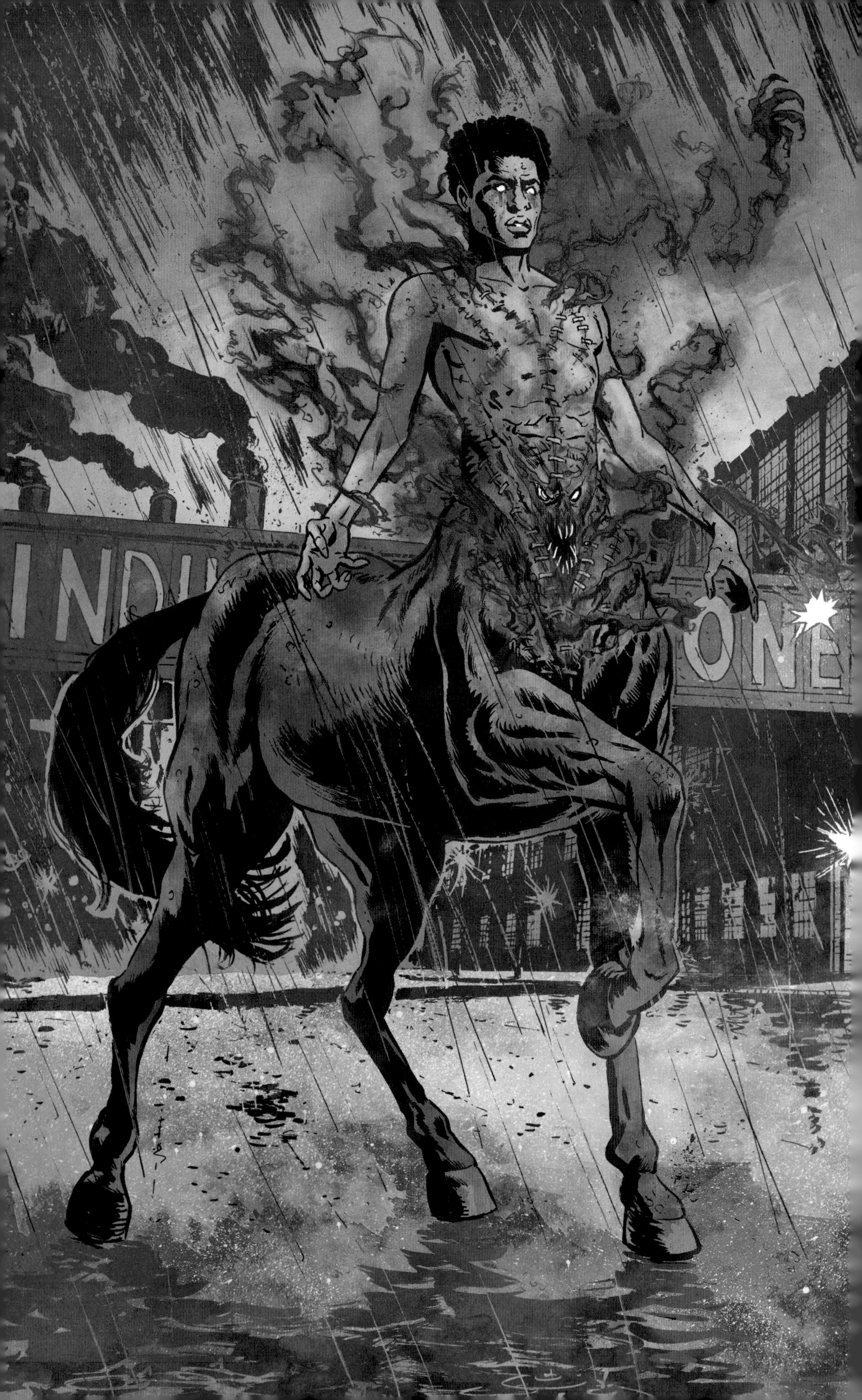
INDU
ONE

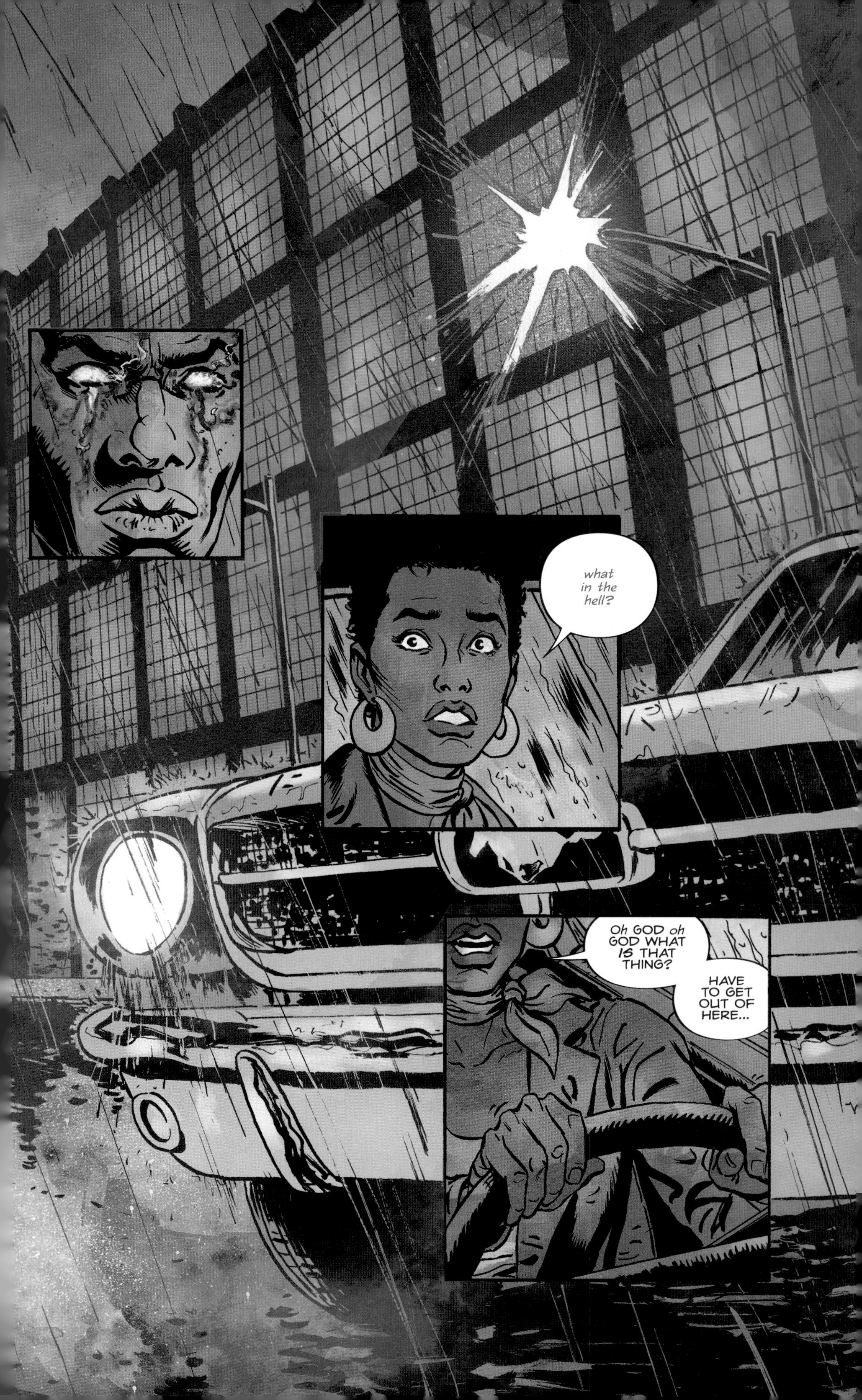
what in the hell?
Oh GOD oh GOD WHAT IS THAT THING?
HAVE TO GET OUT OF HERE...

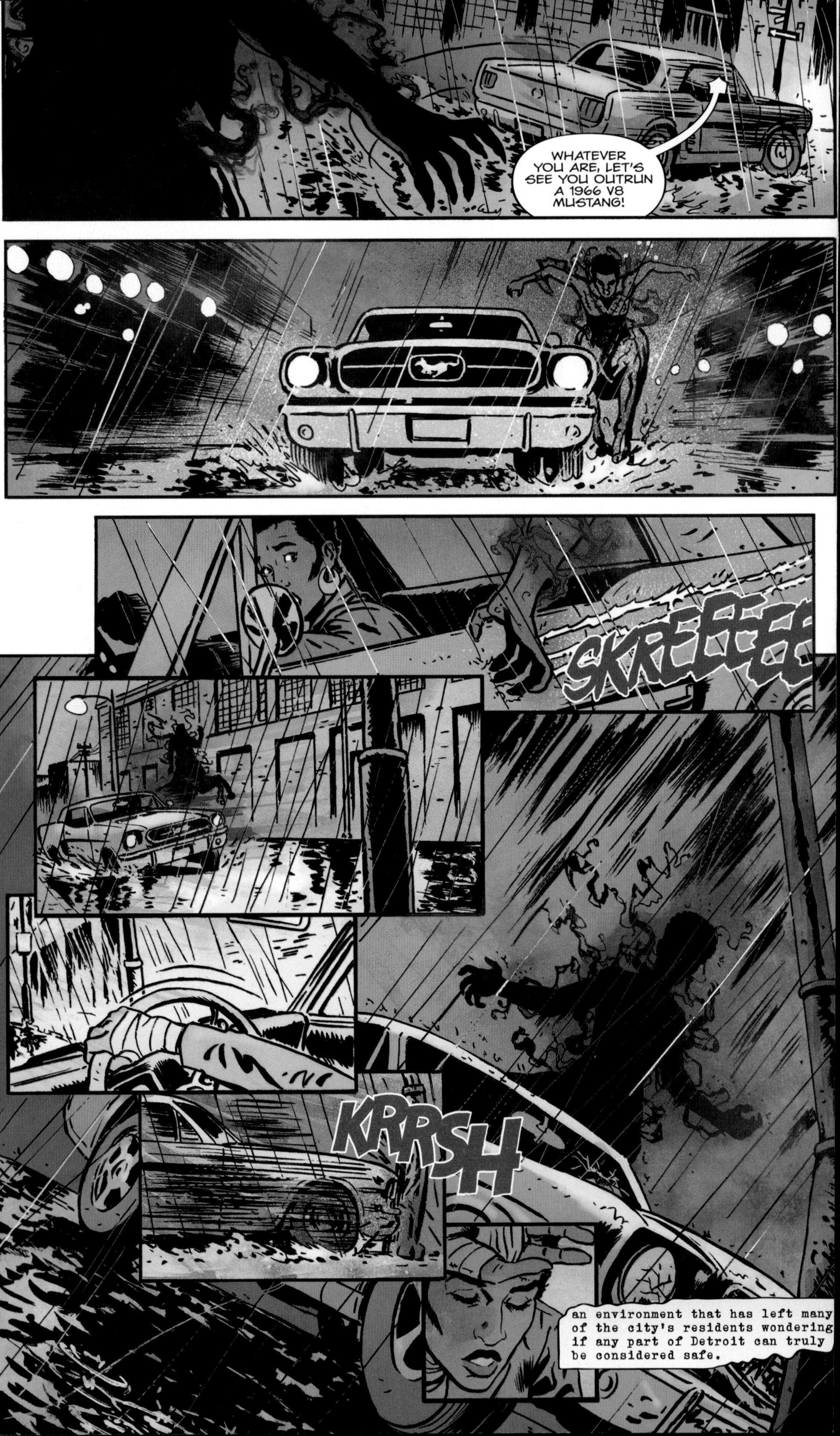
WHATEVER YOU ARE, LET'S SEE YOU OUTRUN A 1966 V8 MUSTANG!
SKREEEEEE
KRRSH
an environment that has left many of the city's residents wondering if any part of Detroit can truly be considered safe.

Issue Two Cover by
Taj Tenfold

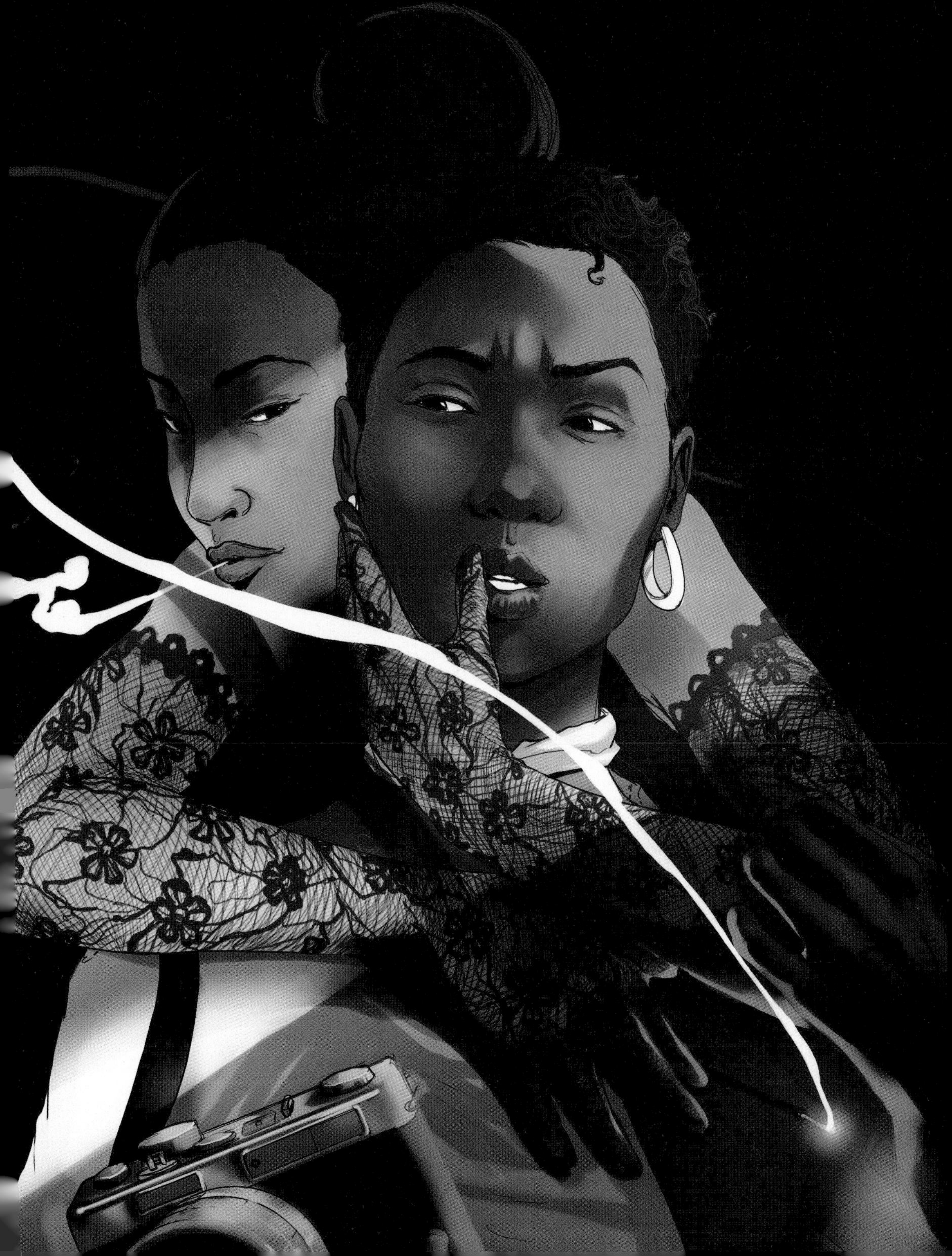

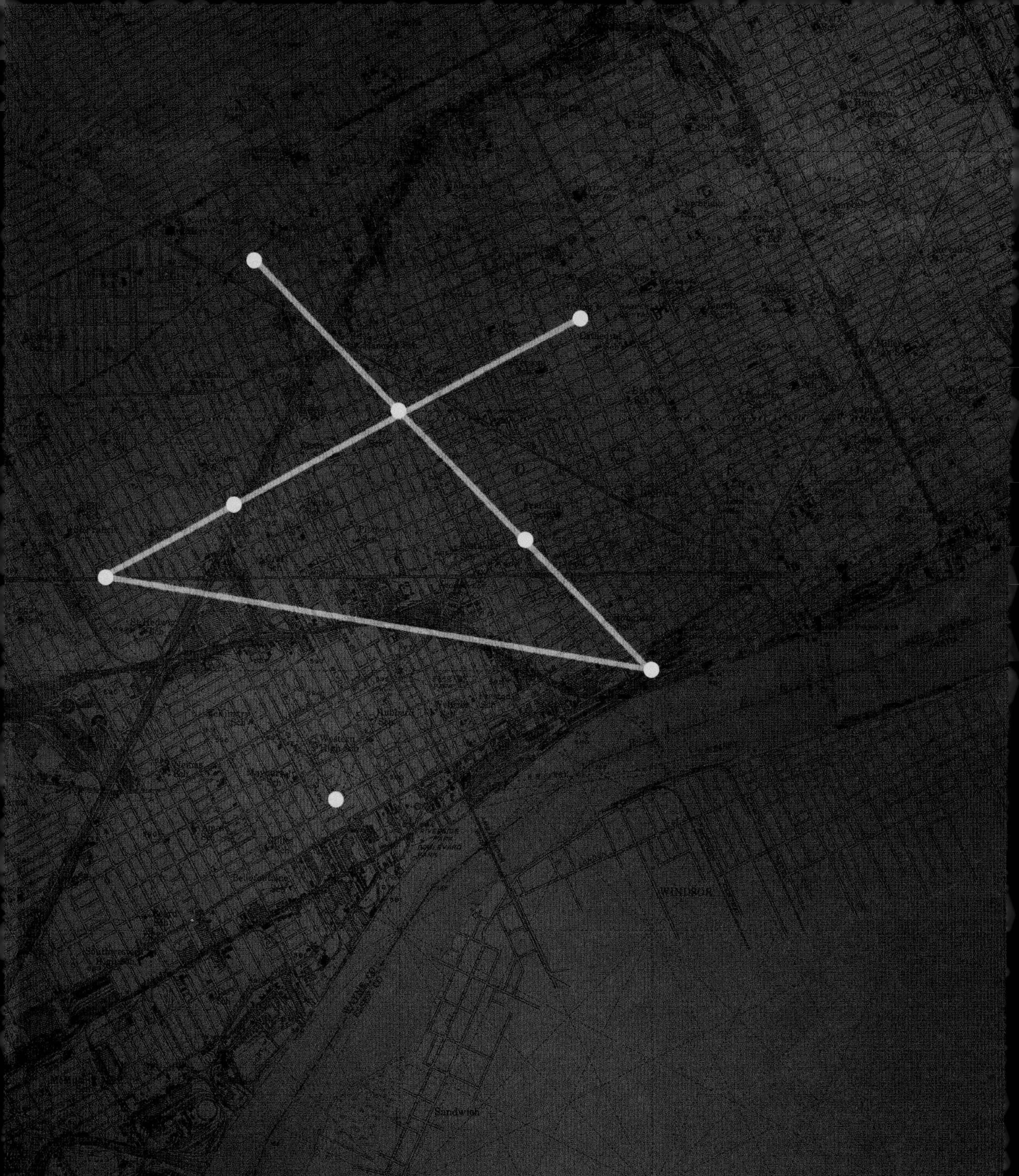
WINDSOR
Sandwich

BALL OF CONFUSION

Chapter Three

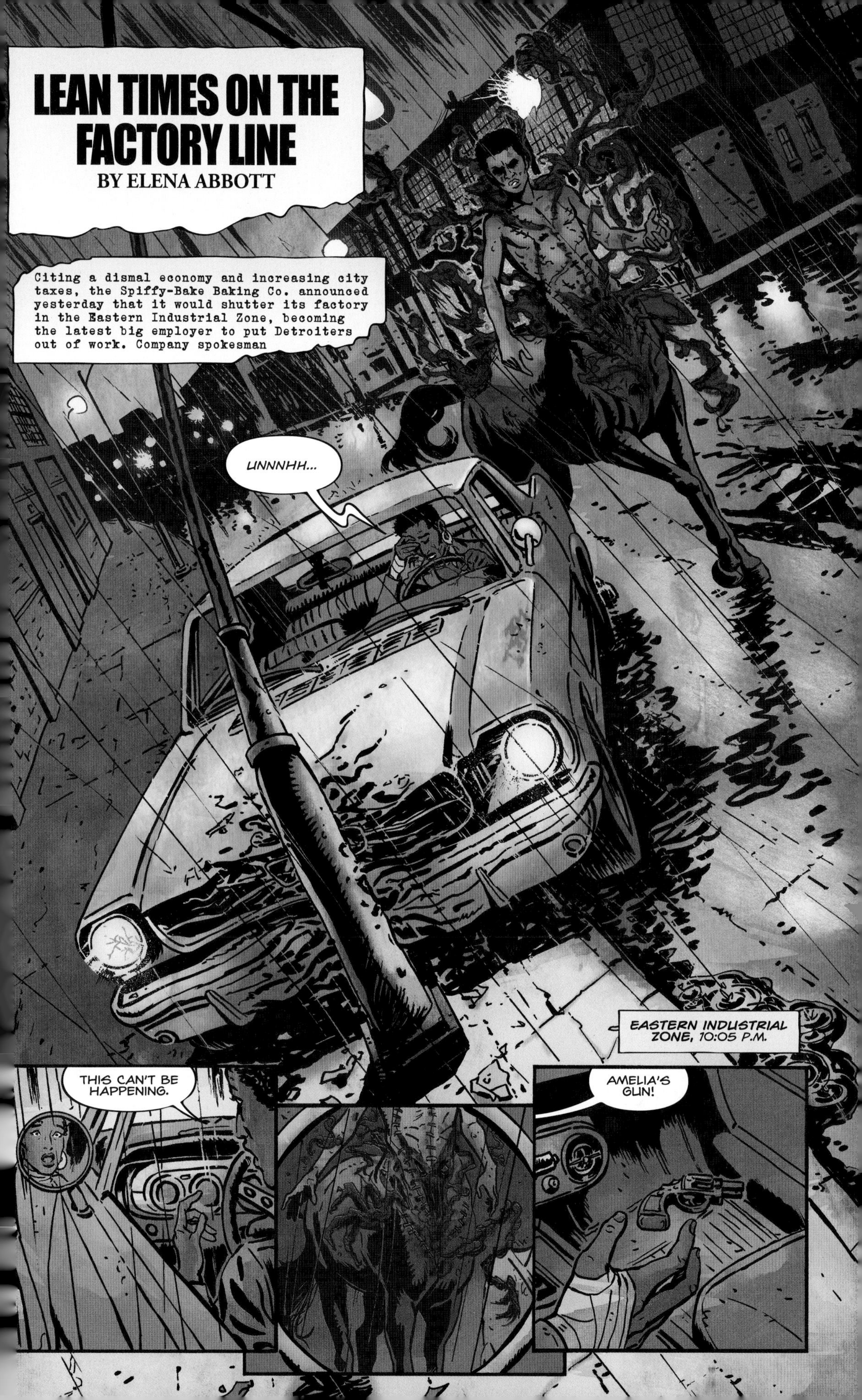
LEAN TIMES ON THE FACTORY LINE
BY ELENA ABBOTT
Citing a dismal economy and increasing city taxes, the Spiffy-Bake Baking Co. announced yesterday that it would shutter its factory in the Eastern Industrial Zone, becoming the latest big employer to put Detroiters out of work. Company spokesman
UNNNHH...
EASTERN INDUSTRIAL ZONE, 10:05 P.M.
THIS CAN'T BE HAPPENING.
AMELIA'S GUN!

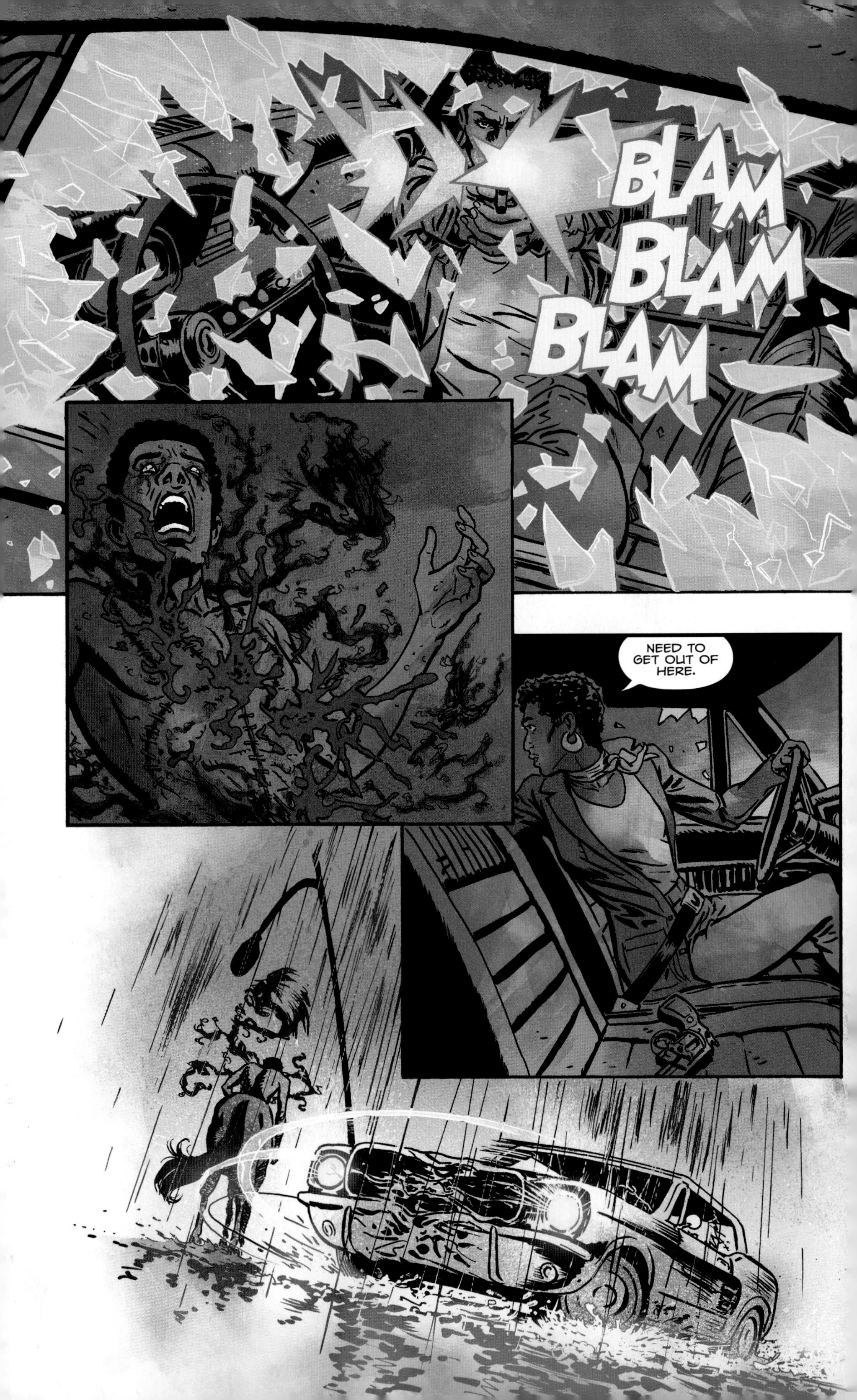
BLAM
BLAM
BLAM
NEED TO GET OUT OF HERE.

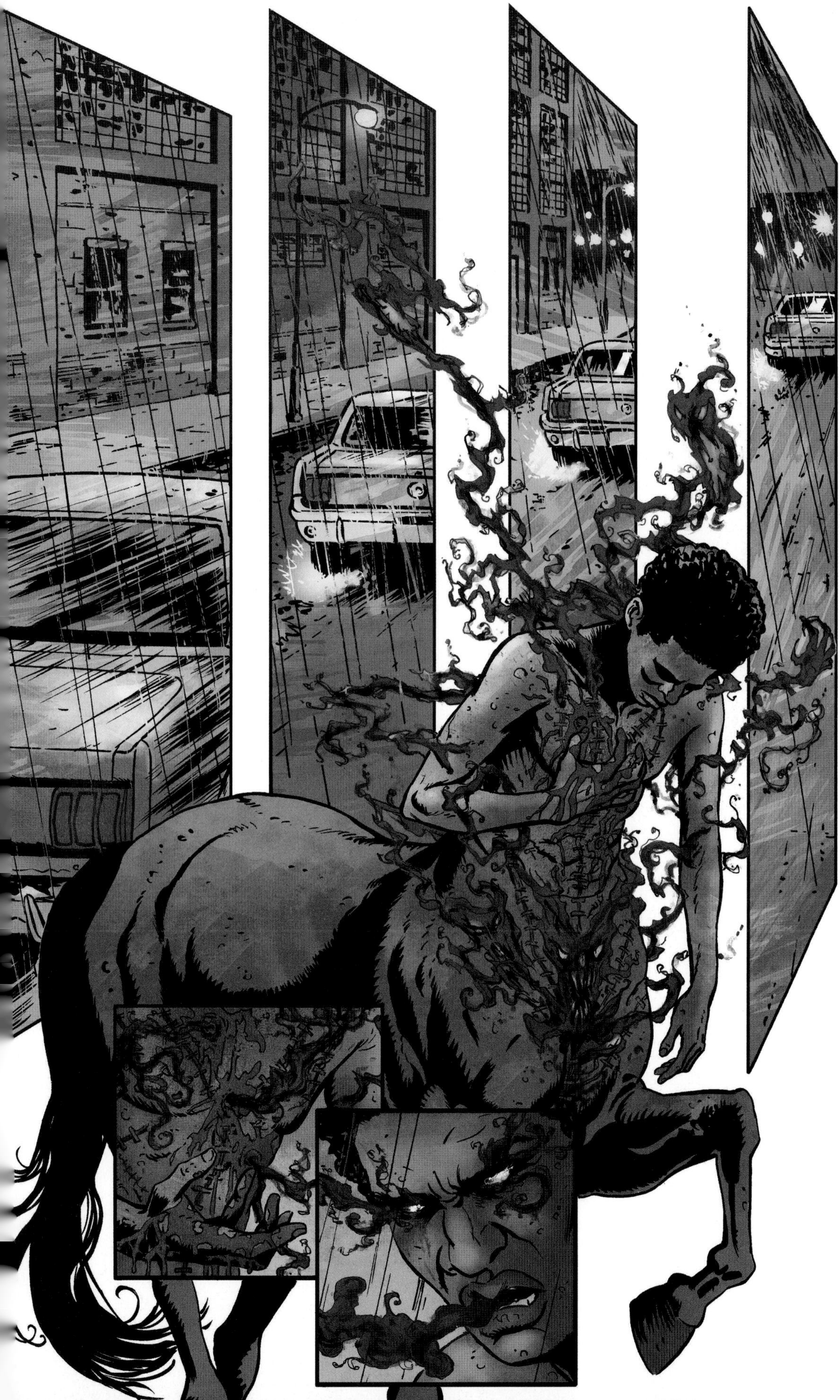

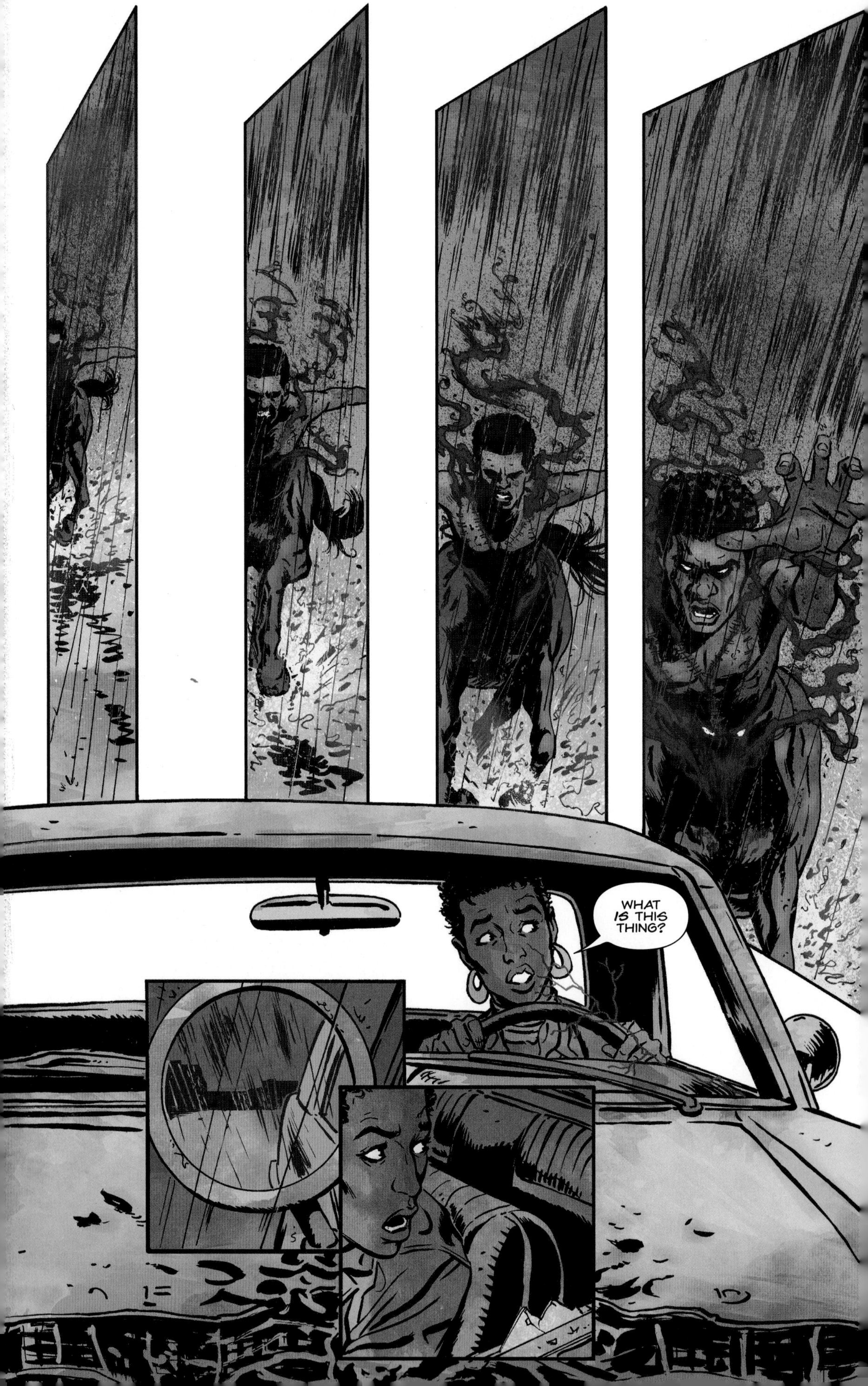
WHAT IS THIS THING?

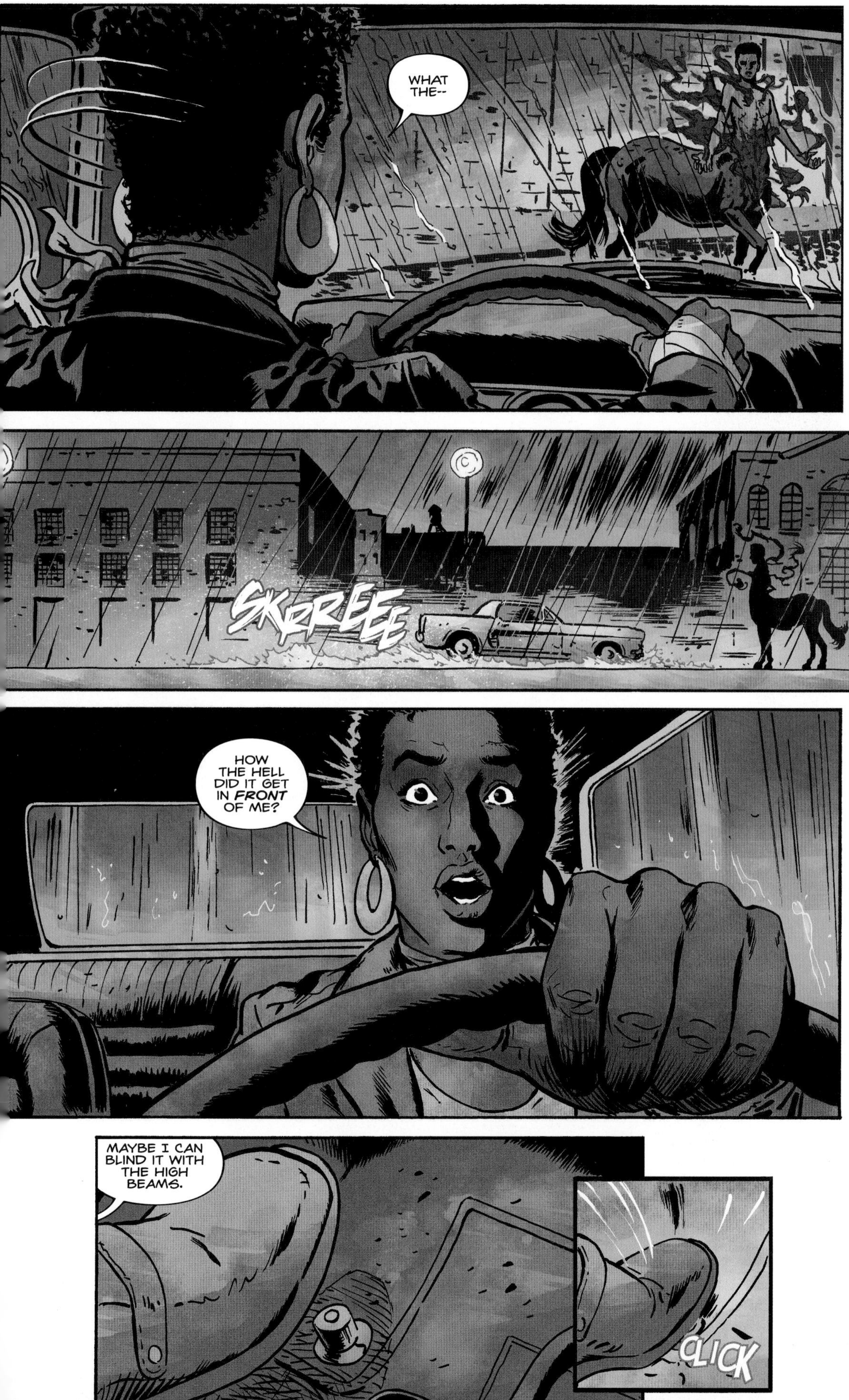
WHAT THE--
SKRREEEE
HOW THE HELL DID IT GET IN *FRONT* OF ME?
MAYBE I CAN BLIND IT WITH THE HIGH BEAMS.
CLICK

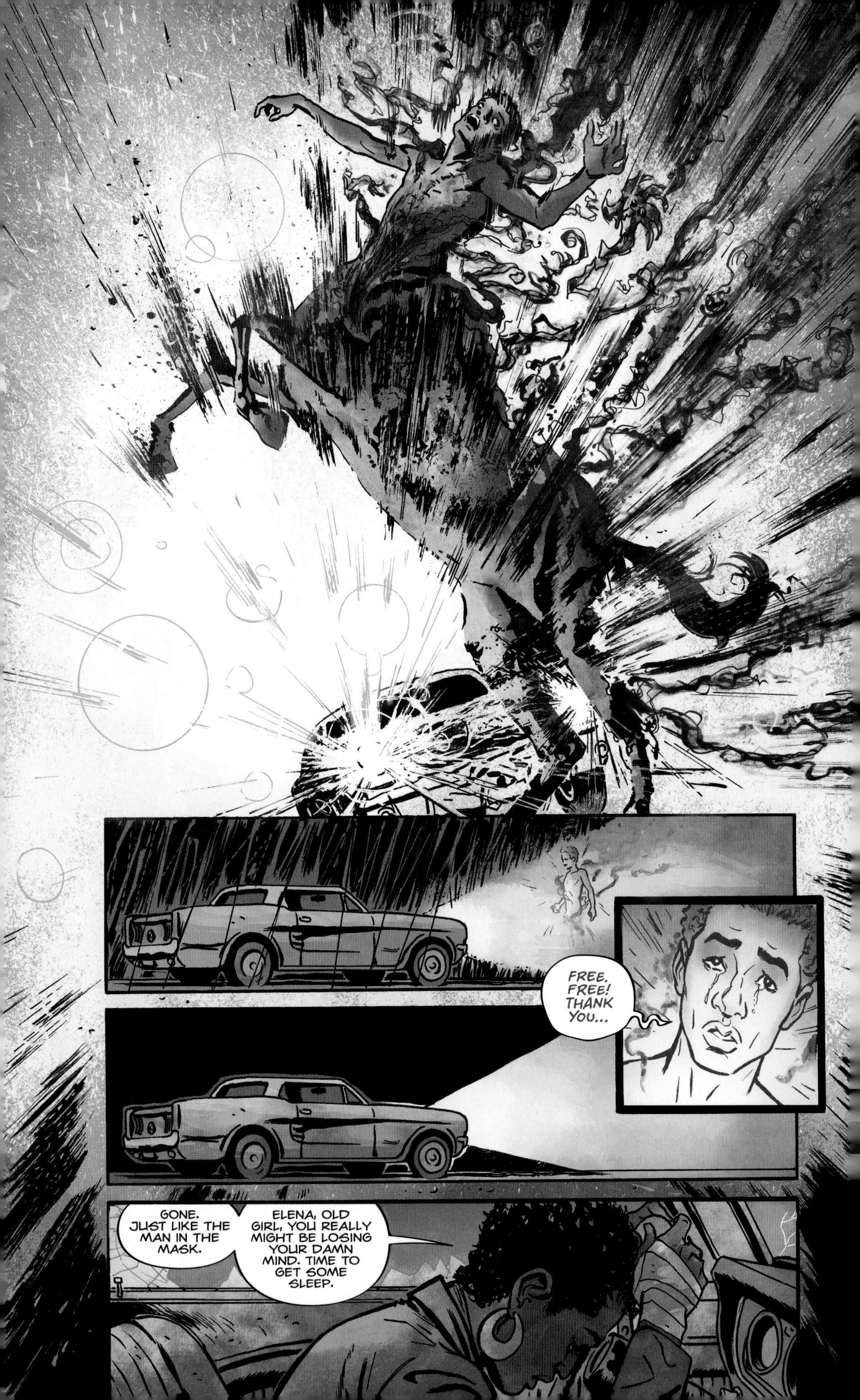

FREE, FREE! THANK YOU...
GONE. JUST LIKE THE MAN IN THE MASK.
ELENA, OLD GIRL, YOU REALLY MIGHT BE LOSING YOUR DAMN MIND. TIME TO GET SOME SLEEP.

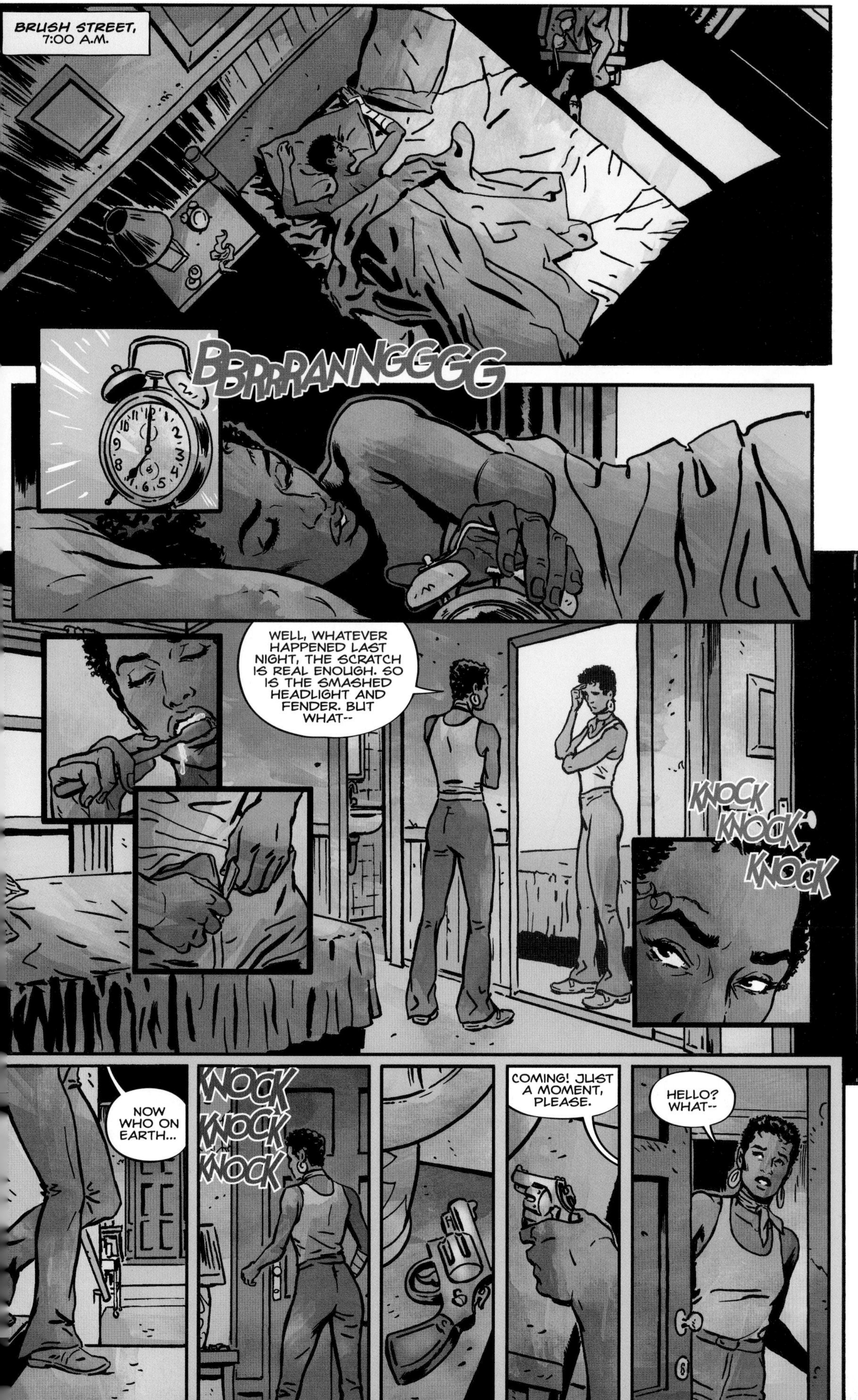
BRUSH STREET, 7:00 A.M.
BBRRRANNGGGG
WELL, WHATEVER HAPPENED LAST NIGHT, THE SCRATCH IS REAL ENOUGH. SO IS THE SMASHED HEADLIGHT AND FENDER. BUT WHAT--
KNOCK KNOCK KNOCK
NOW WHO ON EARTH...
KNOCK KNOCK KNOCK
COMING! JUST A MOMENT, PLEASE.
HELLO? WHAT--

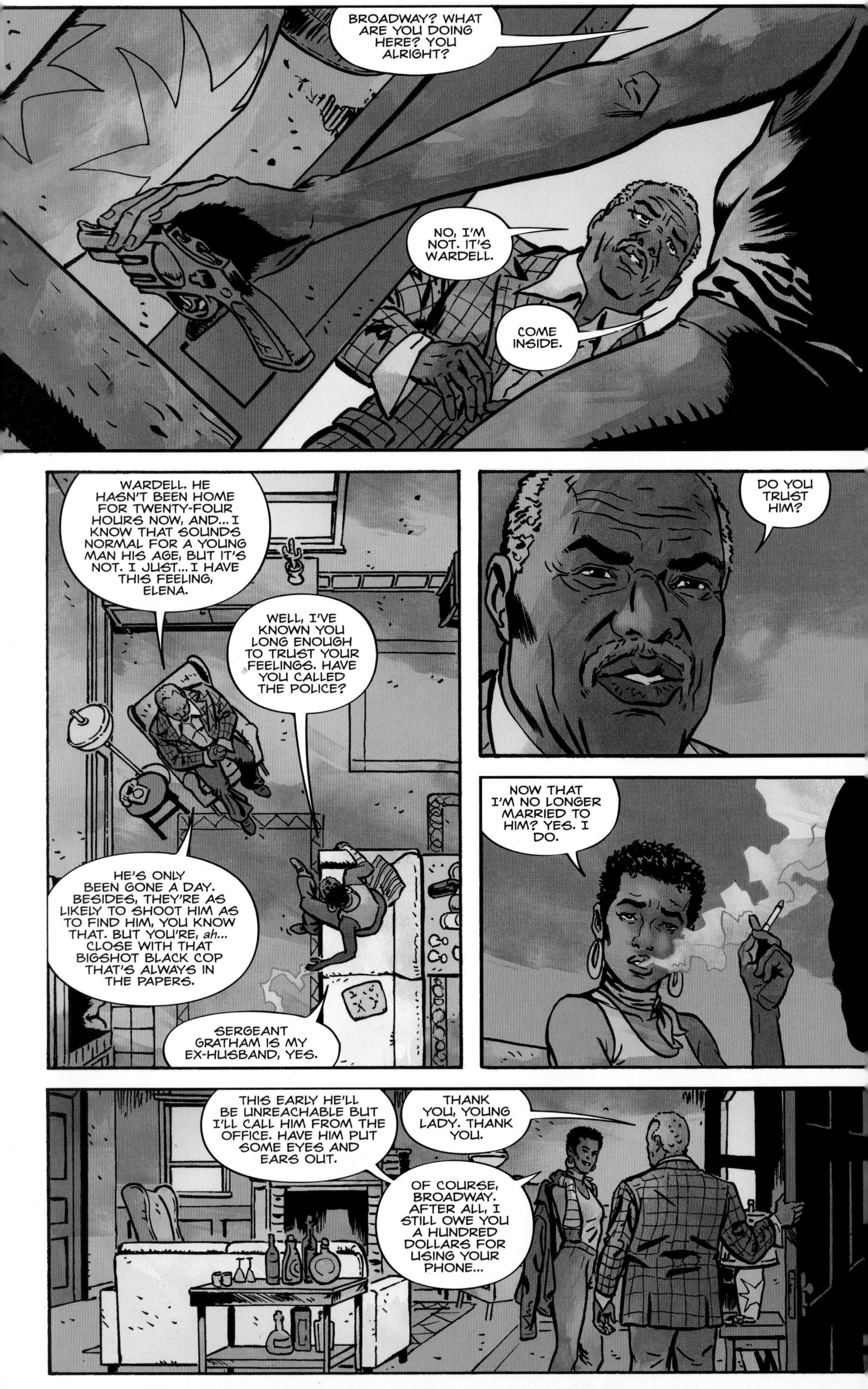
BROADWAY? WHAT ARE YOU DOING HERE? YOU ALRIGHT?
NO, I'M NOT. IT'S WARDELL.
COME INSIDE.
WARDELL. HE HASN'T BEEN HOME FOR TWENTY-FOUR HOURS NOW, AND... I KNOW THAT SOUNDS NORMAL FOR A YOUNG MAN HIS AGE, BUT IT'S NOT. I JUST... I HAVE THIS FEELING, ELENA.
WELL, I'VE KNOWN YOU LONG ENOUGH TO TRUST YOUR FEELINGS. HAVE YOU CALLED THE POLICE?
HE'S ONLY BEEN GONE A DAY. BESIDES, THEY'RE AS LIKELY TO SHOOT HIM AS TO FIND HIM, YOU KNOW THAT. BUT YOU'RE, *ah*... CLOSE WITH THAT BIGSHOT BLACK COP THAT'S ALWAYS IN THE PAPERS.
SERGEANT GRATHAM IS MY EX-HUSBAND, YES.
DO YOU TRUST HIM?
NOW THAT I'M NO LONGER MARRIED TO HIM? YES. I DO.
THIS EARLY HE'LL BE UNREACHABLE BUT I'LL CALL HIM FROM THE OFFICE. HAVE HIM PUT SOME EYES AND EARS OUT.
THANK YOU, YOUNG LADY. THANK YOU.
OF COURSE, BROADWAY. AFTER ALL, I STILL OWE YOU A HUNDRED DOLLARS FOR USING YOUR PHONE...

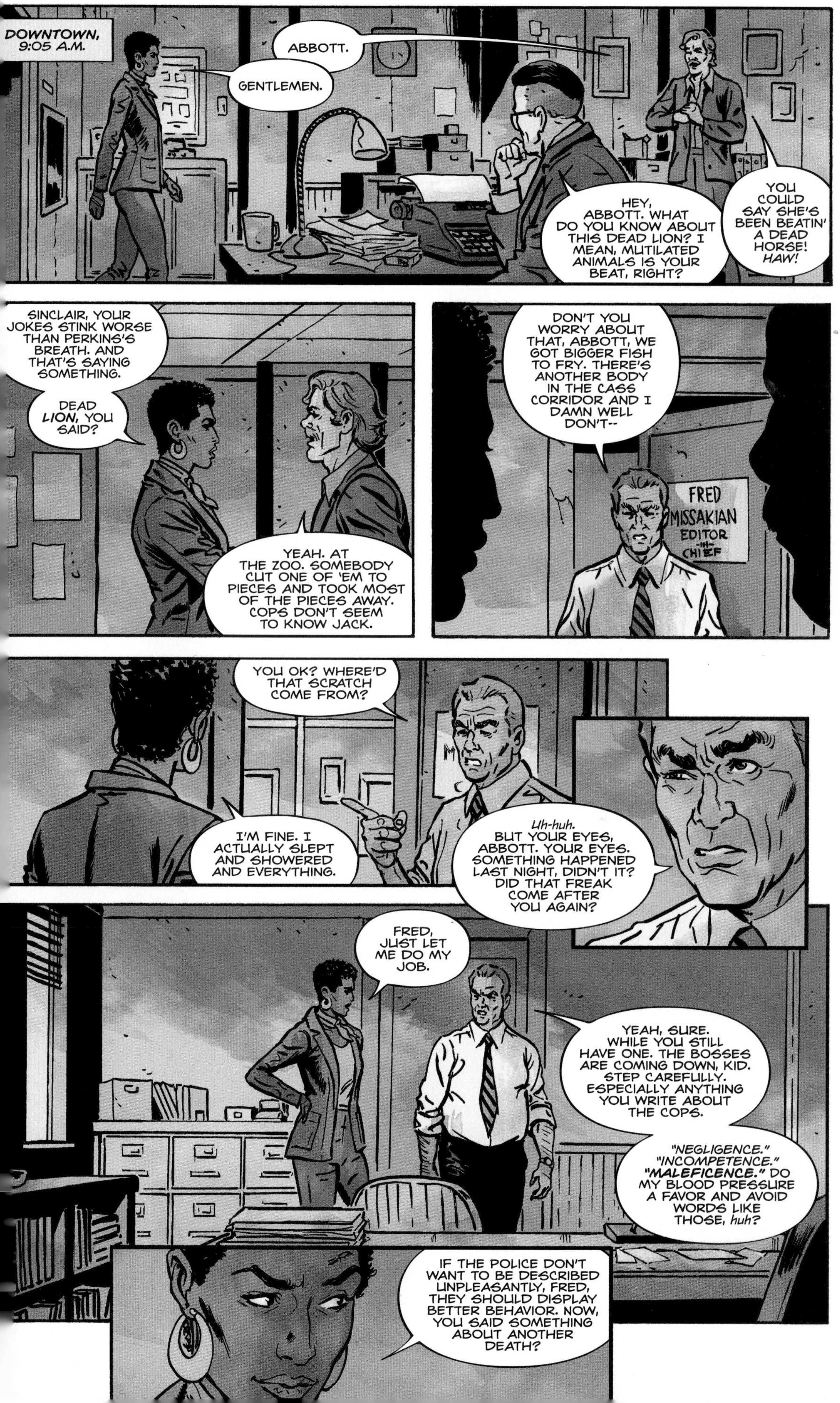
DOWNTOWN, 9:05 A.M.
ABBOTT.
GENTLEMEN.
HEY, ABBOTT. WHAT DO YOU KNOW ABOUT THIS DEAD LION? I MEAN, MUTILATED ANIMALS IS YOUR BEAT, RIGHT?
YOU COULD SAY SHE'S BEEN BEATIN' A DEAD HORSE! HAW!
SINCLAIR, YOUR JOKES STINK WORSE THAN PERKINS'S BREATH. AND THAT'S SAYING SOMETHING.
DEAD LION, YOU SAID?
YEAH. AT THE ZOO. SOMEBODY CUT ONE OF 'EM TO PIECES AND TOOK MOST OF THE PIECES AWAY. COPS DON'T SEEM TO KNOW JACK.
DON'T YOU WORRY ABOUT THAT, ABBOTT, WE GOT BIGGER FISH TO FRY. THERE'S ANOTHER BODY IN THE CASS CORRIDOR AND I DAMN WELL DON'T--
FRED MISSAKIAN EDITOR -IN- CHIEF
YOU OK? WHERE'D THAT SCRATCH COME FROM?
I'M FINE. I ACTUALLY SLEPT AND SHOWERED AND EVERYTHING.
Uh-huh. BUT YOUR EYES, ABBOTT. YOUR EYES. SOMETHING HAPPENED LAST NIGHT, DIDN'T IT? DID THAT FREAK COME AFTER YOU AGAIN?
FRED, JUST LET ME DO MY JOB.
YEAH, SURE. WHILE YOU STILL HAVE ONE. THE BOSSES ARE COMING DOWN, KID. STEP CAREFULLY. ESPECIALLY ANYTHING YOU WRITE ABOUT THE COPS.
"NEGLIGENCE." "INCOMPETENCE." "MALEFICENCE." DO MY BLOOD PRESSURE A FAVOR AND AVOID WORDS LIKE THOSE, huh?
IF THE POLICE DON'T WANT TO BE DESCRIBED UNPLEASANTLY, FRED, THEY SHOULD DISPLAY BETTER BEHAVIOR. NOW, YOU SAID SOMETHING ABOUT ANOTHER DEATH?

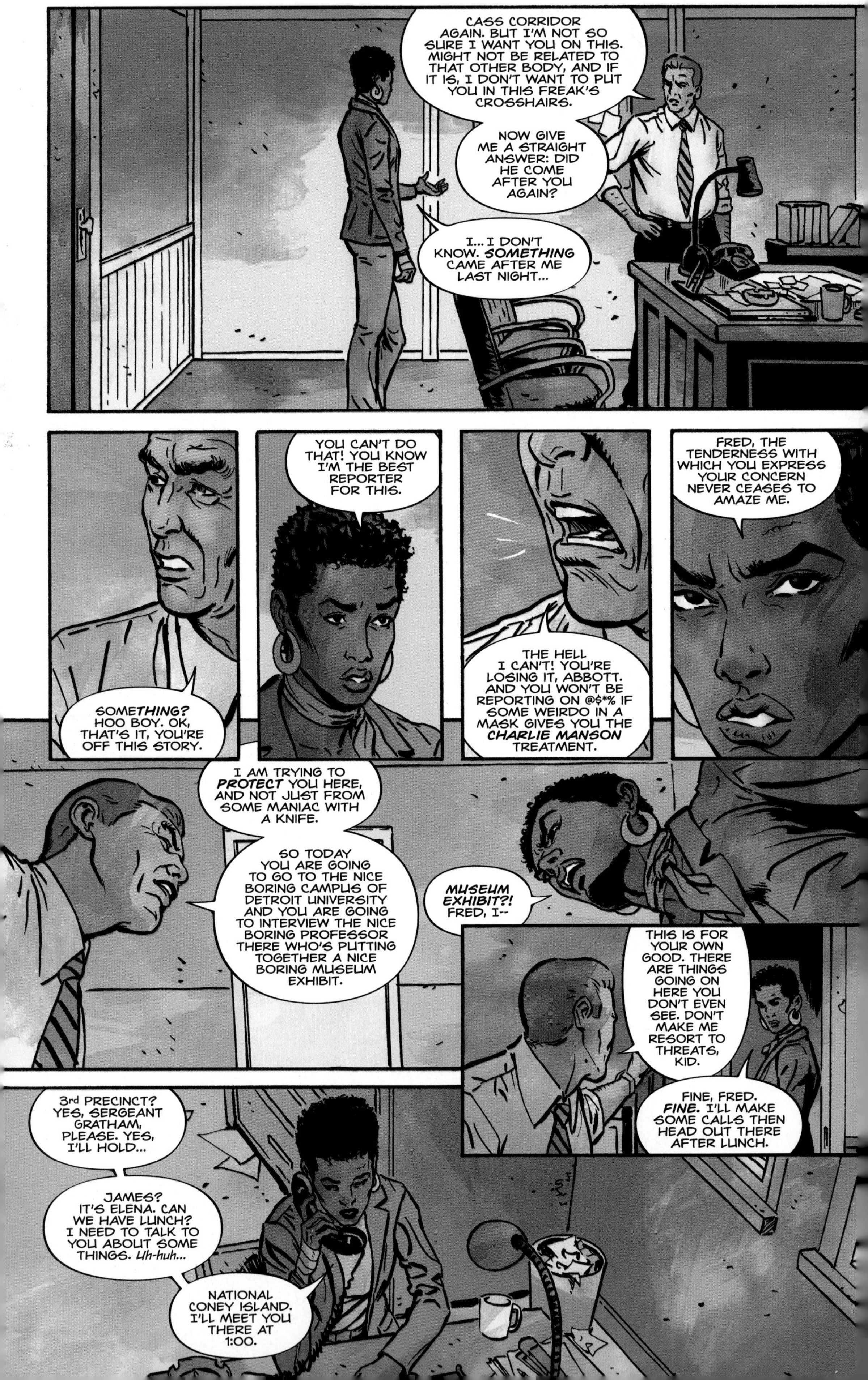
CASS CORRIDOR AGAIN. BUT I'M NOT SO SURE I WANT YOU ON THIS. MIGHT NOT BE RELATED TO THAT OTHER BODY, AND IF IT IS, I DON'T WANT TO PUT YOU IN THIS FREAK'S CROSSHAIRS.
NOW GIVE ME A STRAIGHT ANSWER: DID HE COME AFTER YOU AGAIN?
I... I DON'T KNOW. *SOMETHING* CAME AFTER ME LAST NIGHT...
SOME*THING*? HOO BOY. OK, THAT'S IT, YOU'RE OFF THIS STORY.
YOU CAN'T DO THAT! YOU KNOW I'M THE BEST REPORTER FOR THIS.
THE HELL I CAN'T! YOU'RE LOSING IT, ABBOTT. AND YOU WON'T BE REPORTING ON @$*% IF SOME WEIRDO IN A MASK GIVES YOU THE *CHARLIE MANSON* TREATMENT.
FRED, THE TENDERNESS WITH WHICH YOU EXPRESS YOUR CONCERN NEVER CEASES TO AMAZE ME.
I AM TRYING TO *PROTECT* YOU HERE, AND NOT JUST FROM SOME MANIAC WITH A KNIFE.
SO TODAY YOU ARE GOING TO GO TO THE NICE BORING CAMPUS OF DETROIT UNIVERSITY AND YOU ARE GOING TO INTERVIEW THE NICE BORING PROFESSOR THERE WHO'S PUTTING TOGETHER A NICE BORING MUSEUM EXHIBIT.
MUSEUM EXHIBIT?! FRED, I--
THIS IS FOR YOUR OWN GOOD. THERE ARE THINGS GOING ON HERE YOU DON'T EVEN SEE. DON'T MAKE ME RESORT TO THREATS, KID.
FINE, FRED. *FINE.* I'LL MAKE SOME CALLS THEN HEAD OUT THERE AFTER LUNCH.
3rd PRECINCT? YES, SERGEANT GRATHAM, PLEASE. YES, I'LL HOLD...
JAMES? IT'S ELENA. CAN WE HAVE LUNCH? I NEED TO TALK TO YOU ABOUT SOME THINGS. *Uh-huh...*
NATIONAL CONEY ISLAND. I'LL MEET YOU THERE AT 1:00.

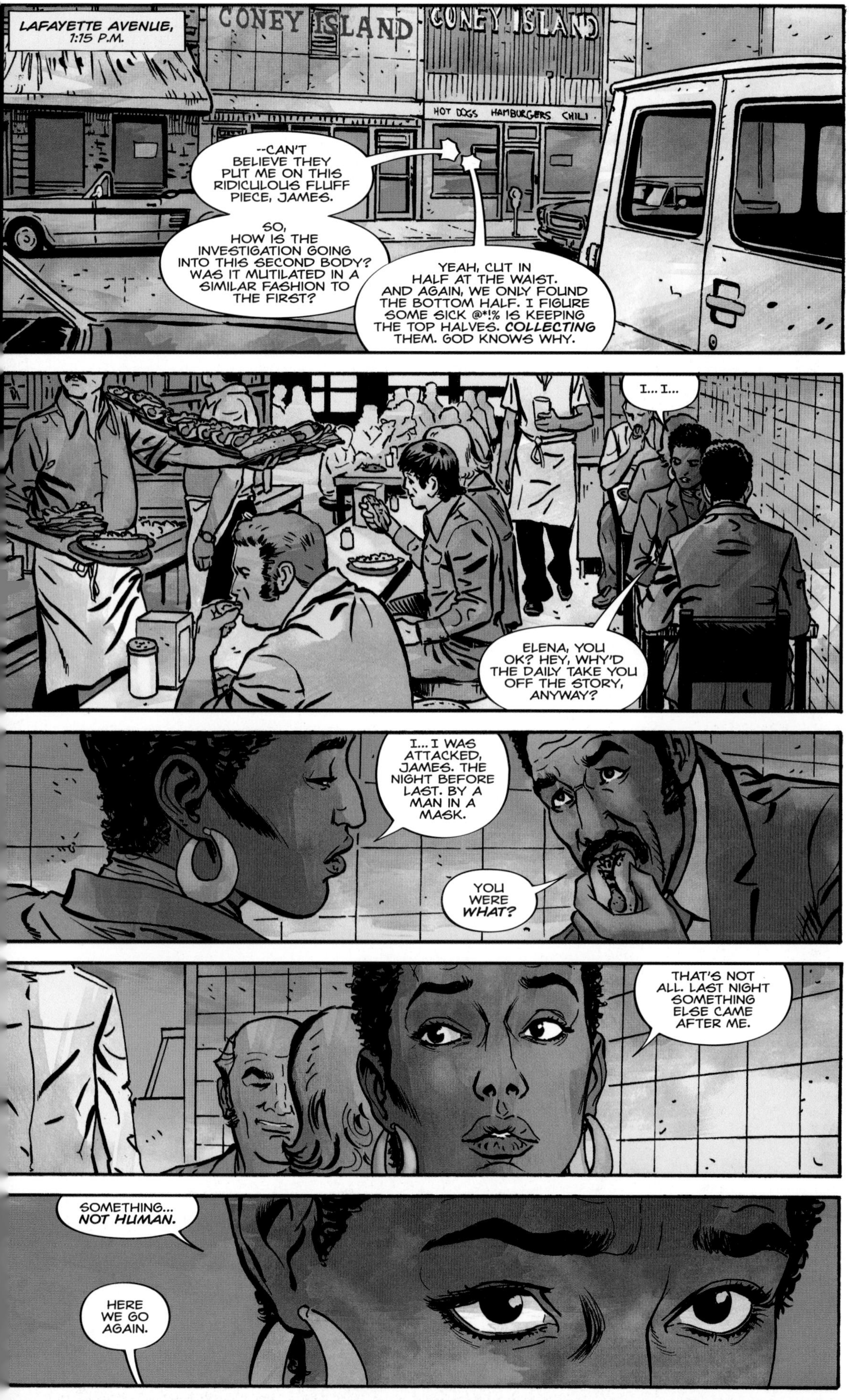
LAFAYETTE AVENUE, 7:15 P.M.
CONEY ISLAND
CONEY ISLAND
HOT DOGS HAMBURGERS CHILI
--CAN'T BELIEVE THEY PUT ME ON THIS RIDICULOUS FLUFF PIECE, JAMES.
SO, HOW IS THE INVESTIGATION GOING INTO THIS SECOND BODY? WAS IT MUTILATED IN A SIMILAR FASHION TO THE FIRST?
YEAH, CUT IN HALF AT THE WAIST. AND AGAIN, WE ONLY FOUND THE BOTTOM HALF. I FIGURE SOME SICK @*!% IS KEEPING THE TOP HALVES. *COLLECTING* THEM. GOD KNOWS WHY.
I... I...
ELENA, YOU OK? HEY, WHY'D THE DAILY TAKE YOU OFF THE STORY, ANYWAY?
I... I WAS ATTACKED, JAMES. THE NIGHT BEFORE LAST. BY A MAN IN A MASK.
YOU WERE *WHAT?*
THAT'S NOT ALL. LAST NIGHT SOMETHING ELSE CAME AFTER ME.
SOMETHING... *NOT HUMAN.*
HERE WE GO AGAIN.

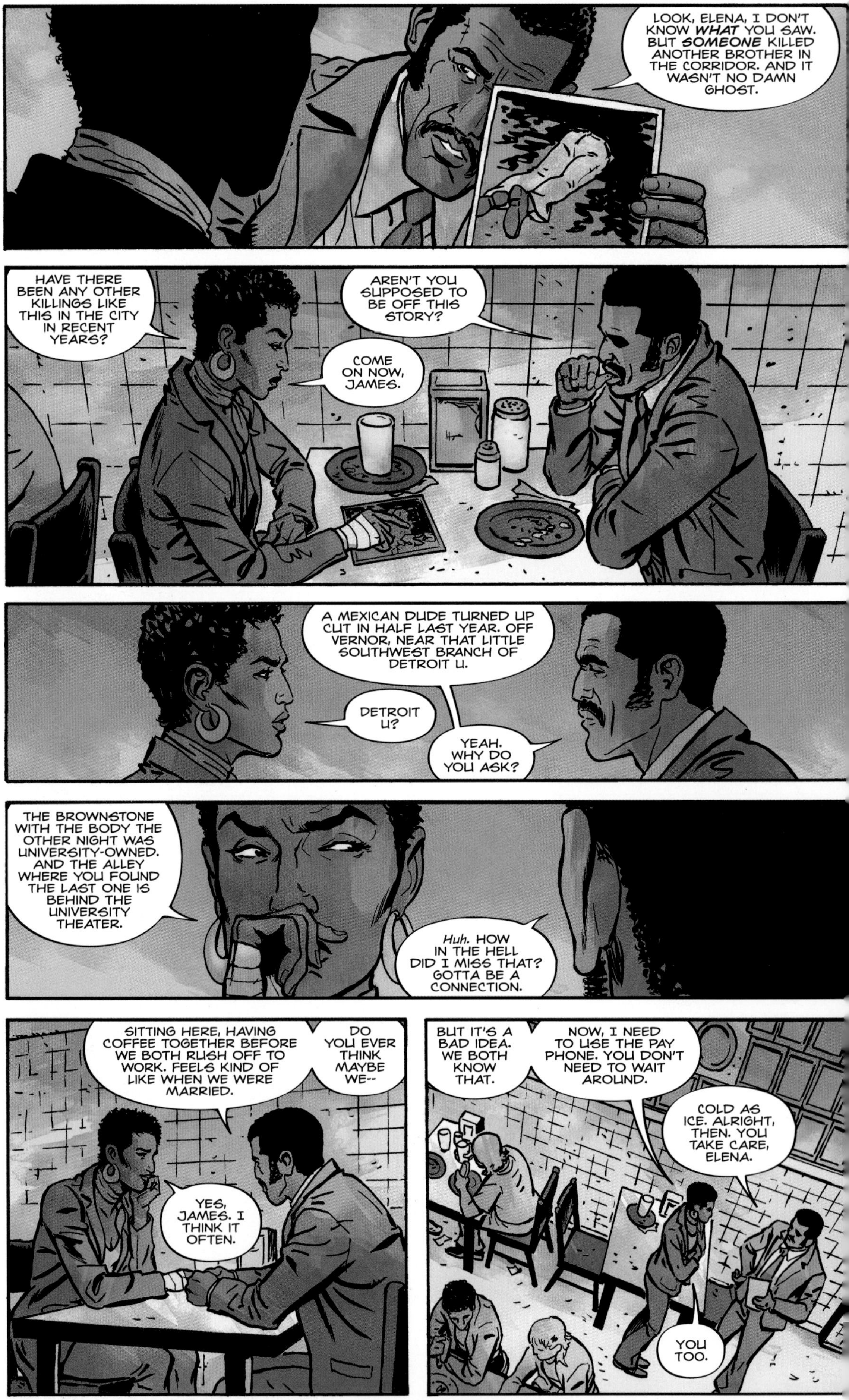
LOOK, ELENA, I DON'T KNOW *WHAT* YOU SAW. BUT *SOMEONE* KILLED ANOTHER BROTHER IN THE CORRIDOR. AND IT WASN'T NO DAMN GHOST.
HAVE THERE BEEN ANY OTHER KILLINGS LIKE THIS IN THE CITY IN RECENT YEARS?
AREN'T YOU SUPPOSED TO BE OFF THIS STORY?
COME ON NOW, JAMES.
A MEXICAN DUDE TURNED UP CUT IN HALF LAST YEAR. OFF VERNOR, NEAR THAT LITTLE SOUTHWEST BRANCH OF DETROIT U.
DETROIT U?
YEAH. WHY DO YOU ASK?
THE BROWNSTONE WITH THE BODY THE OTHER NIGHT WAS UNIVERSITY-OWNED. AND THE ALLEY WHERE YOU FOUND THE LAST ONE IS BEHIND THE UNIVERSITY THEATER.
Huh. HOW IN THE HELL DID I MISS THAT? GOTTA BE A CONNECTION.
SITTING HERE, HAVING COFFEE TOGETHER BEFORE WE BOTH RUSH OFF TO WORK. FEELS KIND OF LIKE WHEN WE WERE MARRIED.
DO YOU EVER THINK MAYBE WE--
YES, JAMES. I THINK IT OFTEN.
BUT IT'S A BAD IDEA. WE BOTH KNOW THAT.
NOW, I NEED TO USE THE PAY PHONE. YOU DON'T NEED TO WAIT AROUND.
COLD AS ICE. ALRIGHT, THEN. YOU TAKE CARE, ELENA.
YOU TOO.

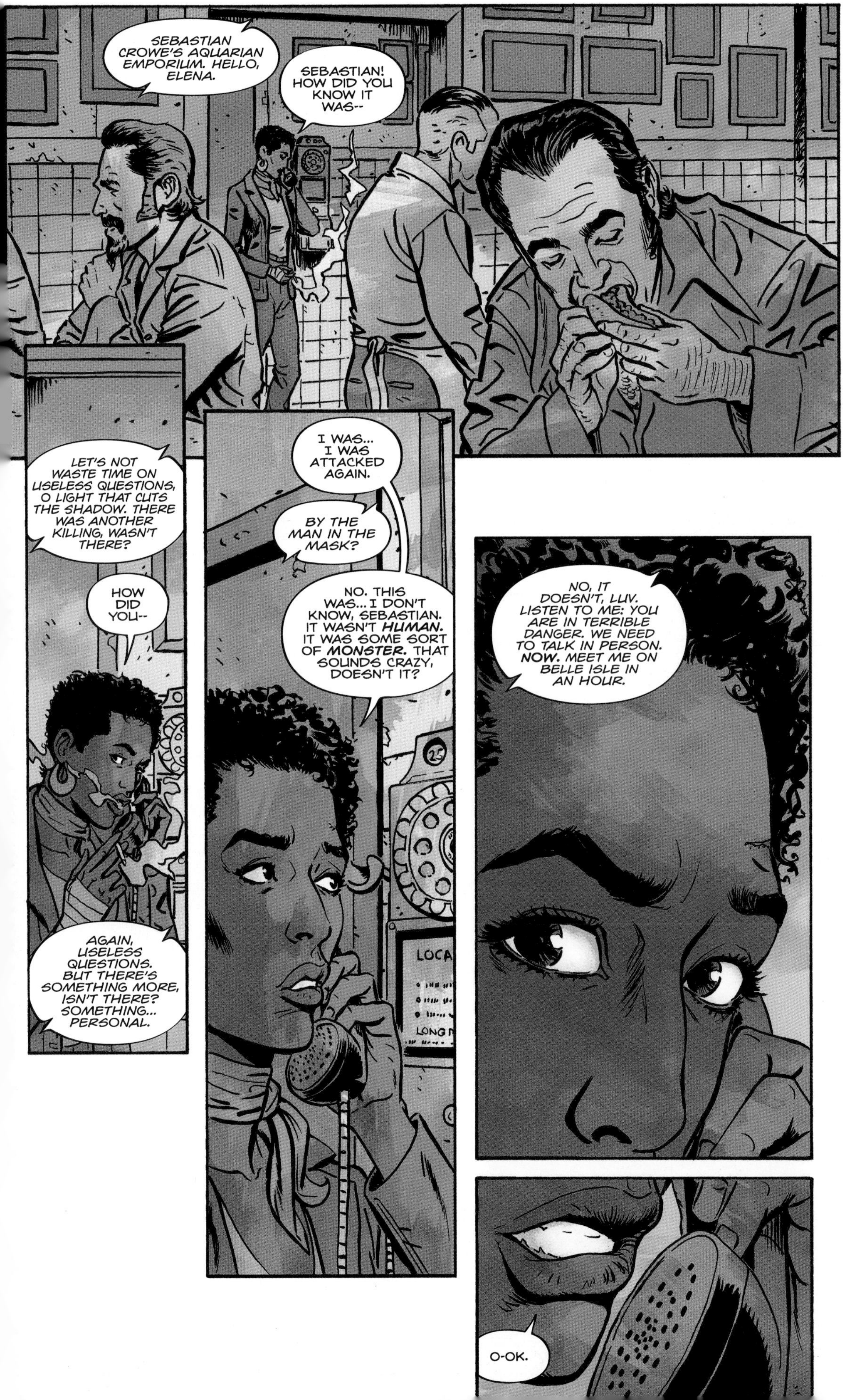
SEBASTIAN CROWE'S AQUARIAN EMPORIUM. HELLO, ELENA.
SEBASTIAN! HOW DID YOU KNOW IT WAS--
LET'S NOT WASTE TIME ON USELESS QUESTIONS, O LIGHT THAT CUTS THE SHADOW. THERE WAS ANOTHER KILLING, WASN'T THERE?
HOW DID YOU--
AGAIN, USELESS QUESTIONS. BUT THERE'S SOMETHING MORE, ISN'T THERE? SOMETHING... PERSONAL.
I WAS... I WAS ATTACKED AGAIN.
BY THE MAN IN THE MASK?
NO. THIS WAS... I DON'T KNOW, SEBASTIAN. IT WASN'T HUMAN. IT WAS SOME SORT OF MONSTER. THAT SOUNDS CRAZY, DOESN'T IT?
NO, IT DOESN'T, LUV. LISTEN TO ME: YOU ARE IN TERRIBLE DANGER. WE NEED TO TALK IN PERSON. NOW. MEET ME ON BELLE ISLE IN AN HOUR.
O-OK.

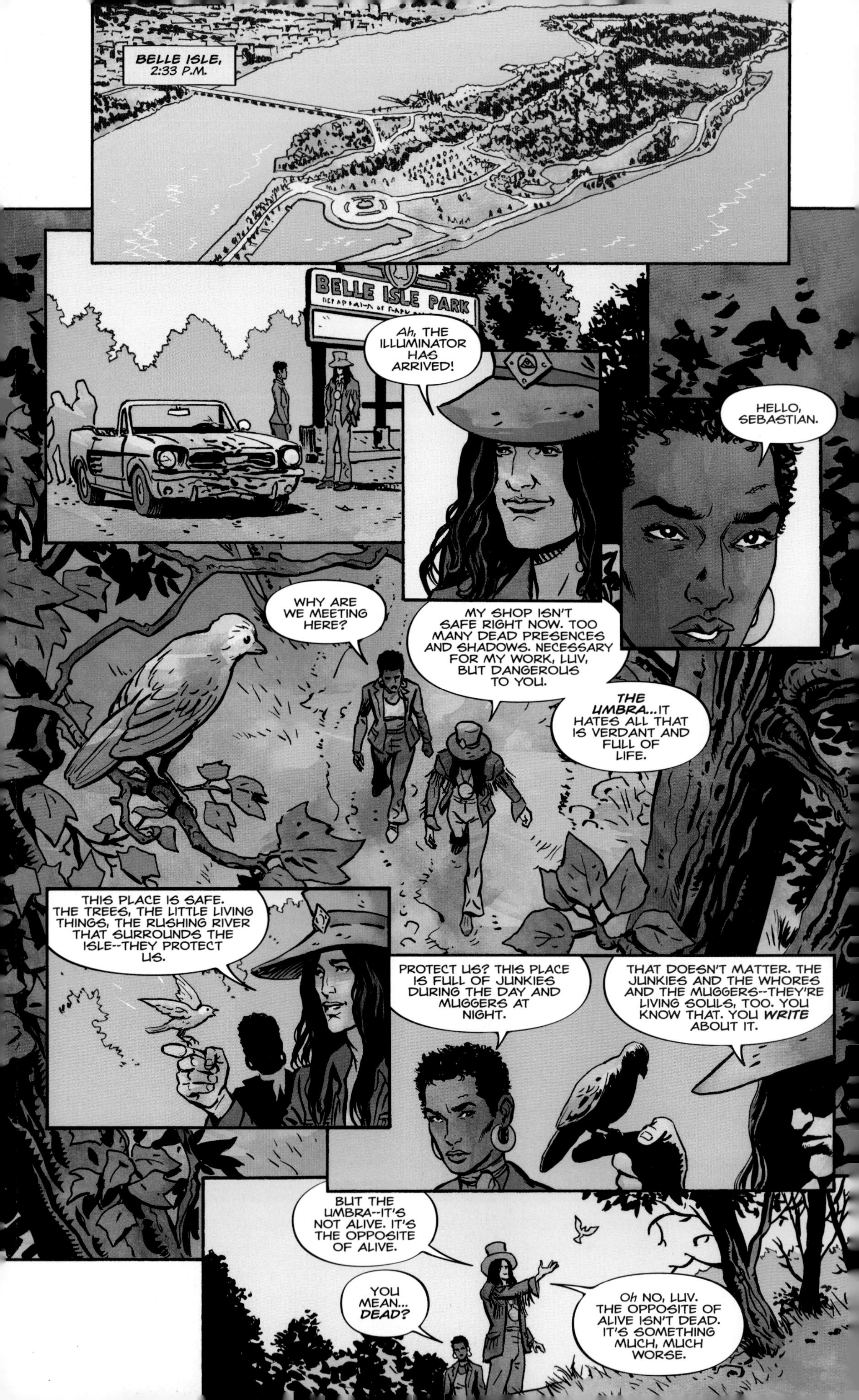
BELLE ISLE, 2:33 P.M.
BELLE ISLE PARK
Ah, THE ILLUMINATOR HAS ARRIVED!
HELLO, SEBASTIAN.
WHY ARE WE MEETING HERE?
MY SHOP ISN'T SAFE RIGHT NOW. TOO MANY DEAD PRESENCES AND SHADOWS. NECESSARY FOR MY WORK, LUV, BUT DANGEROUS TO YOU.
THE UMBRA...IT HATES ALL THAT IS VERDANT AND FULL OF LIFE.
THIS PLACE IS SAFE. THE TREES, THE LITTLE LIVING THINGS, THE RUSHING RIVER THAT SURROUNDS THE ISLE--THEY PROTECT US.
PROTECT US? THIS PLACE IS FULL OF JUNKIES DURING THE DAY AND MUGGERS AT NIGHT.
THAT DOESN'T MATTER. THE JUNKIES AND THE WHORES AND THE MUGGERS--THEY'RE LIVING SOULS, TOO. YOU KNOW THAT. YOU WRITE ABOUT IT.
BUT THE UMBRA--IT'S NOT ALIVE. IT'S THE OPPOSITE OF ALIVE.
YOU MEAN... DEAD?
Oh NO, LUV. THE OPPOSITE OF ALIVE ISN'T DEAD. IT'S SOMETHING MUCH, MUCH WORSE.

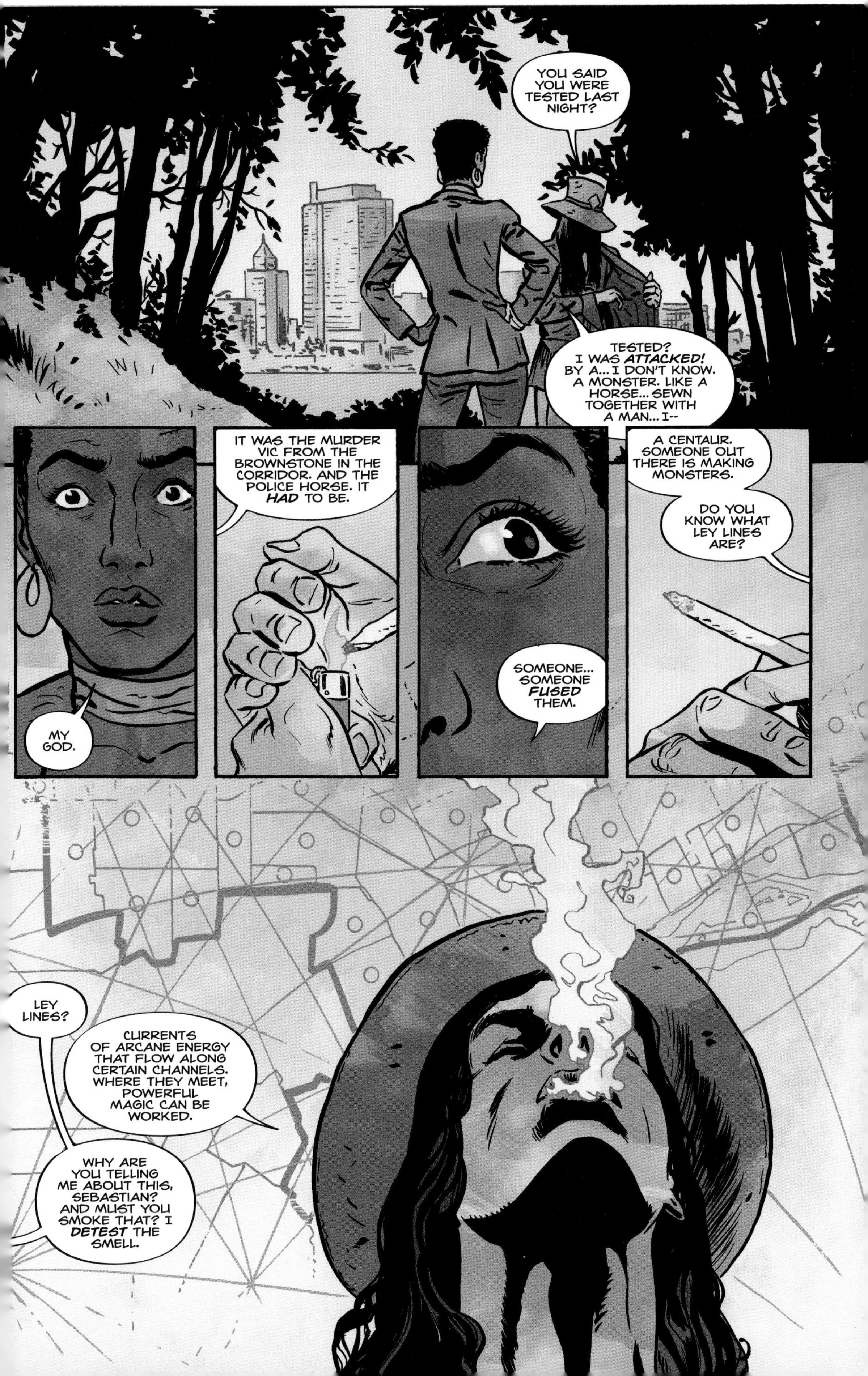
YOU SAID YOU WERE TESTED LAST NIGHT?
TESTED? I WAS ATTACKED! BY A... I DON'T KNOW. A MONSTER. LIKE A HORSE... SEWN TOGETHER WITH A MAN... I--
MY GOD.
IT WAS THE MURDER VIC FROM THE BROWNSTONE IN THE CORRIDOR. AND THE POLICE HORSE. IT HAD TO BE.
SOMEONE... SOMEONE FUSED THEM.
A CENTAUR. SOMEONE OUT THERE IS MAKING MONSTERS.
DO YOU KNOW WHAT LEY LINES ARE?
LEY LINES?
CURRENTS OF ARCANE ENERGY THAT FLOW ALONG CERTAIN CHANNELS. WHERE THEY MEET, POWERFUL MAGIC CAN BE WORKED.
WHY ARE YOU TELLING ME ABOUT THIS, SEBASTIAN? AND MUST YOU SMOKE THAT? I DETEST THE SMELL.

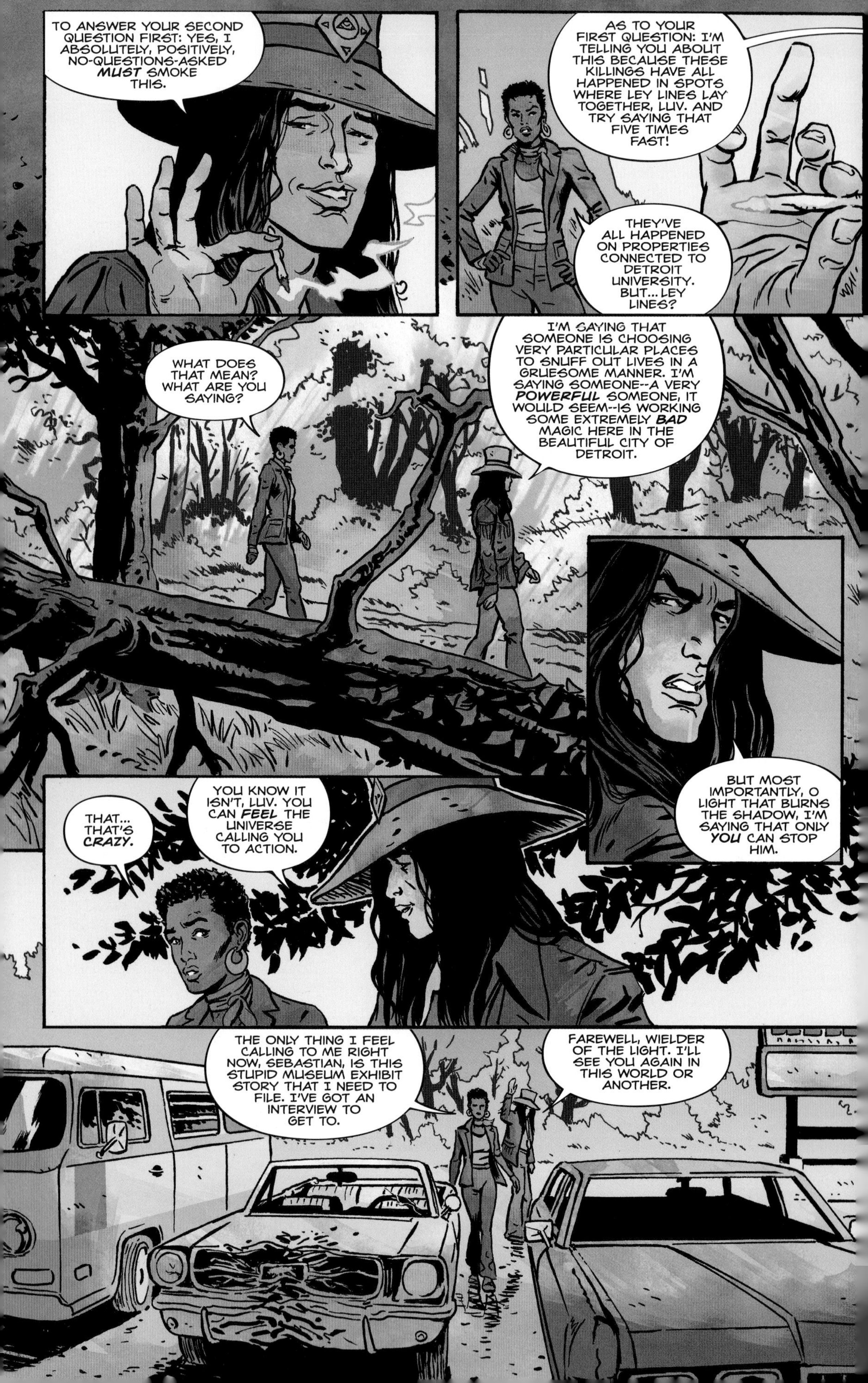
TO ANSWER YOUR SECOND QUESTION FIRST: YES, I ABSOLUTELY, POSITIVELY, NO-QUESTIONS-ASKED MUST SMOKE THIS.
AS TO YOUR FIRST QUESTION: I'M TELLING YOU ABOUT THIS BECAUSE THESE KILLINGS HAVE ALL HAPPENED IN SPOTS WHERE LEY LINES LAY TOGETHER, LUV. AND TRY SAYING THAT FIVE TIMES FAST!
THEY'VE ALL HAPPENED ON PROPERTIES CONNECTED TO DETROIT UNIVERSITY. BUT... LEY LINES?
WHAT DOES THAT MEAN? WHAT ARE YOU SAYING?
I'M SAYING THAT SOMEONE IS CHOOSING VERY PARTICULAR PLACES TO SNUFF OUT LIVES IN A GRUESOME MANNER. I'M SAYING SOMEONE--A VERY POWERFUL SOMEONE, IT WOULD SEEM--IS WORKING SOME EXTREMELY BAD MAGIC HERE IN THE BEAUTIFUL CITY OF DETROIT.
BUT MOST IMPORTANTLY, O LIGHT THAT BURNS THE SHADOW, I'M SAYING THAT ONLY YOU CAN STOP HIM.
THAT... THAT'S CRAZY.
YOU KNOW IT ISN'T, LUV. YOU CAN FEEL THE UNIVERSE CALLING YOU TO ACTION.
THE ONLY THING I FEEL CALLING TO ME RIGHT NOW, SEBASTIAN, IS THIS STUPID MUSEUM EXHIBIT STORY THAT I NEED TO FILE. I'VE GOT AN INTERVIEW TO GET TO.
FAREWELL, WIELDER OF THE LIGHT. I'LL SEE YOU AGAIN IN THIS WORLD OR ANOTHER.

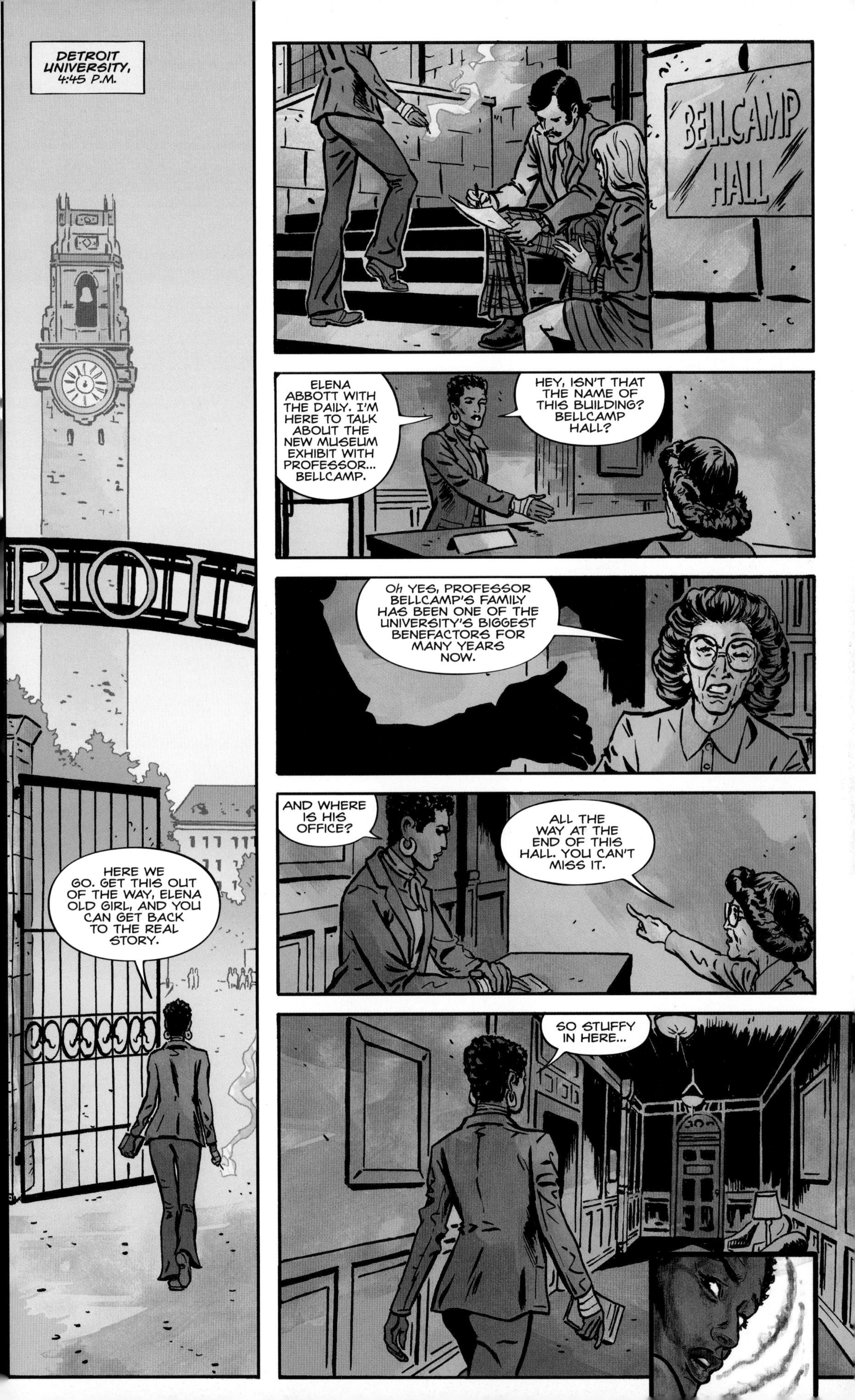
DETROIT UNIVERSITY, 4:45 P.M.
ROIT
HERE WE GO. GET THIS OUT OF THE WAY, ELENA OLD GIRL, AND YOU CAN GET BACK TO THE REAL STORY.
BELLCAMP HALL
ELENA ABBOTT WITH THE DAILY. I'M HERE TO TALK ABOUT THE NEW MUSEUM EXHIBIT WITH PROFESSOR... BELLCAMP.
HEY, ISN'T THAT THE NAME OF THIS BUILDING? BELLCAMP HALL?
Oh YES, PROFESSOR BELLCAMP'S FAMILY HAS BEEN ONE OF THE UNIVERSITY'S BIGGEST BENEFACTORS FOR MANY YEARS NOW.
AND WHERE IS HIS OFFICE?
ALL THE WAY AT THE END OF THIS HALL. YOU CAN'T MISS IT.
SO STUFFY IN HERE...

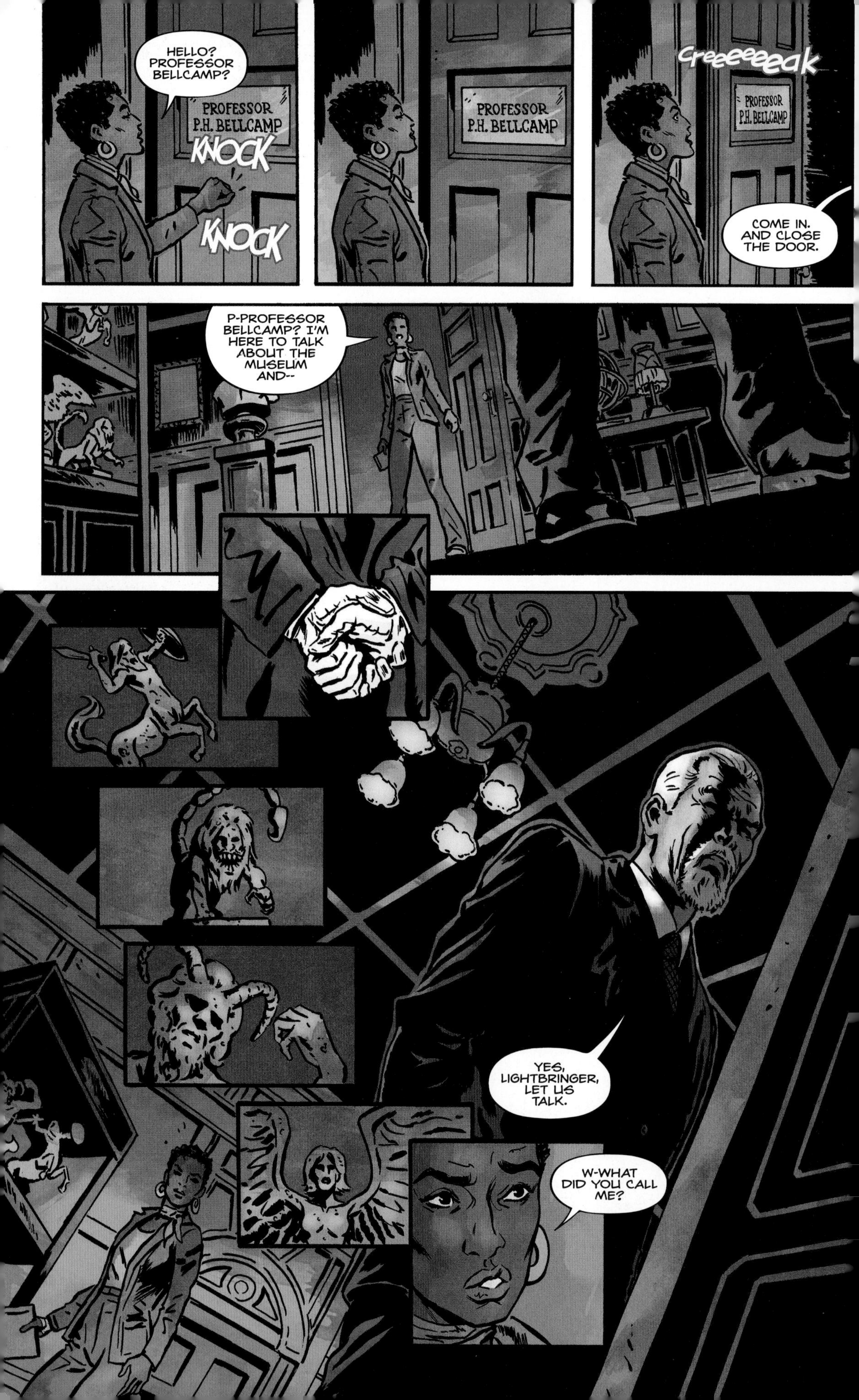
HELLO? PROFESSOR BELLCAMP?
PROFESSOR P.H. BELLCAMP
KNOCK
KNOCK
PROFESSOR P.H. BELLCAMP
CREEEEEEAK
PROFESSOR P.H. BELLCAMP
COME IN. AND CLOSE THE DOOR.
P-PROFESSOR BELLCAMP? I'M HERE TO TALK ABOUT THE MUSEUM AND--
YES, LIGHTBRINGER, LET US TALK.
W-WHAT DID YOU CALL ME?

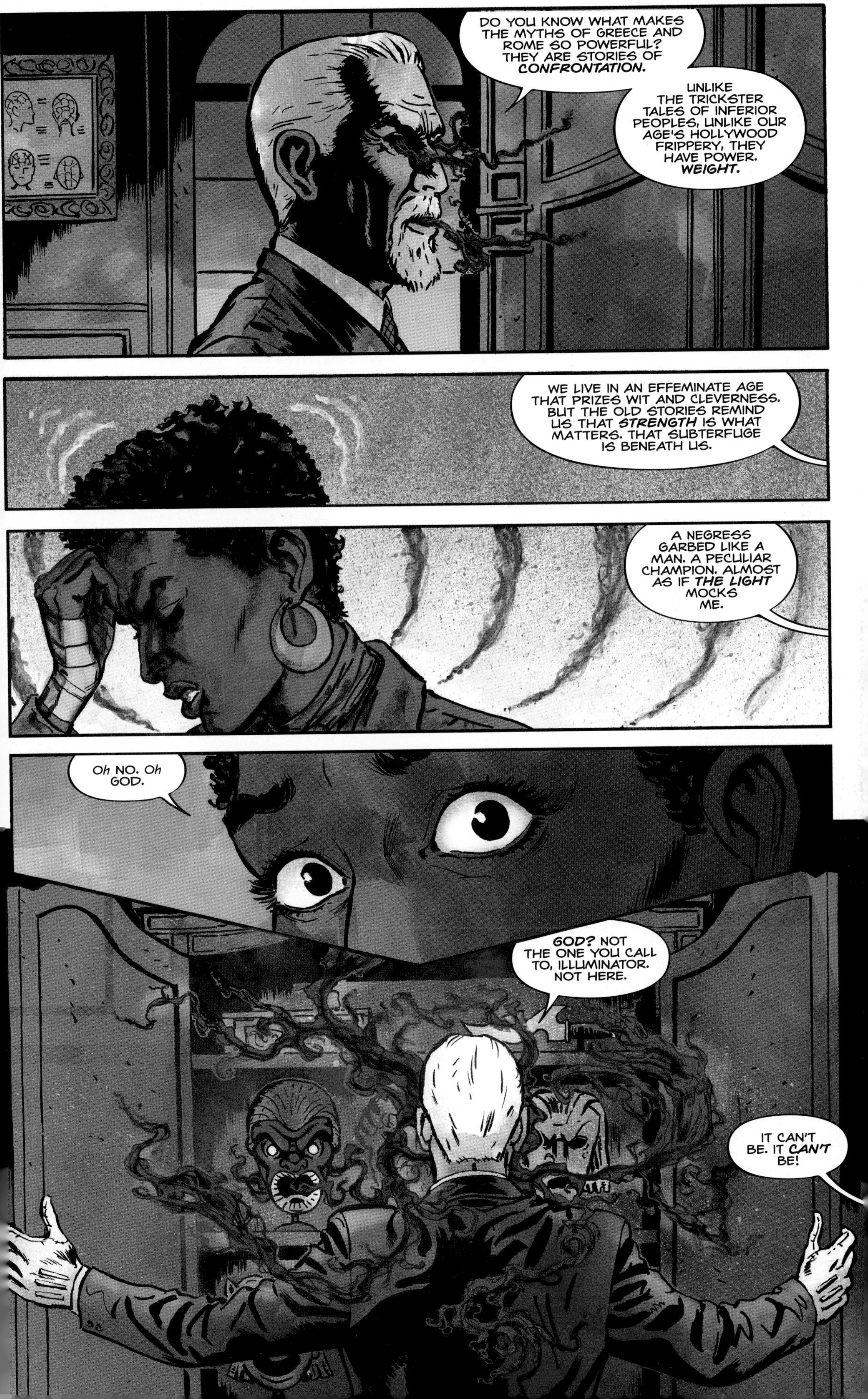
DO YOU KNOW WHAT MAKES THE MYTHS OF GREECE AND ROME SO POWERFUL? THEY ARE STORIES OF *CONFRONTATION.*
UNLIKE THE TRICKSTER TALES OF INFERIOR PEOPLES, UNLIKE OUR AGE'S HOLLYWOOD FRIPPERY, THEY HAVE POWER. *WEIGHT.*
WE LIVE IN AN EFFEMINATE AGE THAT PRIZES WIT AND CLEVERNESS. BUT THE OLD STORIES REMIND US THAT *STRENGTH* IS WHAT MATTERS. THAT SUBTERFUGE IS BENEATH US.
A NEGRESS GARBED LIKE A MAN. A PECULIAR CHAMPION. ALMOST AS IF *THE LIGHT* MOCKS ME.
Oh NO. *Oh* GOD.
GOD? NOT THE ONE YOU CALL TO, ILLUMINATOR. NOT HERE.
IT CAN'T BE. IT *CAN'T* BE!

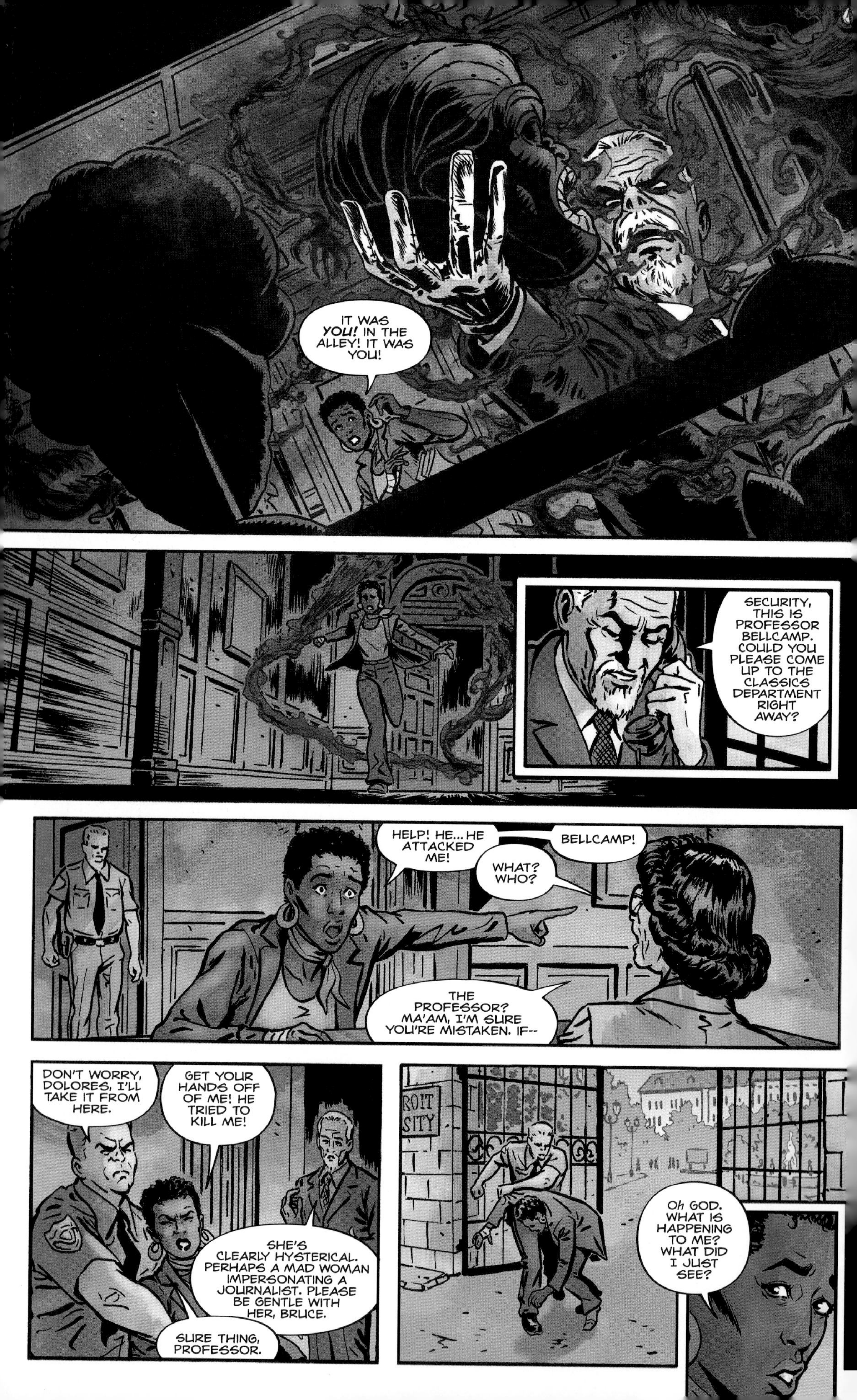
IT WAS *YOU!* IN THE ALLEY! IT WAS YOU!
SECURITY, THIS IS PROFESSOR BELLCAMP. COULD YOU PLEASE COME UP TO THE CLASSICS DEPARTMENT RIGHT AWAY?
HELP! HE... HE ATTACKED ME!
WHAT? WHO?
BELLCAMP!
THE PROFESSOR? MA'AM, I'M SURE YOU'RE MISTAKEN. IF--
DON'T WORRY, DOLORES, I'LL TAKE IT FROM HERE.
GET YOUR HANDS OFF OF ME! HE TRIED TO KILL ME!
SHE'S CLEARLY HYSTERICAL. PERHAPS A MAD WOMAN IMPERSONATING A JOURNALIST. PLEASE BE GENTLE WITH HER, BRUCE.
SURE THING, PROFESSOR.
ROIT
SITY
OH GOD. WHAT IS HAPPENING TO ME? WHAT DID I JUST SEE?

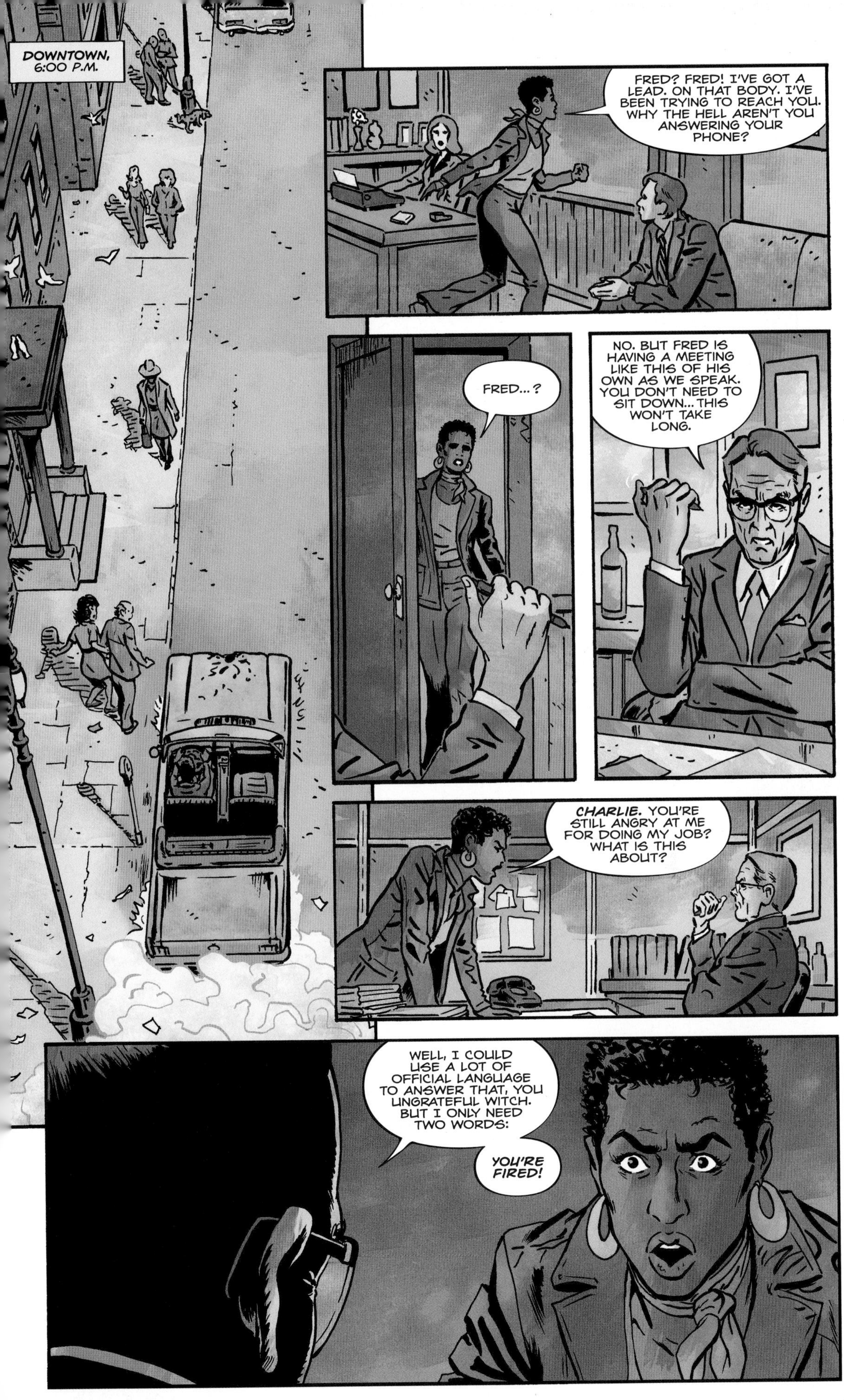
DOWNTOWN, 6:00 P.M.
FRED? FRED! I'VE GOT A LEAD. ON THAT BODY. I'VE BEEN TRYING TO REACH YOU. WHY THE HELL AREN'T YOU ANSWERING YOUR PHONE?
FRED...?
NO. BUT FRED IS HAVING A MEETING LIKE THIS OF HIS OWN AS WE SPEAK. YOU DON'T NEED TO SIT DOWN... THIS WON'T TAKE LONG.
CHARLIE. YOU'RE STILL ANGRY AT ME FOR DOING MY JOB? WHAT IS THIS ABOUT?
WELL, I COULD USE A LOT OF OFFICIAL LANGUAGE TO ANSWER THAT, YOU UNGRATEFUL WITCH. BUT I ONLY NEED TWO WORDS:
YOU'RE FIRED!

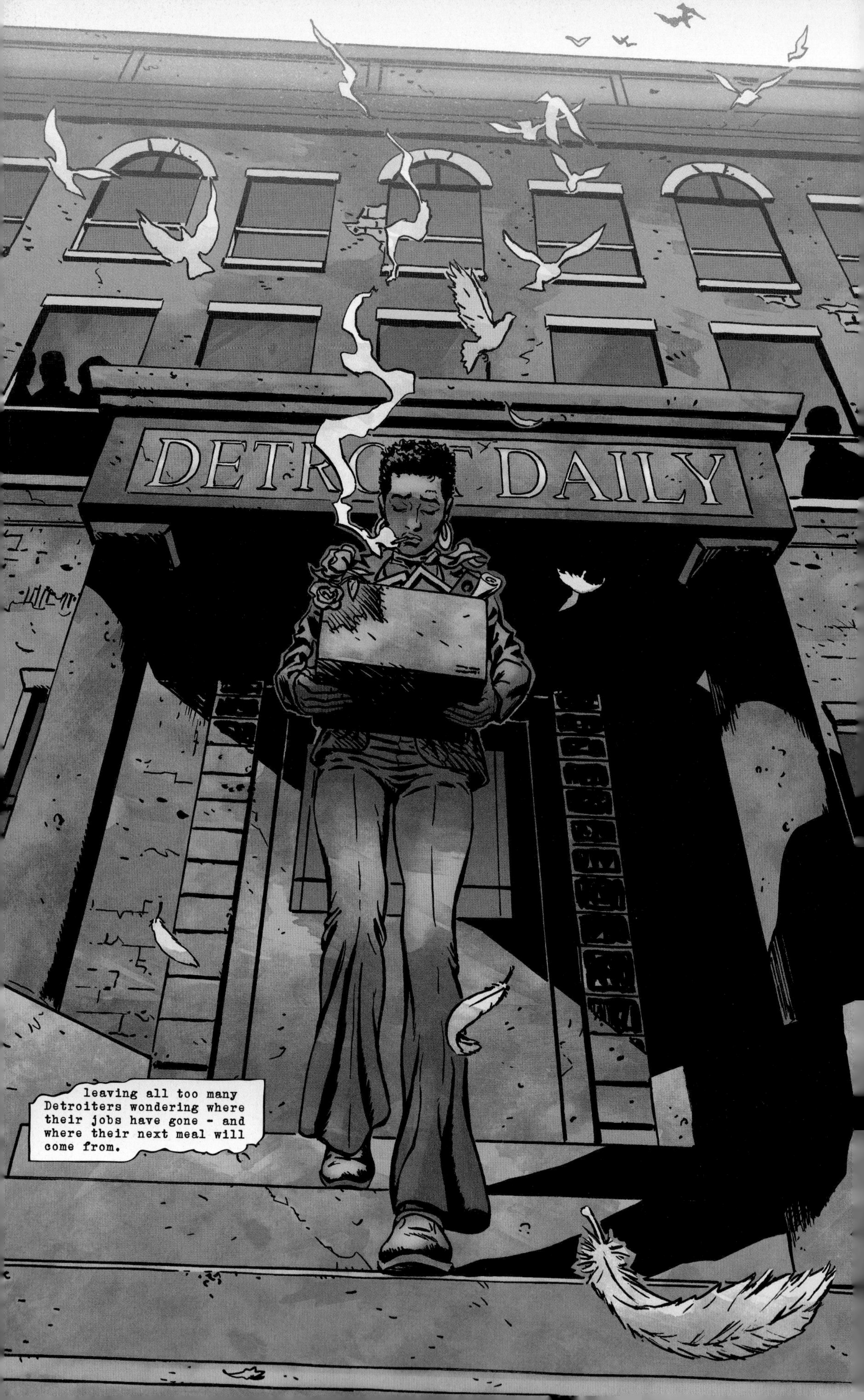
DETROIT DAILY
leaving all too many Detroiters wondering where their jobs have gone - and where their next meal will come from.

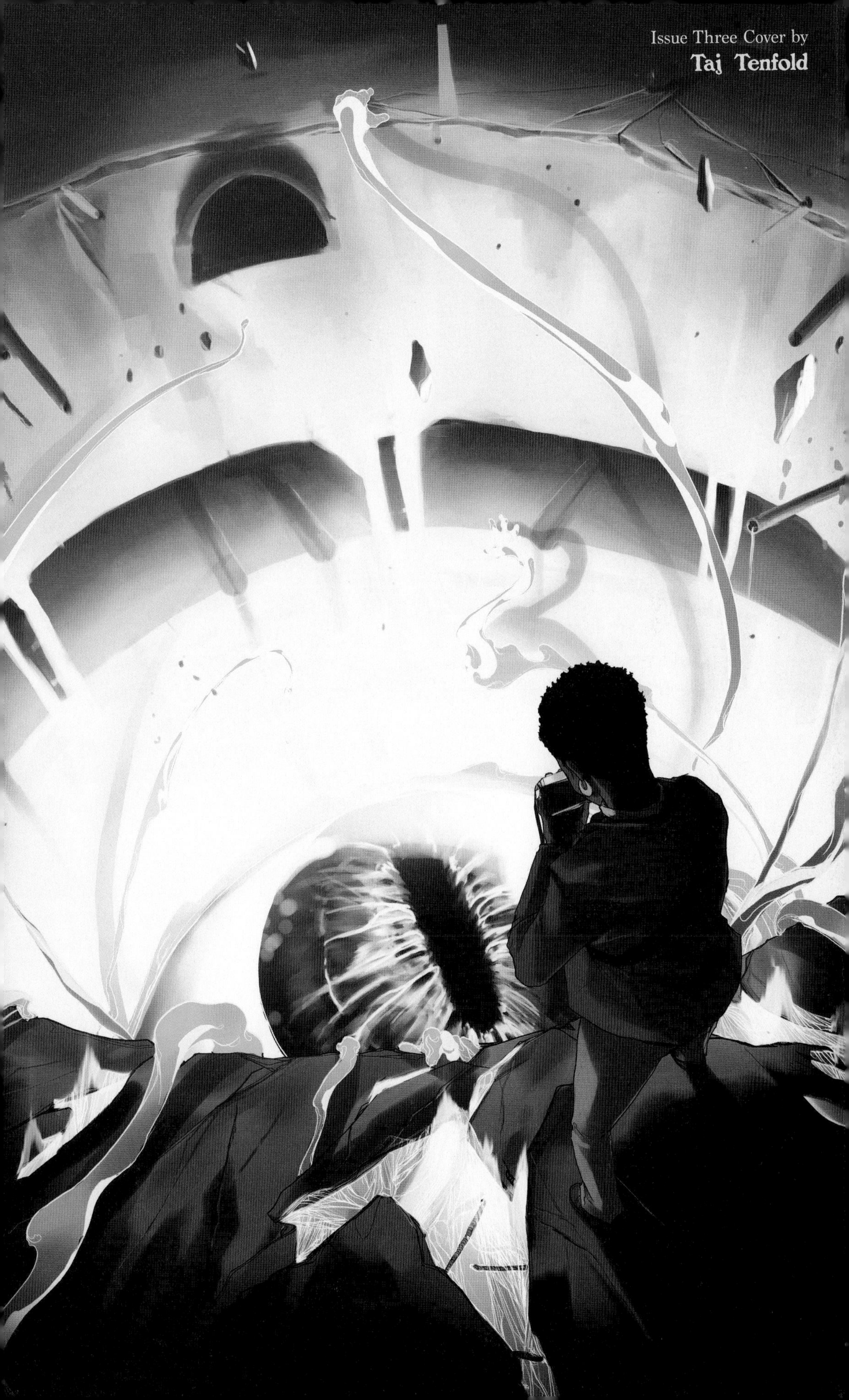

Issue Three Cover by
Taj Tenfold

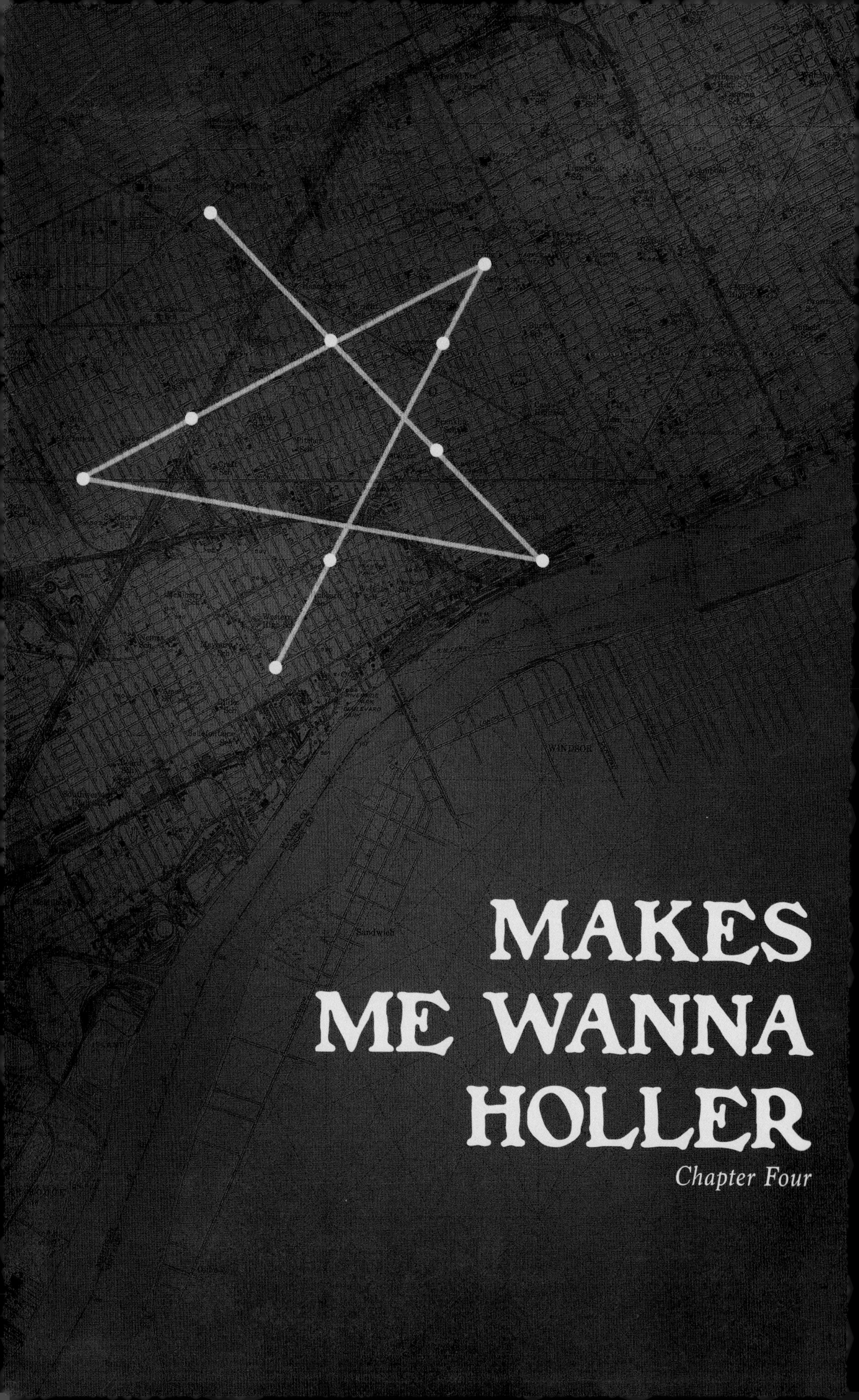
WINDSOR
Sandwich

MAKES ME WANNA HOLLER

Chapter Four

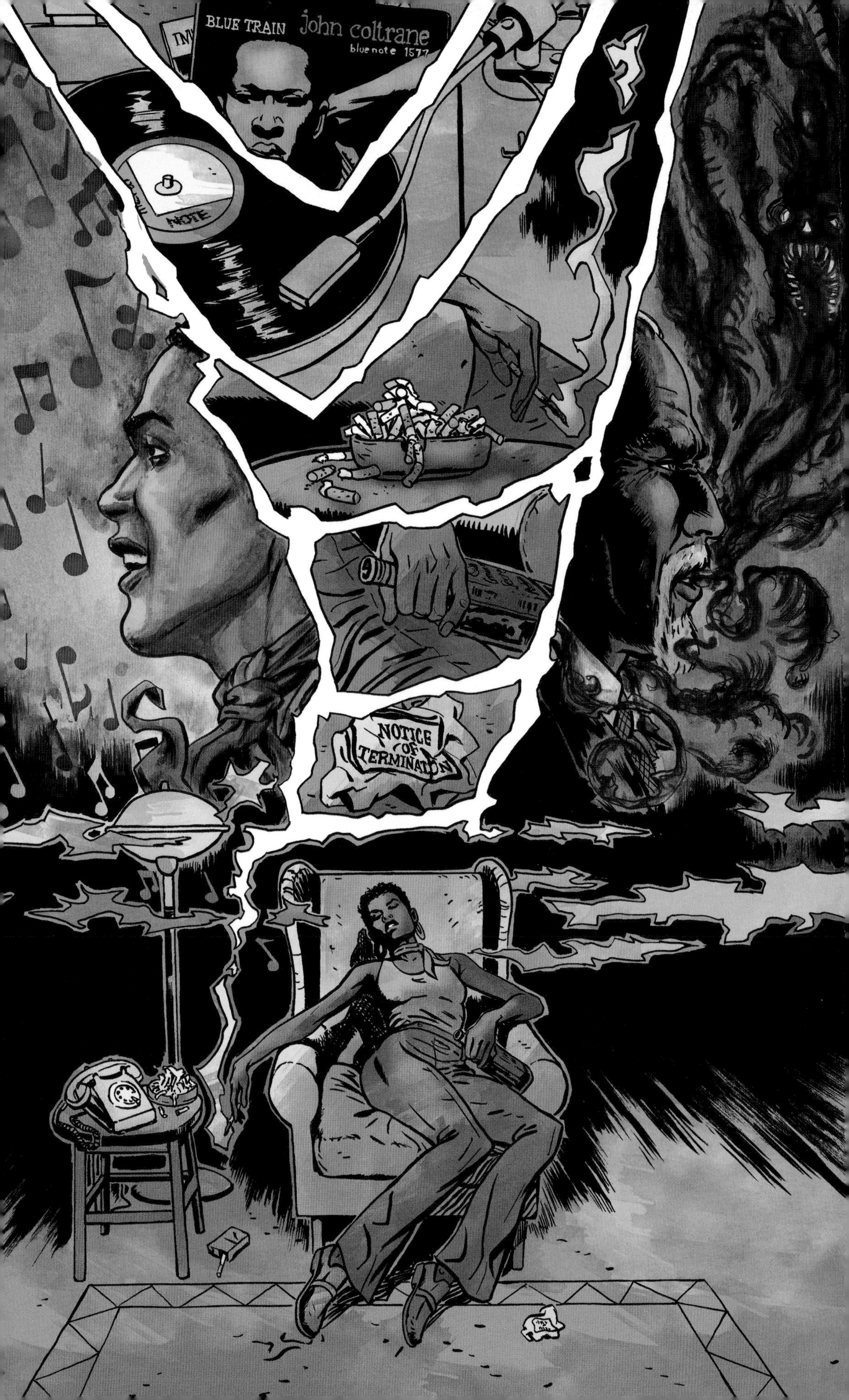
BLUE TRAIN
john coltrane
blue note 1577
NOTE
NOTICE OF TERMINATION

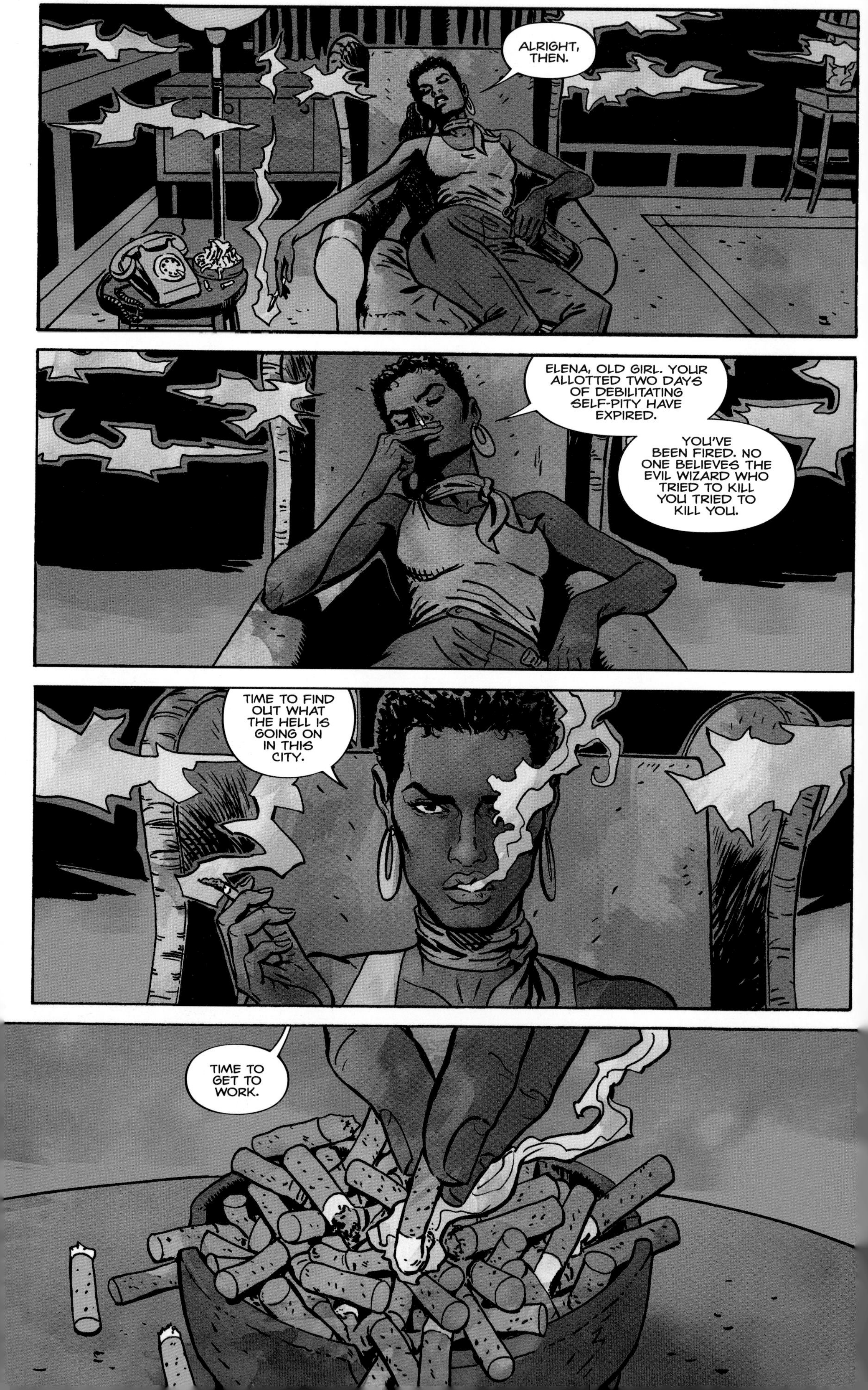
ALRIGHT, THEN.
ELENA, OLD GIRL. YOUR ALLOTTED TWO DAYS OF DEBILITATING SELF-PITY HAVE EXPIRED.
YOU'VE BEEN FIRED. NO ONE BELIEVES THE EVIL WIZARD WHO TRIED TO KILL YOU TRIED TO KILL YOU.
TIME TO FIND OUT WHAT THE HELL IS GOING ON IN THIS CITY.
TIME TO GET TO WORK.

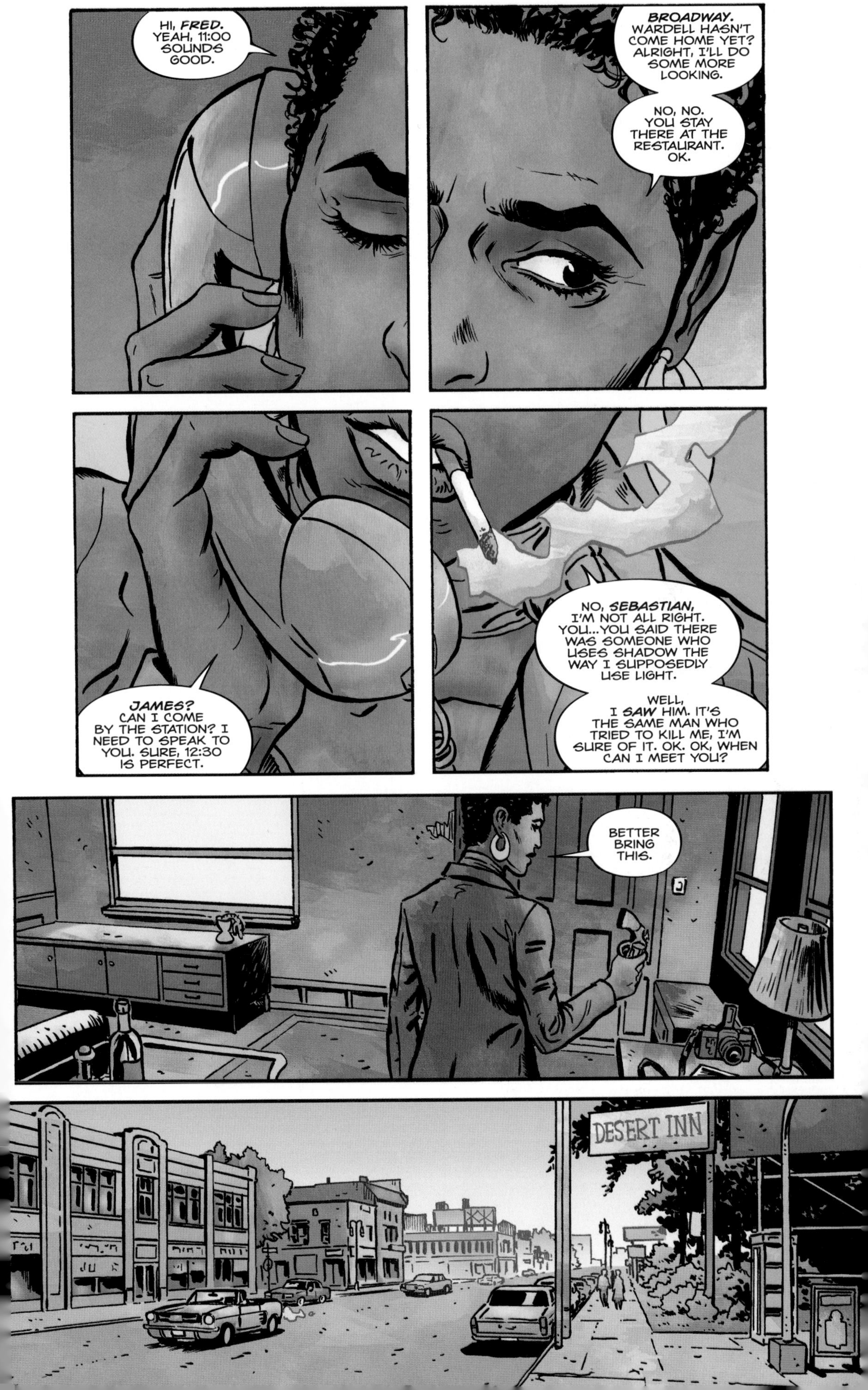
HI, FRED. YEAH, 11:00 SOUNDS GOOD.
BROADWAY. WARDELL HASN'T COME HOME YET? ALRIGHT, I'LL DO SOME MORE LOOKING.
NO, NO. YOU STAY THERE AT THE RESTAURANT. OK.
JAMES? CAN I COME BY THE STATION? I NEED TO SPEAK TO YOU. SURE, 12:30 IS PERFECT.
NO, SEBASTIAN, I'M NOT ALL RIGHT. YOU...YOU SAID THERE WAS SOMEONE WHO USES SHADOW THE WAY I SUPPOSEDLY USE LIGHT.
WELL, I SAW HIM. IT'S THE SAME MAN WHO TRIED TO KILL ME, I'M SURE OF IT. OK. OK, WHEN CAN I MEET YOU?
BETTER BRING THIS.
DESERT INN

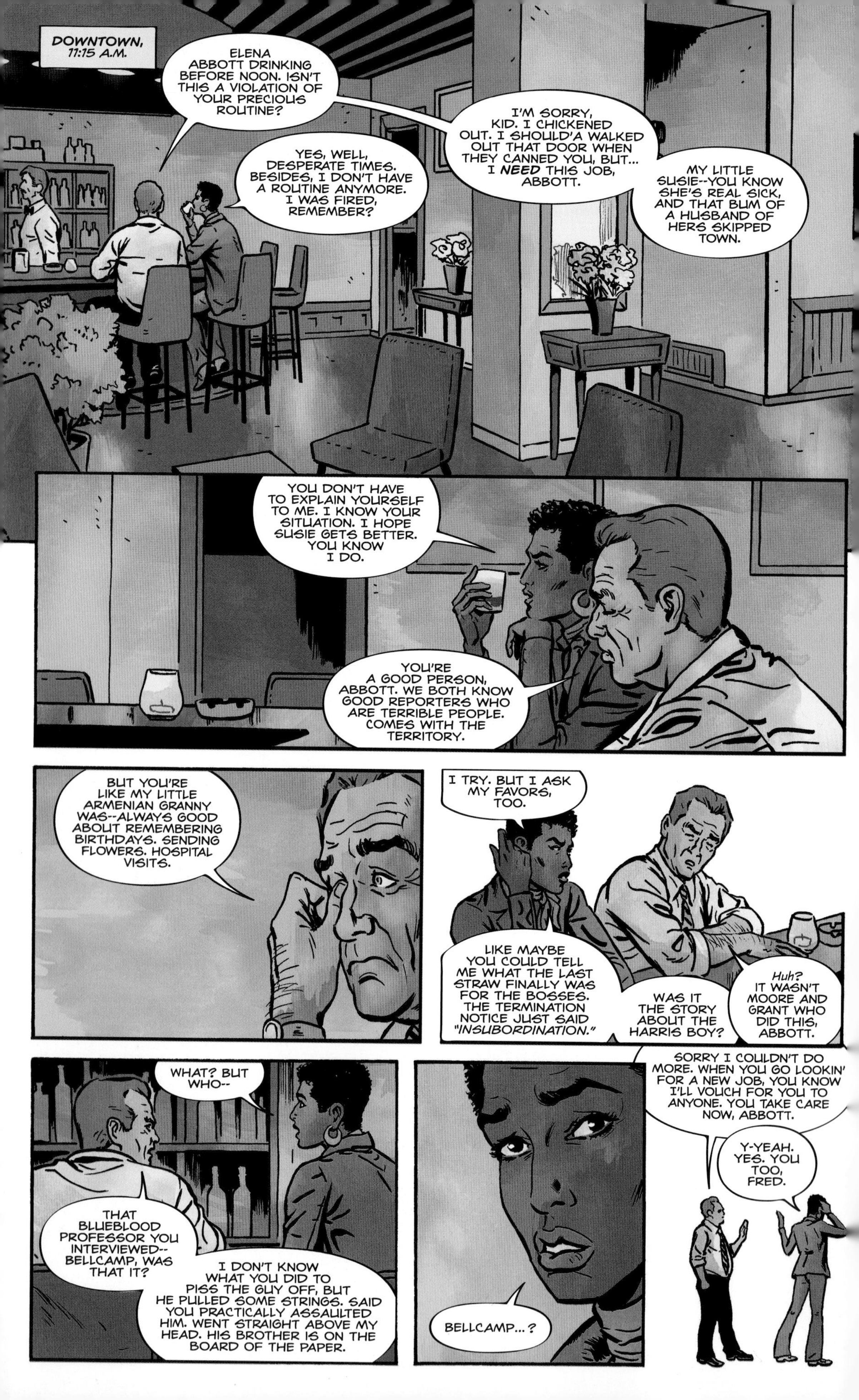
DOWNTOWN, 11:15 A.M.
ELENA ABBOTT DRINKING BEFORE NOON. ISN'T THIS A VIOLATION OF YOUR PRECIOUS ROUTINE?
YES, WELL, DESPERATE TIMES. BESIDES, I DON'T HAVE A ROUTINE ANYMORE. I WAS FIRED, REMEMBER?
I'M SORRY, KID. I CHICKENED OUT. I SHOULD'A WALKED OUT THAT DOOR WHEN THEY CANNED YOU, BUT... I NEED THIS JOB, ABBOTT.
MY LITTLE SUSIE--YOU KNOW SHE'S REAL SICK, AND THAT BUM OF A HUSBAND OF HERS SKIPPED TOWN.
YOU DON'T HAVE TO EXPLAIN YOURSELF TO ME. I KNOW YOUR SITUATION. I HOPE SUSIE GETS BETTER. YOU KNOW I DO.
YOU'RE A GOOD PERSON, ABBOTT. WE BOTH KNOW GOOD REPORTERS WHO ARE TERRIBLE PEOPLE. COMES WITH THE TERRITORY.
BUT YOU'RE LIKE MY LITTLE ARMENIAN GRANNY WAS--ALWAYS GOOD ABOUT REMEMBERING BIRTHDAYS. SENDING FLOWERS. HOSPITAL VISITS.
I TRY. BUT I ASK MY FAVORS, TOO.
LIKE MAYBE YOU COULD TELL ME WHAT THE LAST STRAW FINALLY WAS FOR THE BOSSES. THE TERMINATION NOTICE JUST SAID "INSUBORDINATION."
WAS IT THE STORY ABOUT THE HARRIS BOY?
Huh? IT WASN'T MOORE AND GRANT WHO DID THIS, ABBOTT.
WHAT? BUT WHO--
THAT BLUEBLOOD PROFESSOR YOU INTERVIEWED--BELLCAMP, WAS THAT IT?
I DON'T KNOW WHAT YOU DID TO PISS THE GUY OFF, BUT HE PULLED SOME STRINGS. SAID YOU PRACTICALLY ASSAULTED HIM. WENT STRAIGHT ABOVE MY HEAD. HIS BROTHER IS ON THE BOARD OF THE PAPER.
BELLCAMP...?
SORRY I COULDN'T DO MORE. WHEN YOU GO LOOKIN' FOR A NEW JOB, YOU KNOW I'LL VOUCH FOR YOU TO ANYONE. YOU TAKE CARE NOW, ABBOTT.
Y-YEAH. YES. YOU TOO, FRED.

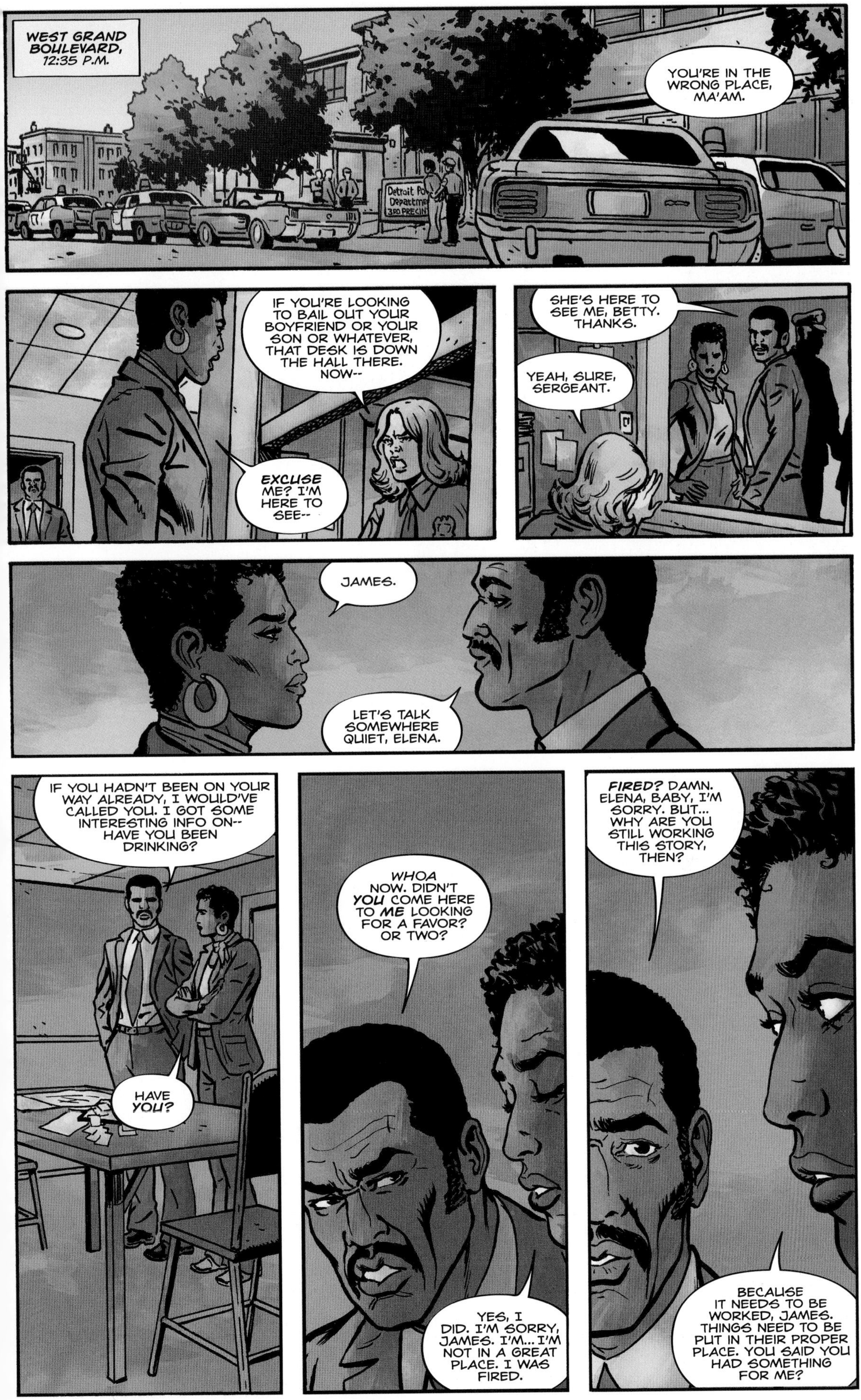
WEST GRAND BOULEVARD, 12:35 P.M.
YOU'RE IN THE WRONG PLACE, MA'AM.
IF YOU'RE LOOKING TO BAIL OUT YOUR BOYFRIEND OR YOUR SON OR WHATEVER, THAT DESK IS DOWN THE HALL THERE. NOW--
EXCUSE ME? I'M HERE TO SEE--
SHE'S HERE TO SEE ME, BETTY. THANKS.
YEAH, SURE, SERGEANT.
JAMES.
LET'S TALK SOMEWHERE QUIET, ELENA.
IF YOU HADN'T BEEN ON YOUR WAY ALREADY, I WOULD'VE CALLED YOU. I GOT SOME INTERESTING INFO ON-- HAVE YOU BEEN DRINKING?
HAVE YOU?
WHOA NOW. DIDN'T YOU COME HERE TO ME LOOKING FOR A FAVOR? OR TWO?
YES, I DID. I'M SORRY, JAMES. I'M... I'M NOT IN A GREAT PLACE. I WAS FIRED.
FIRED? DAMN. ELENA, BABY, I'M SORRY. BUT... WHY ARE YOU STILL WORKING THIS STORY, THEN?
BECAUSE IT NEEDS TO BE WORKED, JAMES. THINGS NEED TO BE PUT IN THEIR PROPER PLACE. YOU SAID YOU HAD SOMETHING FOR ME?

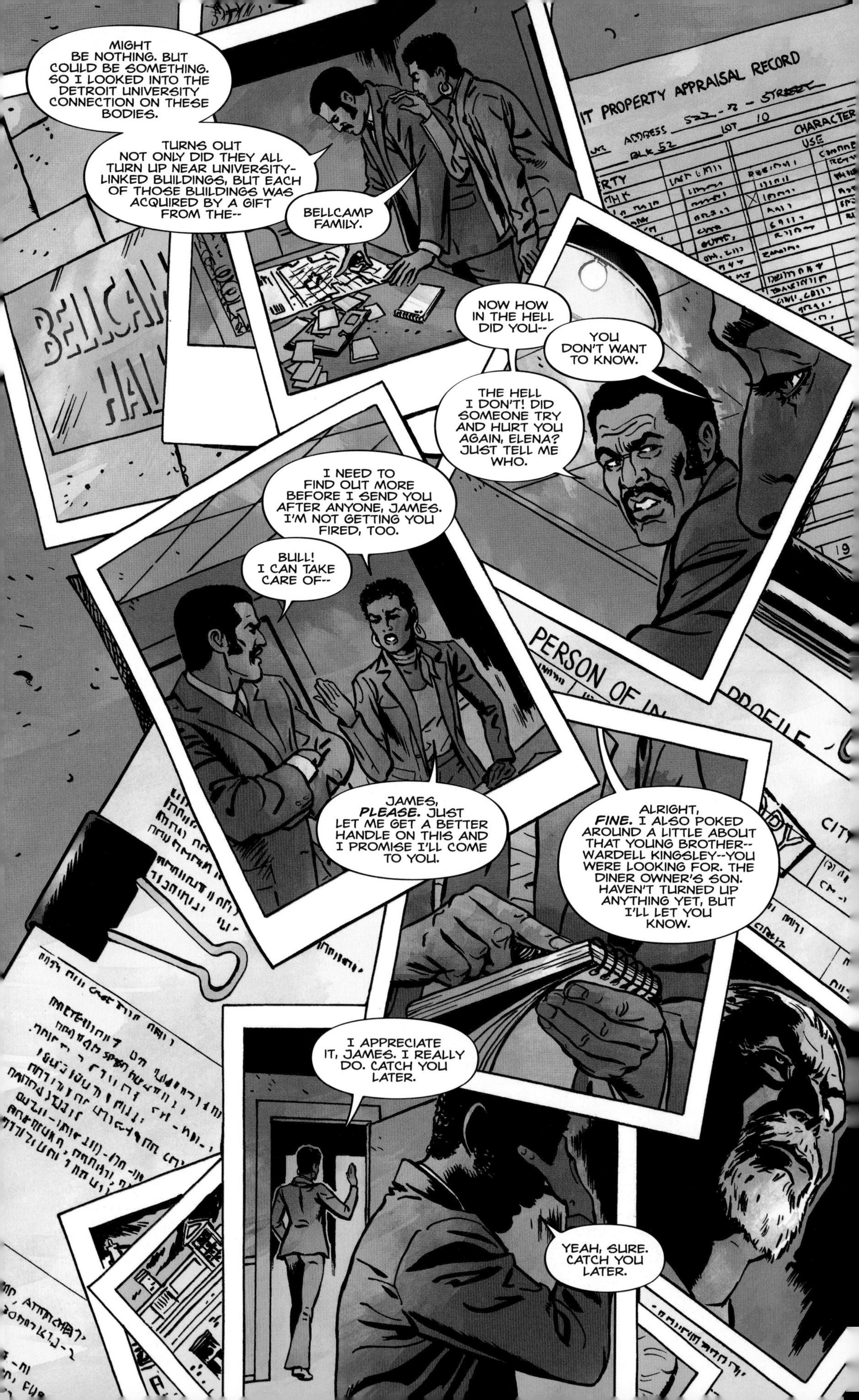
MIGHT BE NOTHING. BUT COULD BE SOMETHING. SO I LOOKED INTO THE DETROIT UNIVERSITY CONNECTION ON THESE BODIES.
TURNS OUT NOT ONLY DID THEY ALL TURN UP NEAR UNIVERSITY-LINKED BUILDINGS, BUT EACH OF THOSE BUILDINGS WAS ACQUIRED BY A GIFT FROM THE--
BELLCAMP FAMILY.
PROPERTY APPRAISAL RECORD
NOW HOW IN THE HELL DID YOU--
YOU DON'T WANT TO KNOW.
THE HELL I DON'T! DID SOMEONE TRY AND HURT YOU AGAIN, ELENA? JUST TELL ME WHO.
I NEED TO FIND OUT MORE BEFORE I SEND YOU AFTER ANYONE, JAMES. I'M NOT GETTING YOU FIRED, TOO.
BULL! I CAN TAKE CARE OF--
JAMES, *PLEASE.* JUST LET ME GET A BETTER HANDLE ON THIS AND I PROMISE I'LL COME TO YOU.
ALRIGHT, *FINE.* I ALSO POKED AROUND A LITTLE ABOUT THAT YOUNG BROTHER--WARDELL KINGSLEY--YOU WERE LOOKING FOR. THE DINER OWNER'S SON. HAVEN'T TURNED UP ANYTHING YET, BUT I'LL LET YOU KNOW.
I APPRECIATE IT, JAMES. I REALLY DO. CATCH YOU LATER.
YEAH, SURE. CATCH YOU LATER.

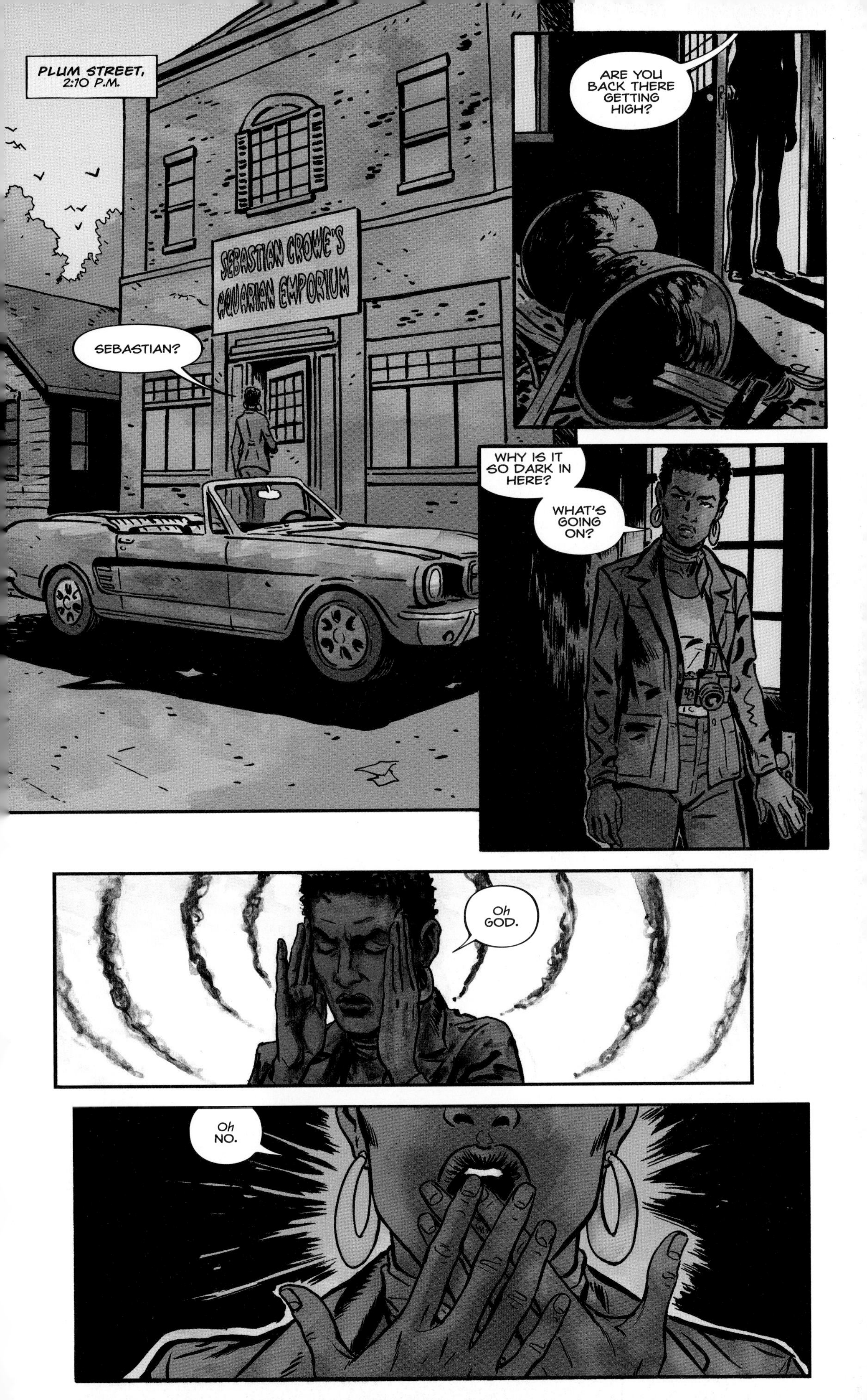
PLUM STREET, 2:10 P.M.
SEBASTIAN CROWE'S AQUARIAN EMPORIUM
SEBASTIAN?
ARE YOU BACK THERE GETTING HIGH?
WHY IS IT SO DARK IN HERE?
WHAT'S GOING ON?
Oh GOD.
Oh NO.

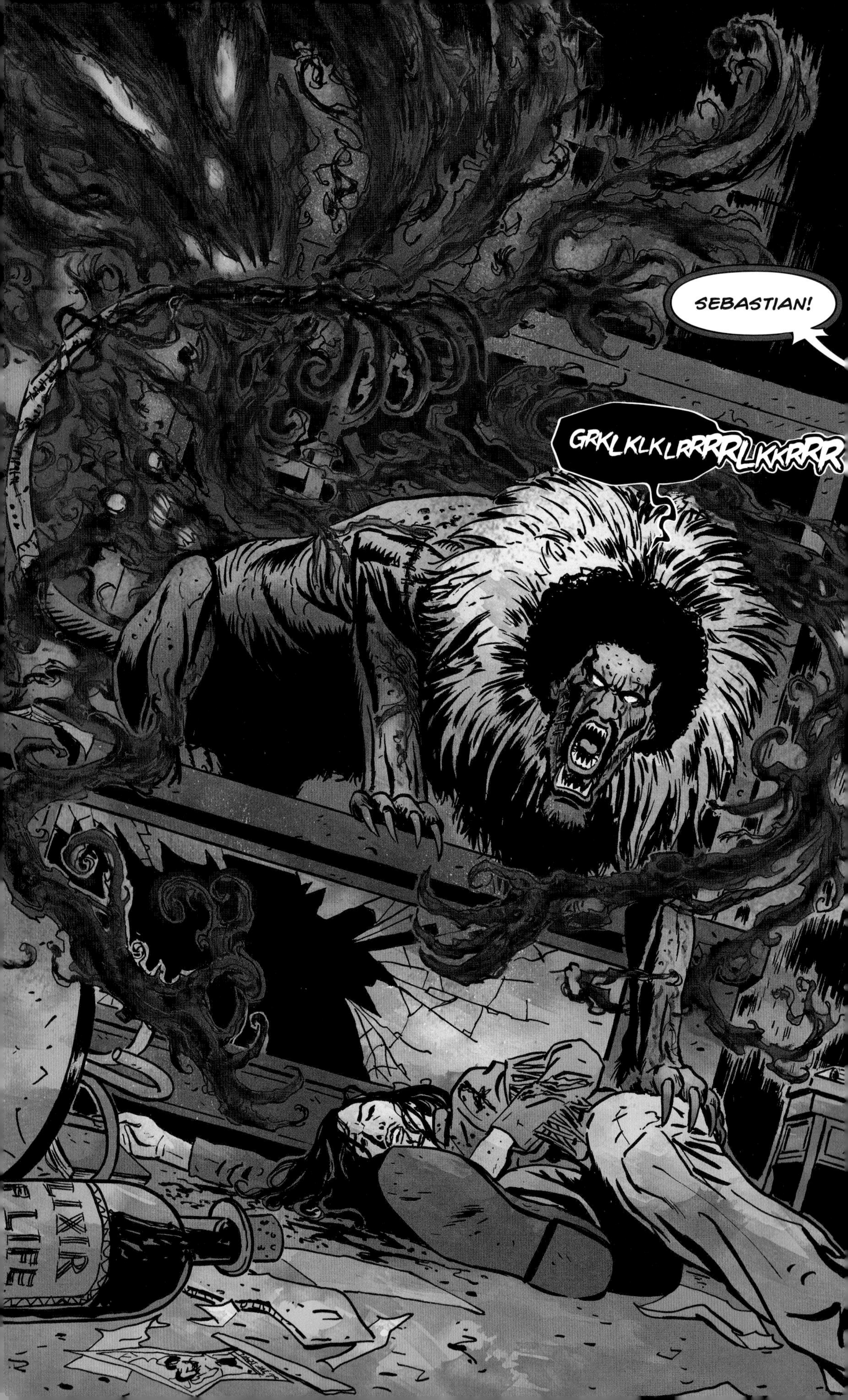
SEBASTIAN!
GRKLKLKLRRRRLKKRRR

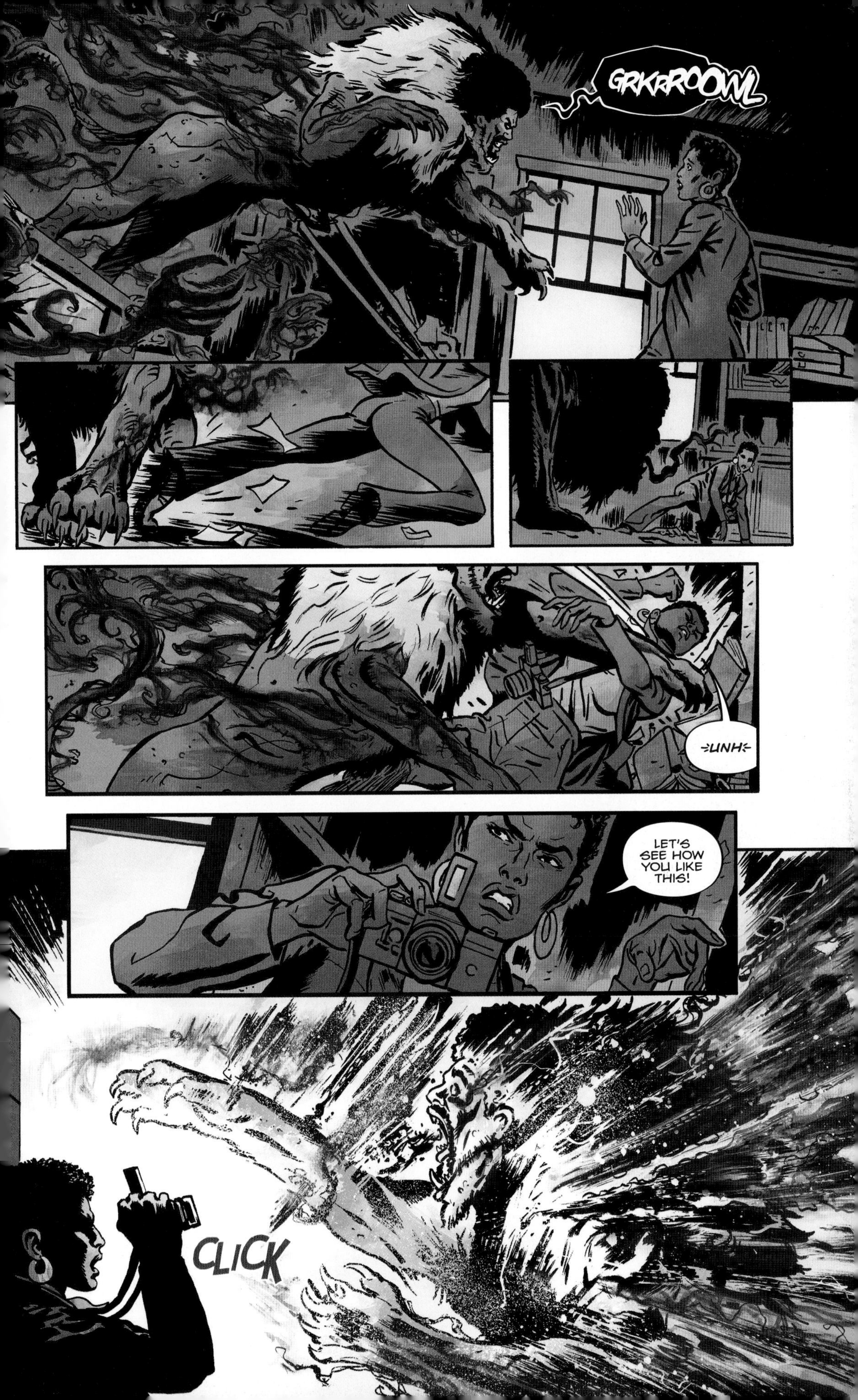
GRKRROOWL
=UNH=
LET'S SEE HOW YOU LIKE THIS!
CLICK

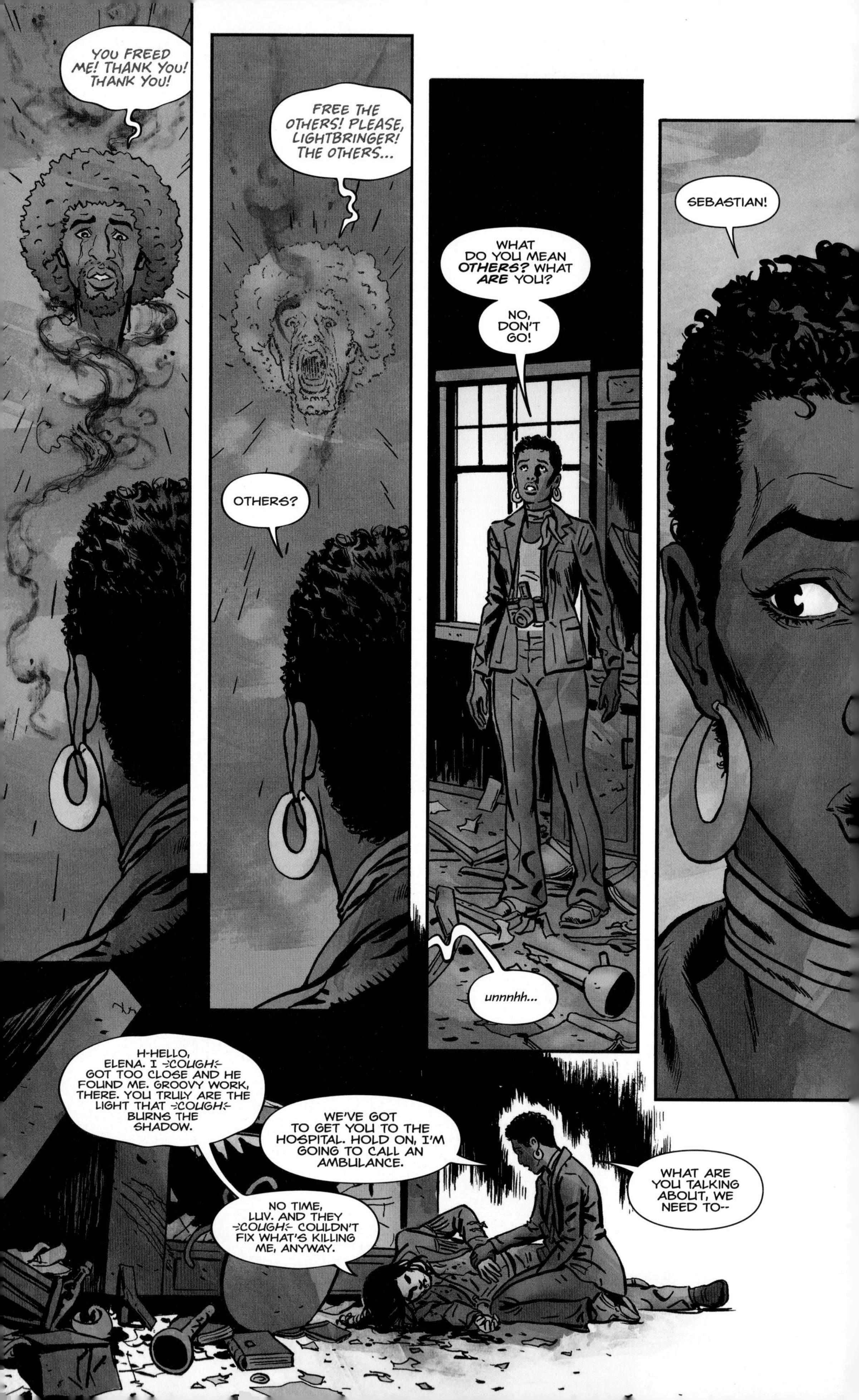
YOU FREED ME! THANK YOU! THANK YOU!
FREE THE OTHERS! PLEASE, LIGHTBRINGER! THE OTHERS...
OTHERS?
WHAT DO YOU MEAN OTHERS? WHAT ARE YOU?
NO, DON'T GO!
unnnhh...
SEBASTIAN!
H-HELLO, ELENA. I -COUGH- GOT TOO CLOSE AND HE FOUND ME. GROOVY WORK, THERE. YOU TRULY ARE THE LIGHT THAT -COUGH- BURNS THE SHADOW.
WE'VE GOT TO GET YOU TO THE HOSPITAL. HOLD ON, I'M GOING TO CALL AN AMBULANCE.
NO TIME, LUV. AND THEY -COUGH- COULDN'T FIX WHAT'S KILLING ME, ANYWAY.
WHAT ARE YOU TALKING ABOUT, WE NEED TO--

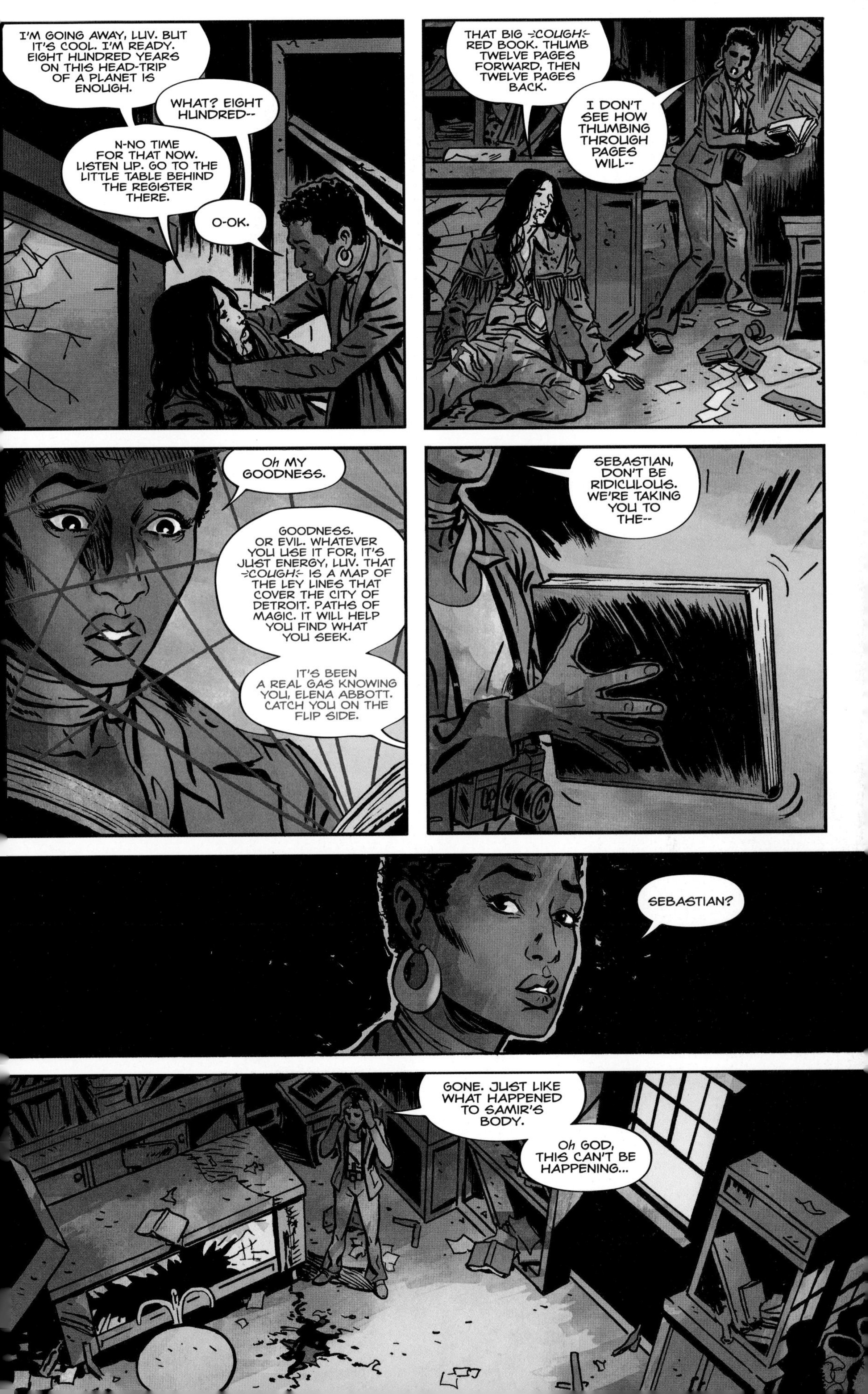
I'M GOING AWAY, LUV. BUT IT'S COOL. I'M READY. EIGHT HUNDRED YEARS ON THIS HEAD-TRIP OF A PLANET IS ENOUGH.
WHAT? EIGHT HUNDRED--
N-NO TIME FOR THAT NOW. LISTEN UP. GO TO THE LITTLE TABLE BEHIND THE REGISTER THERE.
O-OK.
THAT BIG =COUGH= RED BOOK. THUMB TWELVE PAGES FORWARD, THEN TWELVE PAGES BACK.
I DON'T SEE HOW THUMBING THROUGH PAGES WILL--
Oh MY GOODNESS.
GOODNESS. OR EVIL. WHATEVER YOU USE IT FOR, IT'S JUST ENERGY, LUV. THAT =COUGH= IS A MAP OF THE LEY LINES THAT COVER THE CITY OF DETROIT. PATHS OF MAGIC. IT WILL HELP YOU FIND WHAT YOU SEEK.
IT'S BEEN A REAL GAS KNOWING YOU, ELENA ABBOTT. CATCH YOU ON THE FLIP SIDE.
SEBASTIAN, DON'T BE RIDICULOUS. WE'RE TAKING YOU TO THE--
SEBASTIAN?
GONE. JUST LIKE WHAT HAPPENED TO SAMIR'S BODY.
Oh GOD, THIS CAN'T BE HAPPENING...

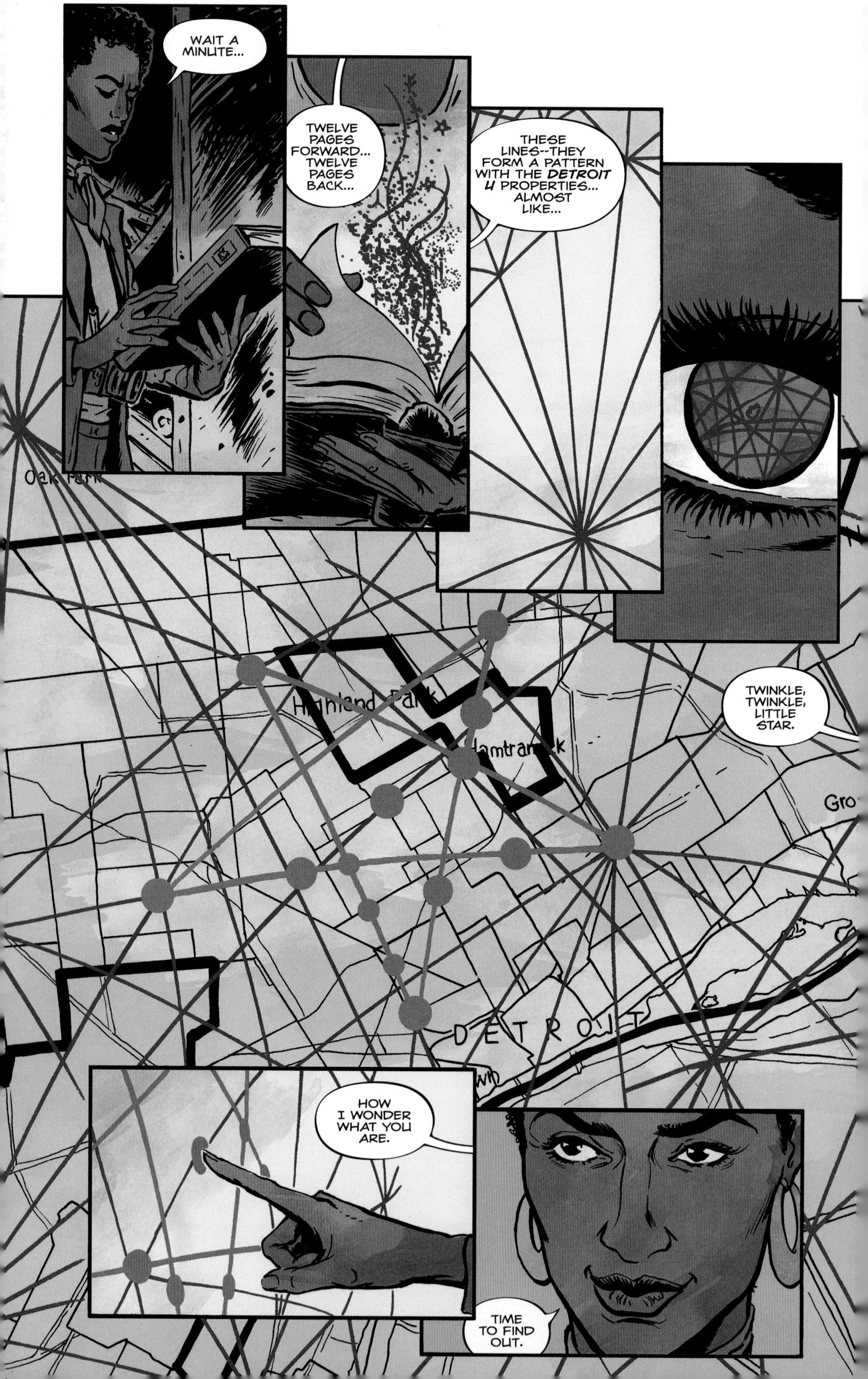
WAIT A MINUTE...
TWELVE PAGES FORWARD... TWELVE PAGES BACK...
THESE LINES--THEY FORM A PATTERN WITH THE DETROIT 4 PROPERTIES... ALMOST LIKE...
Oak Park
Highland Park
Hamtramck
DETROIT
TWINKLE, TWINKLE, LITTLE STAR.
HOW I WONDER WHAT YOU ARE.
TIME TO FIND OUT.

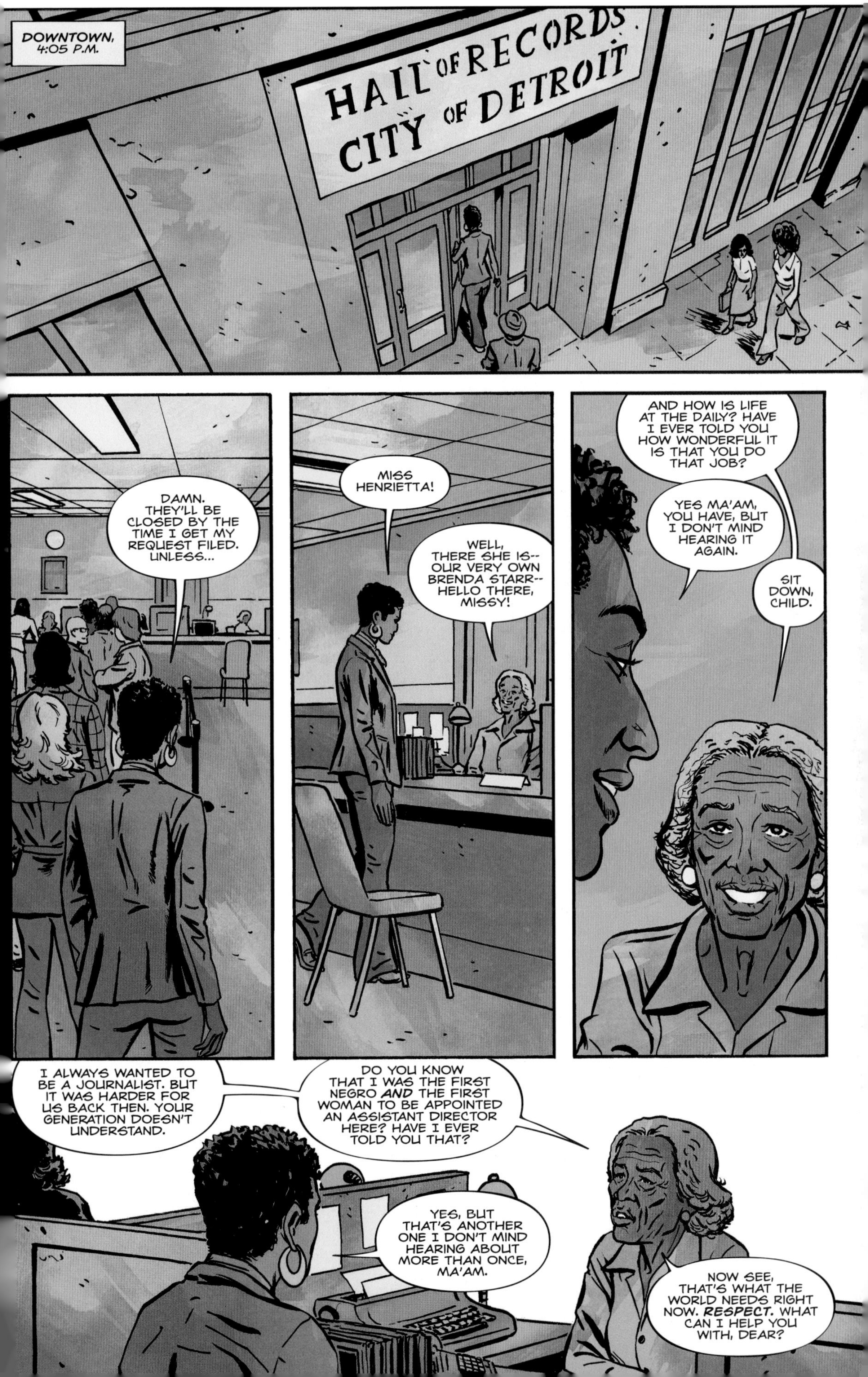
DOWNTOWN, 4:05 P.M.
HALL OF RECORDS CITY OF DETROIT
DAMN. THEY'LL BE CLOSED BY THE TIME I GET MY REQUEST FILED. UNLESS...
MISS HENRIETTA!
WELL, THERE SHE IS-- OUR VERY OWN BRENDA STARR-- HELLO THERE, MISSY!
AND HOW IS LIFE AT THE DAILY? HAVE I EVER TOLD YOU HOW WONDERFUL IT IS THAT YOU DO THAT JOB?
YES MA'AM, YOU HAVE, BUT I DON'T MIND HEARING IT AGAIN.
SIT DOWN, CHILD.
I ALWAYS WANTED TO BE A JOURNALIST. BUT IT WAS HARDER FOR US BACK THEN. YOUR GENERATION DOESN'T UNDERSTAND.
DO YOU KNOW THAT I WAS THE FIRST NEGRO AND THE FIRST WOMAN TO BE APPOINTED AN ASSISTANT DIRECTOR HERE? HAVE I EVER TOLD YOU THAT?
YES, BUT THAT'S ANOTHER ONE I DON'T MIND HEARING ABOUT MORE THAN ONCE, MA'AM.
NOW SEE, THAT'S WHAT THE WORLD NEEDS RIGHT NOW. RESPECT. WHAT CAN I HELP YOU WITH, DEAR?

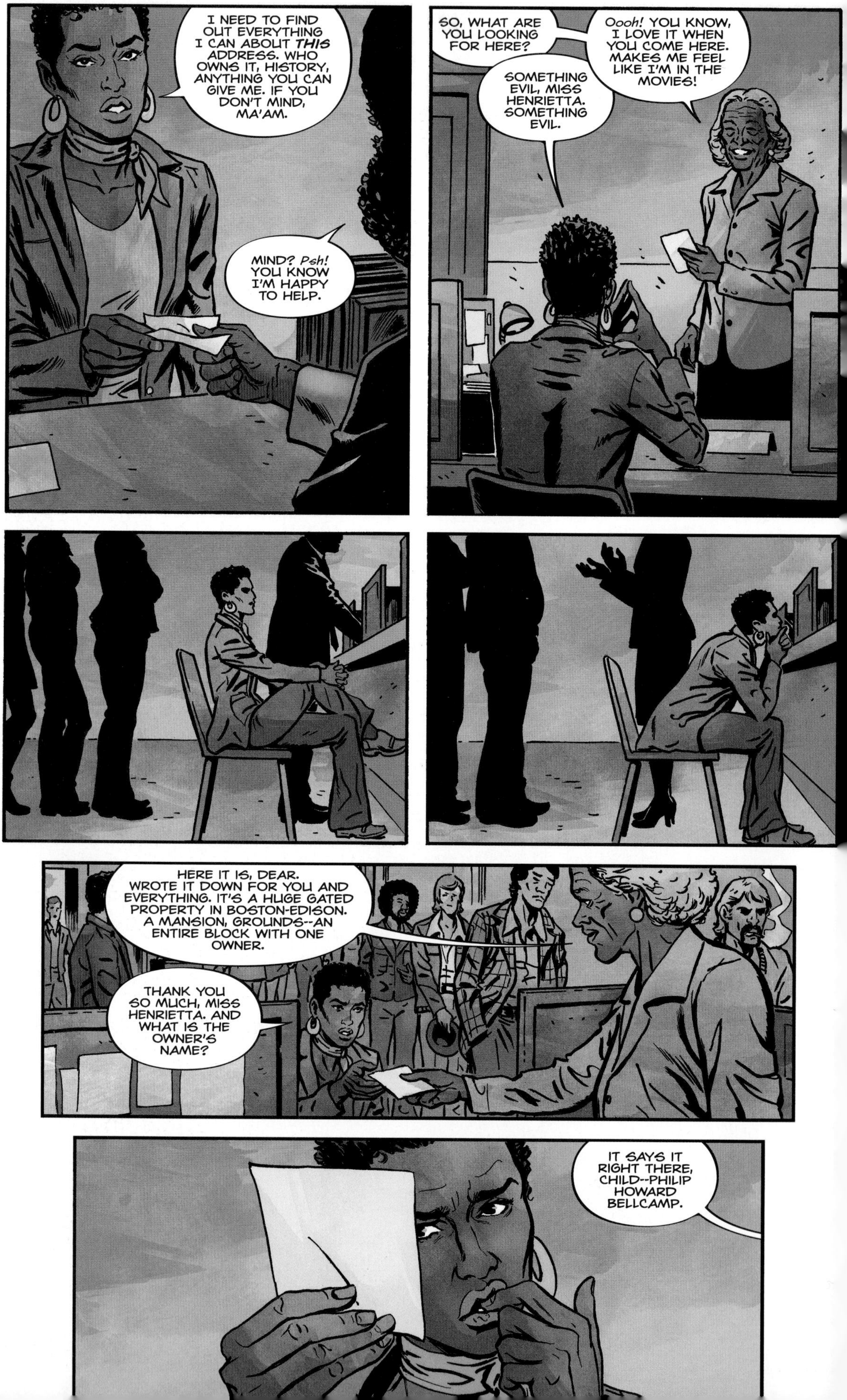
I NEED TO FIND OUT EVERYTHING I CAN ABOUT *THIS* ADDRESS. WHO OWNS IT, HISTORY, ANYTHING YOU CAN GIVE ME. IF YOU DON'T MIND, MA'AM.
MIND? *Psh!* YOU KNOW I'M HAPPY TO HELP.
SO, WHAT ARE YOU LOOKING FOR HERE?
SOMETHING EVIL, MISS HENRIETTA. SOMETHING EVIL.
Oooh! YOU KNOW, I LOVE IT WHEN YOU COME HERE. MAKES ME FEEL LIKE I'M IN THE MOVIES!
HERE IT IS, DEAR. WROTE IT DOWN FOR YOU AND EVERYTHING. IT'S A HUGE GATED PROPERTY IN BOSTON-EDISON. A MANSION, GROUNDS--AN ENTIRE BLOCK WITH ONE OWNER.
THANK YOU SO MUCH, MISS HENRIETTA. AND WHAT IS THE OWNER'S NAME?
IT SAYS IT RIGHT THERE, CHILD--PHILIP HOWARD BELLCAMP.

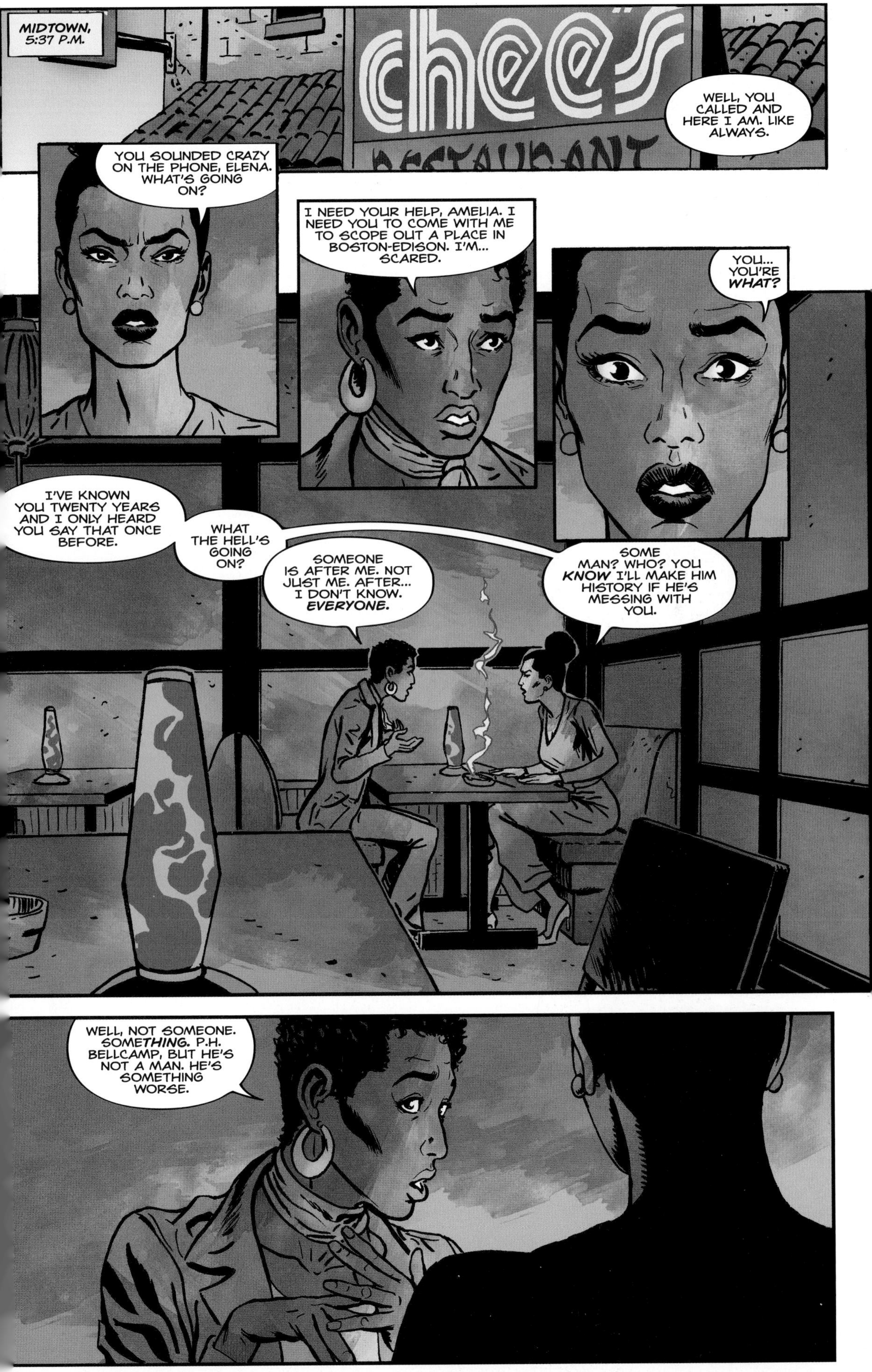
MIDTOWN, 5:37 P.M.
chee's RESTAURANT
WELL, YOU CALLED AND HERE I AM. LIKE ALWAYS.
YOU SOUNDED CRAZY ON THE PHONE, ELENA. WHAT'S GOING ON?
I NEED YOUR HELP, AMELIA. I NEED YOU TO COME WITH ME TO SCOPE OUT A PLACE IN BOSTON-EDISON. I'M... SCARED.
YOU... YOU'RE *WHAT?*
I'VE KNOWN YOU TWENTY YEARS AND I ONLY HEARD YOU SAY THAT ONCE BEFORE.
WHAT THE HELL'S GOING ON?
SOMEONE IS AFTER ME. NOT JUST ME. AFTER... I DON'T KNOW. *EVERYONE.*
SOME MAN? WHO? YOU *KNOW* I'LL MAKE HIM HISTORY IF HE'S MESSING WITH YOU.
WELL, NOT SOMEONE. SOME*THING.* P.H. BELLCAMP, BUT HE'S NOT A MAN. HE'S SOMETHING WORSE.

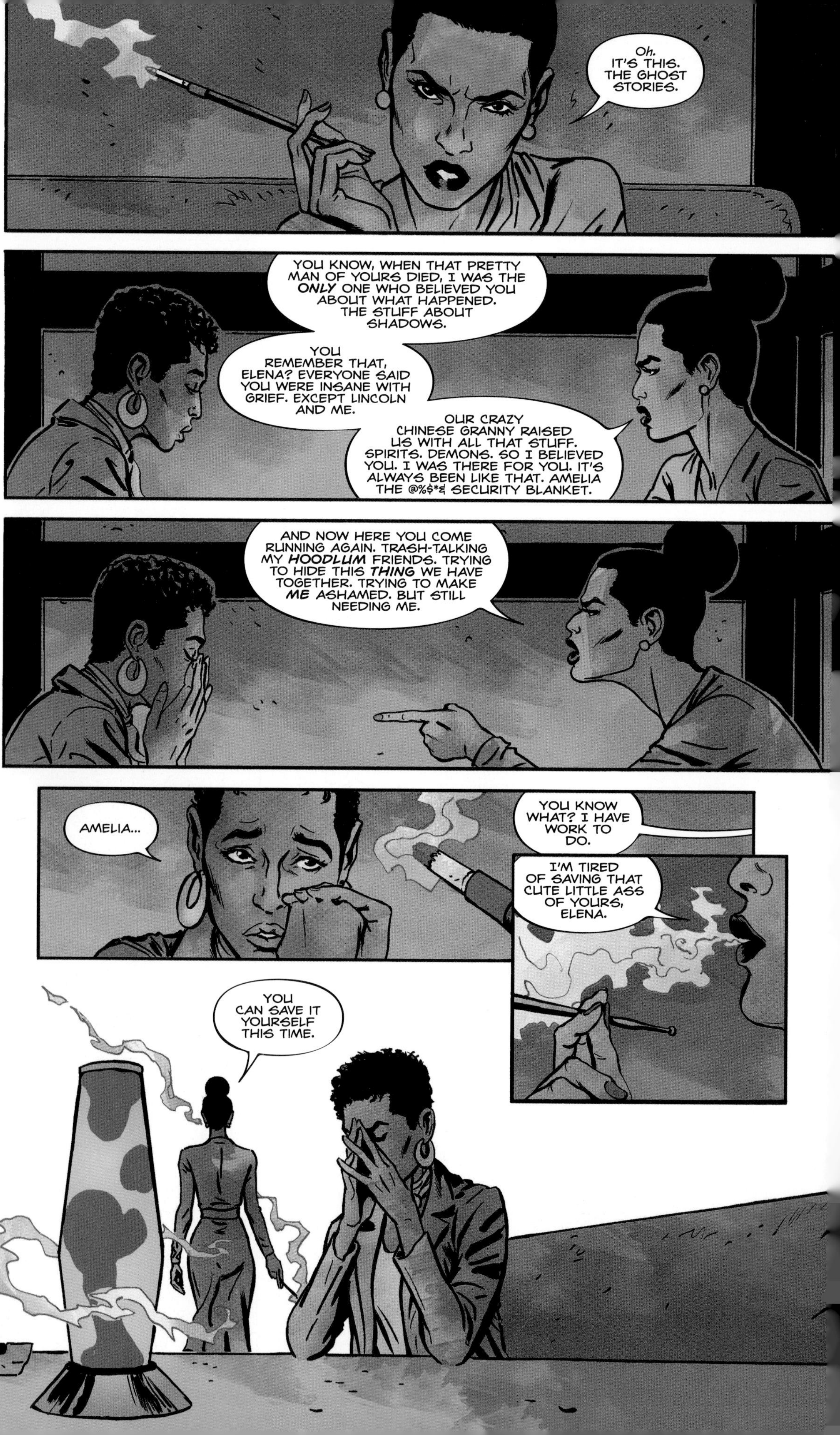
Oh. IT'S THIS. THE GHOST STORIES.
YOU KNOW, WHEN THAT PRETTY MAN OF YOURS DIED, I WAS THE ONLY ONE WHO BELIEVED YOU ABOUT WHAT HAPPENED. THE STUFF ABOUT SHADOWS.
YOU REMEMBER THAT, ELENA? EVERYONE SAID YOU WERE INSANE WITH GRIEF. EXCEPT LINCOLN AND ME.
OUR CRAZY CHINESE GRANNY RAISED US WITH ALL THAT STUFF. SPIRITS. DEMONS. SO I BELIEVED YOU. I WAS THERE FOR YOU. IT'S ALWAYS BEEN LIKE THAT. AMELIA THE @%$*& SECURITY BLANKET.
AND NOW HERE YOU COME RUNNING AGAIN. TRASH-TALKING MY HOODLUM FRIENDS. TRYING TO HIDE THIS THING WE HAVE TOGETHER. TRYING TO MAKE ME ASHAMED. BUT STILL NEEDING ME.
AMELIA...
YOU KNOW WHAT? I HAVE WORK TO DO.
I'M TIRED OF SAVING THAT CUTE LITTLE ASS OF YOURS, ELENA.
YOU CAN SAVE IT YOURSELF THIS TIME.

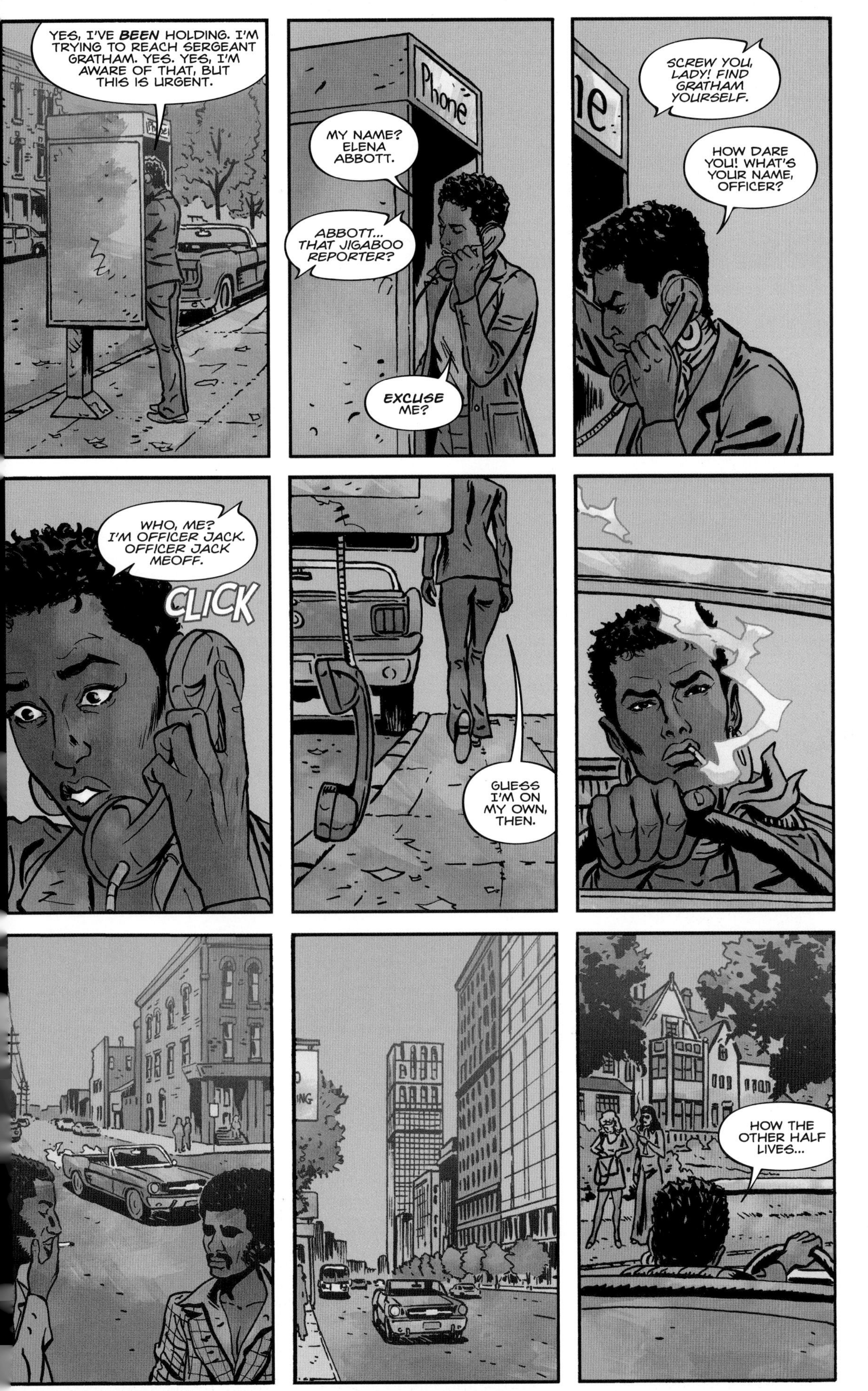
YES, I'VE BEEN HOLDING. I'M TRYING TO REACH SERGEANT GRATHAM. YES. YES, I'M AWARE OF THAT, BUT THIS IS URGENT.
Phone
MY NAME? ELENA ABBOTT.
ABBOTT... THAT JIGABOO REPORTER?
EXCUSE ME?
SCREW YOU, LADY! FIND GRATHAM YOURSELF.
HOW DARE YOU! WHAT'S YOUR NAME, OFFICER?
WHO, ME? I'M OFFICER JACK. OFFICER JACK MEOFF.
CLICK
GUESS I'M ON MY OWN, THEN.
HOW THE OTHER HALF LIVES...

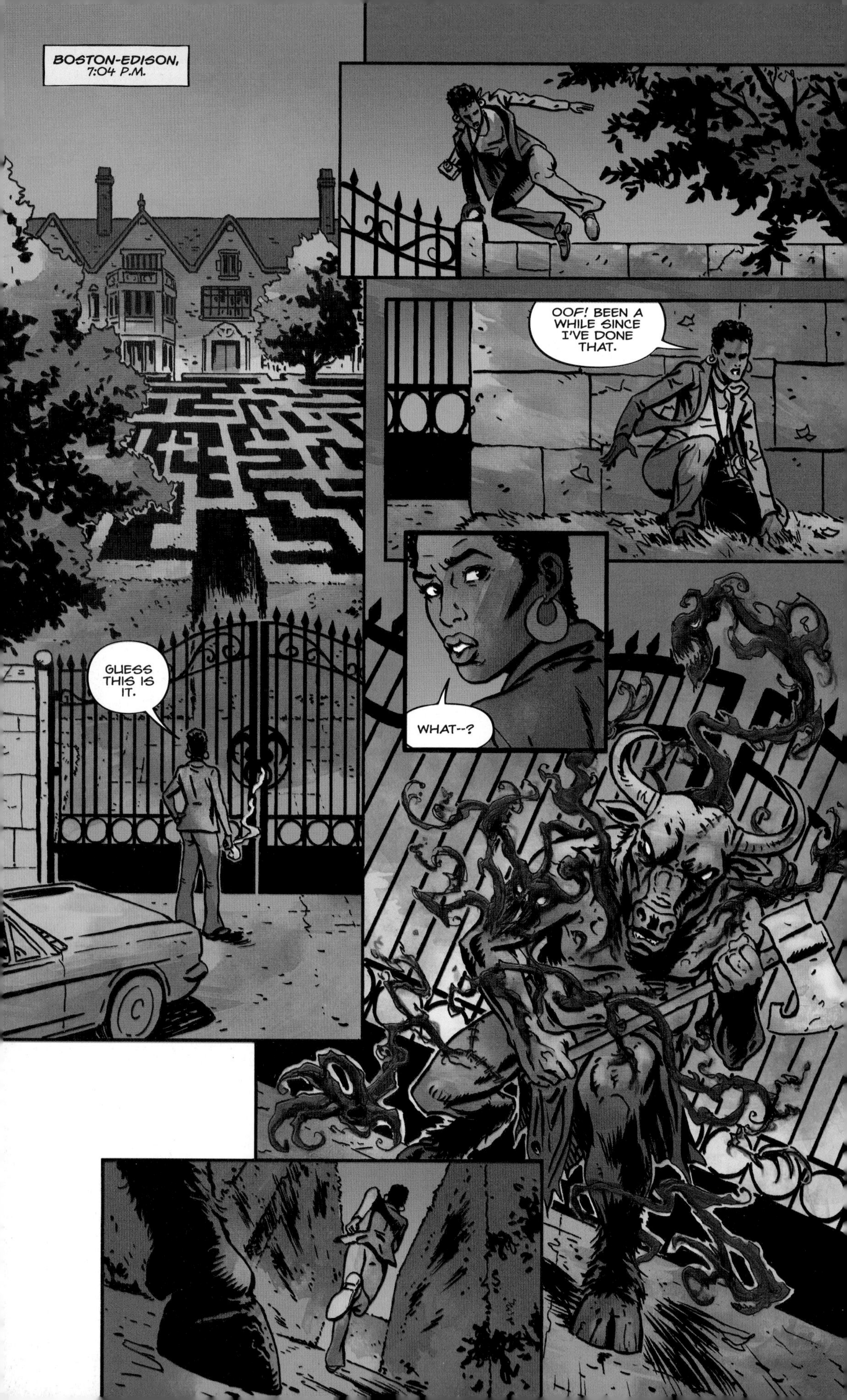
BOSTON-EDISON, 7:04 P.M.
GUESS THIS IS IT.
OOF! BEEN A WHILE SINCE I'VE DONE THAT.
WHAT--?

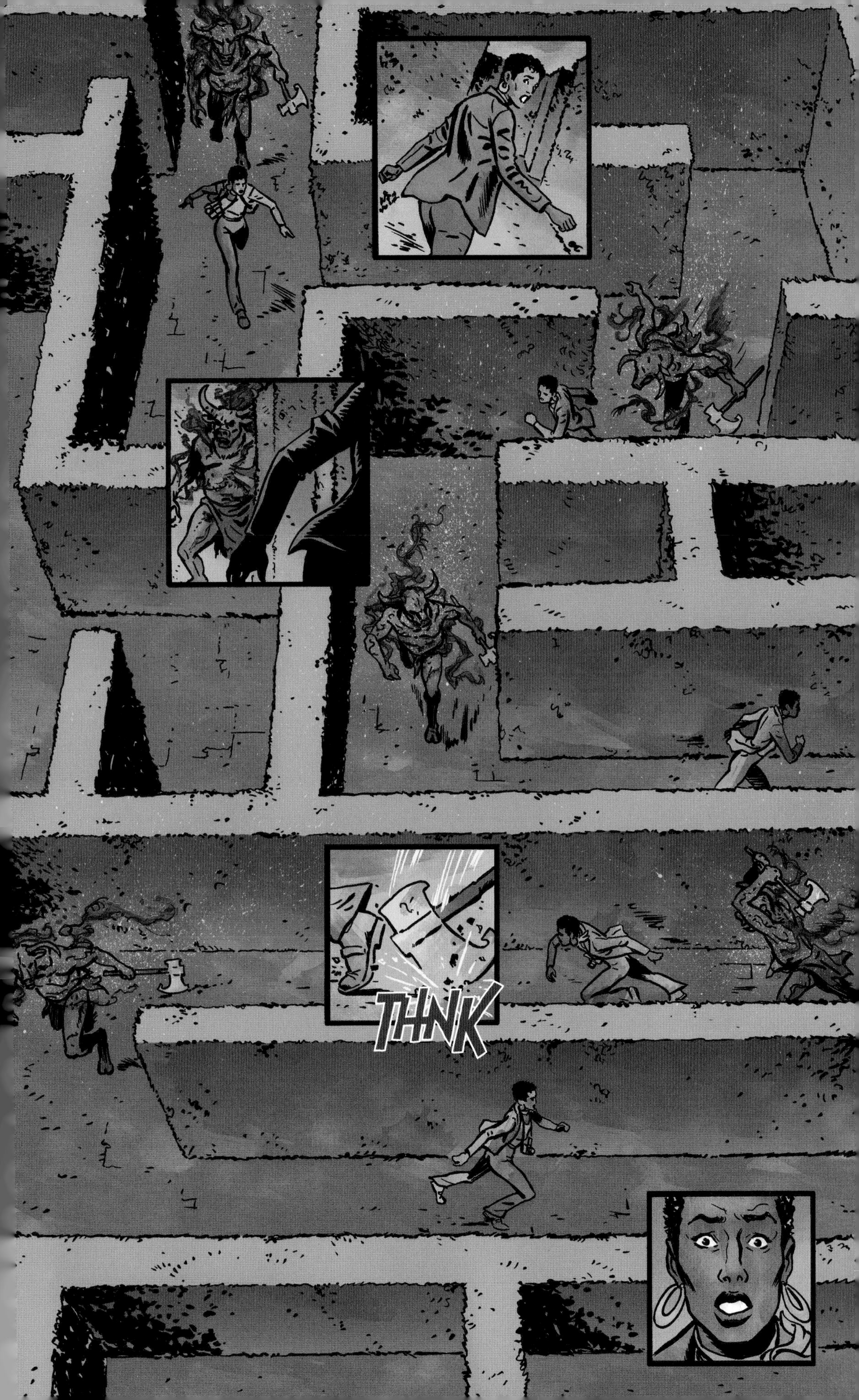
THNK

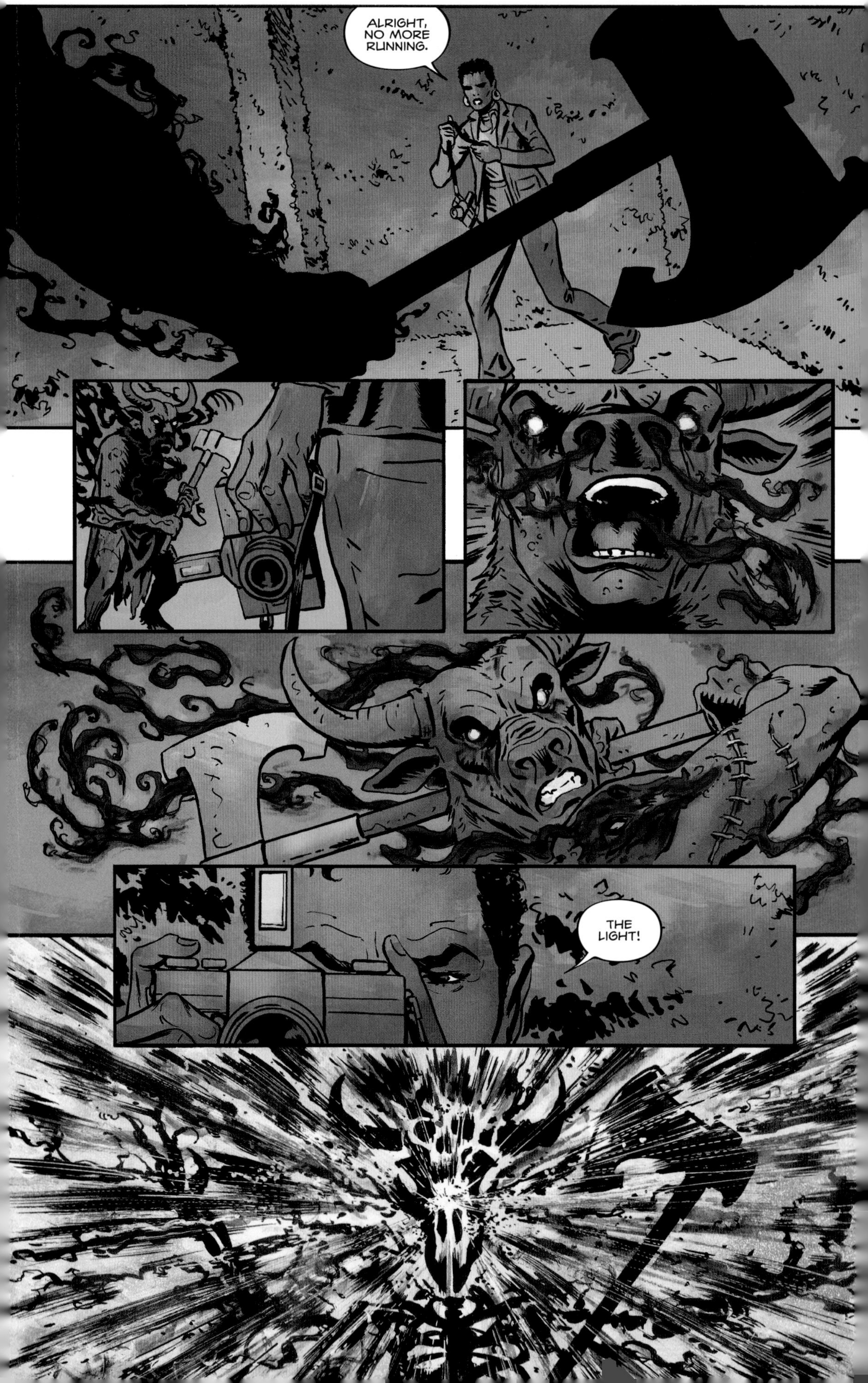
ALRIGHT, NO MORE RUNNING.
THE LIGHT!

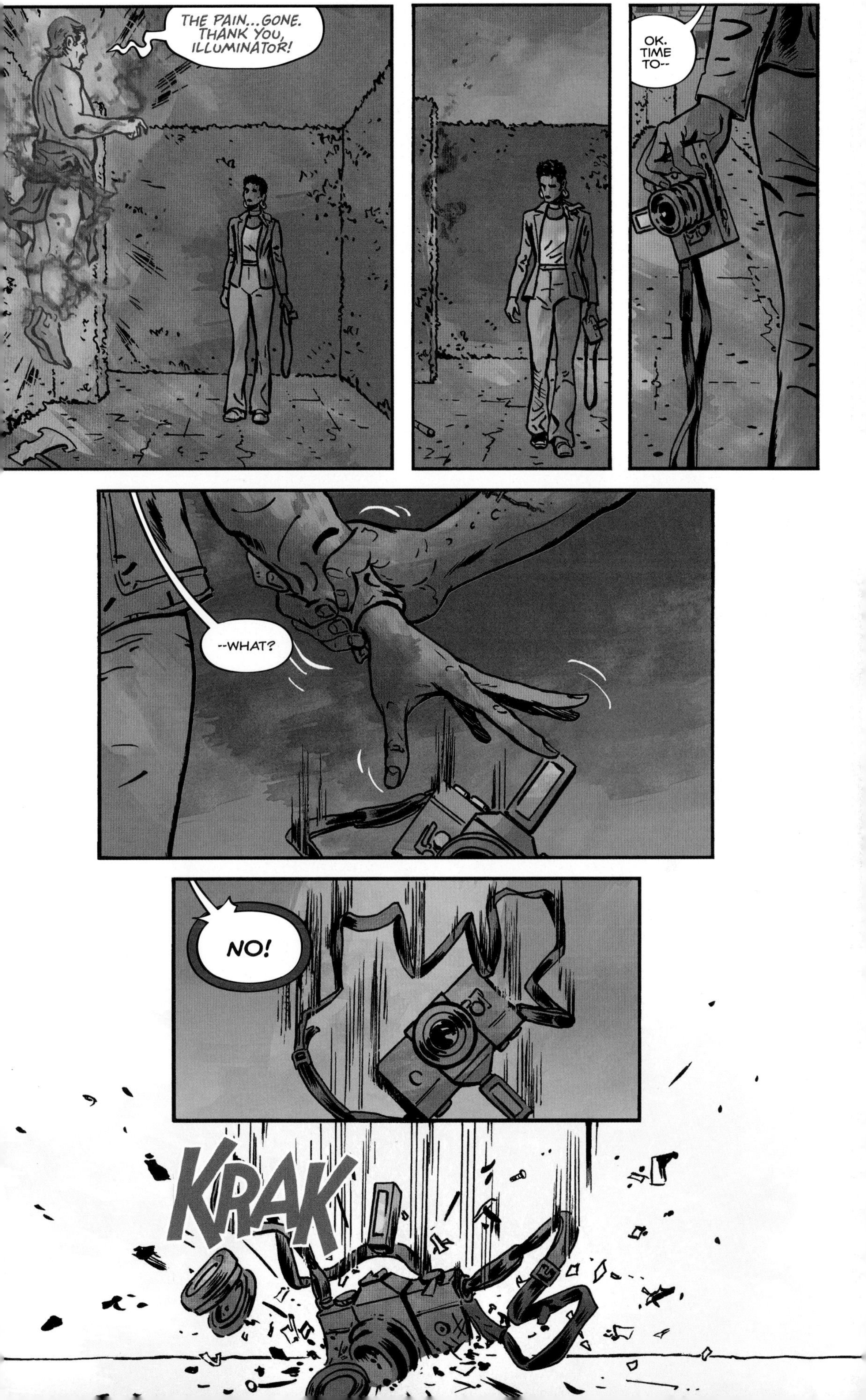
THE PAIN...GONE. THANK YOU, ILLUMINATOR!
OK. TIME TO--
--WHAT?
NO!
KRAK

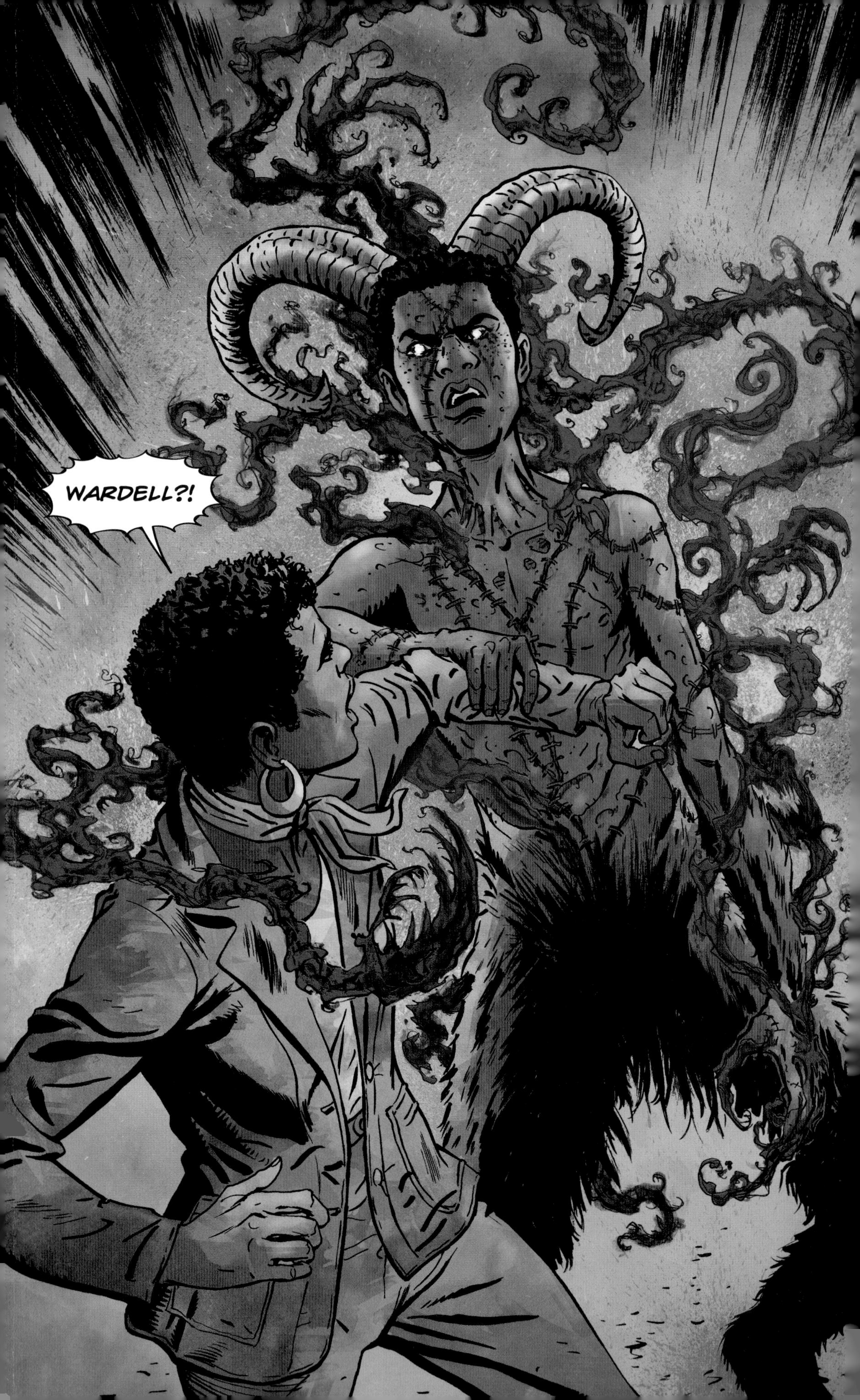
WARDELL?!

Issue Four Cover by
Taj Tenfold

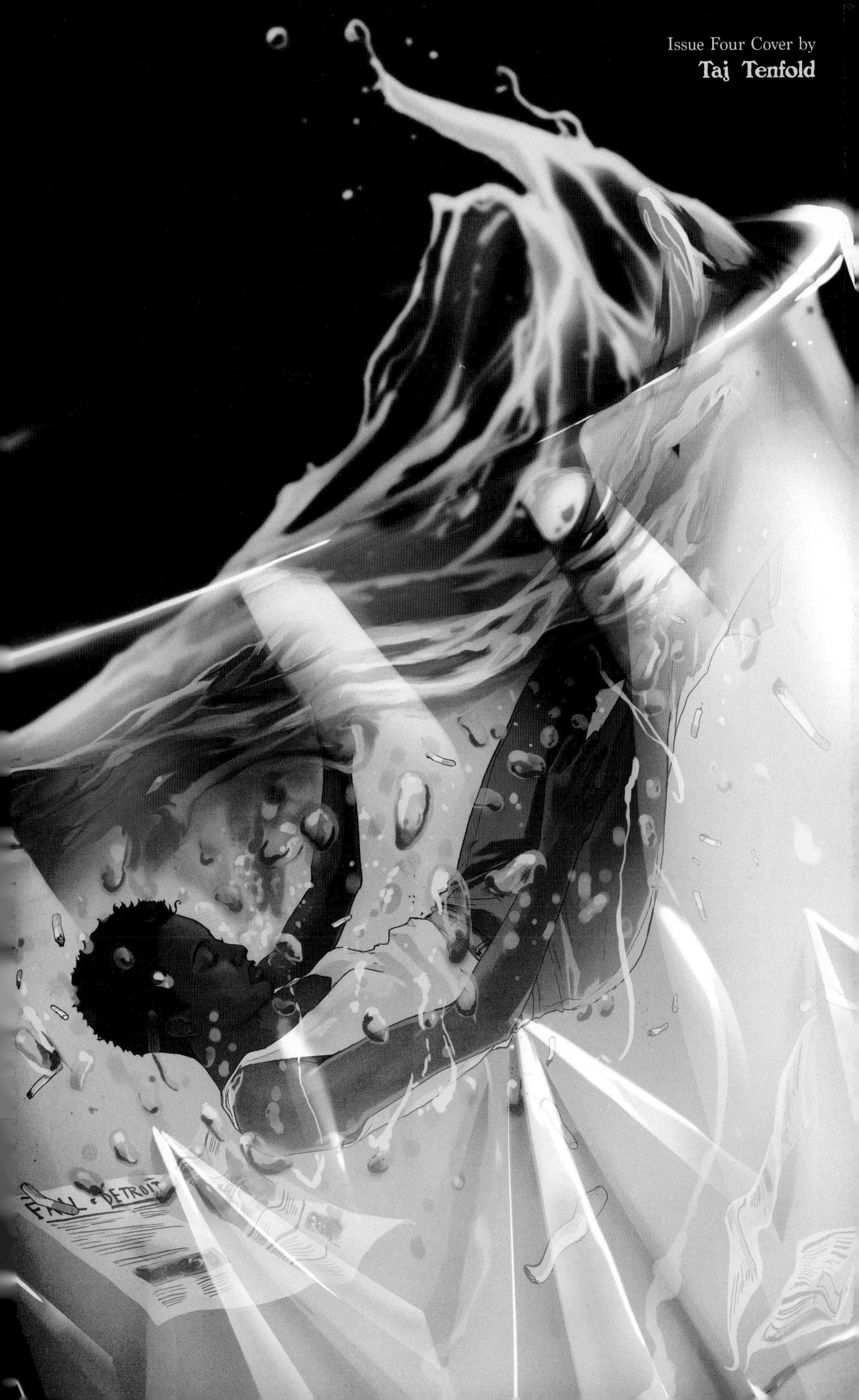
FALL · DETROIT

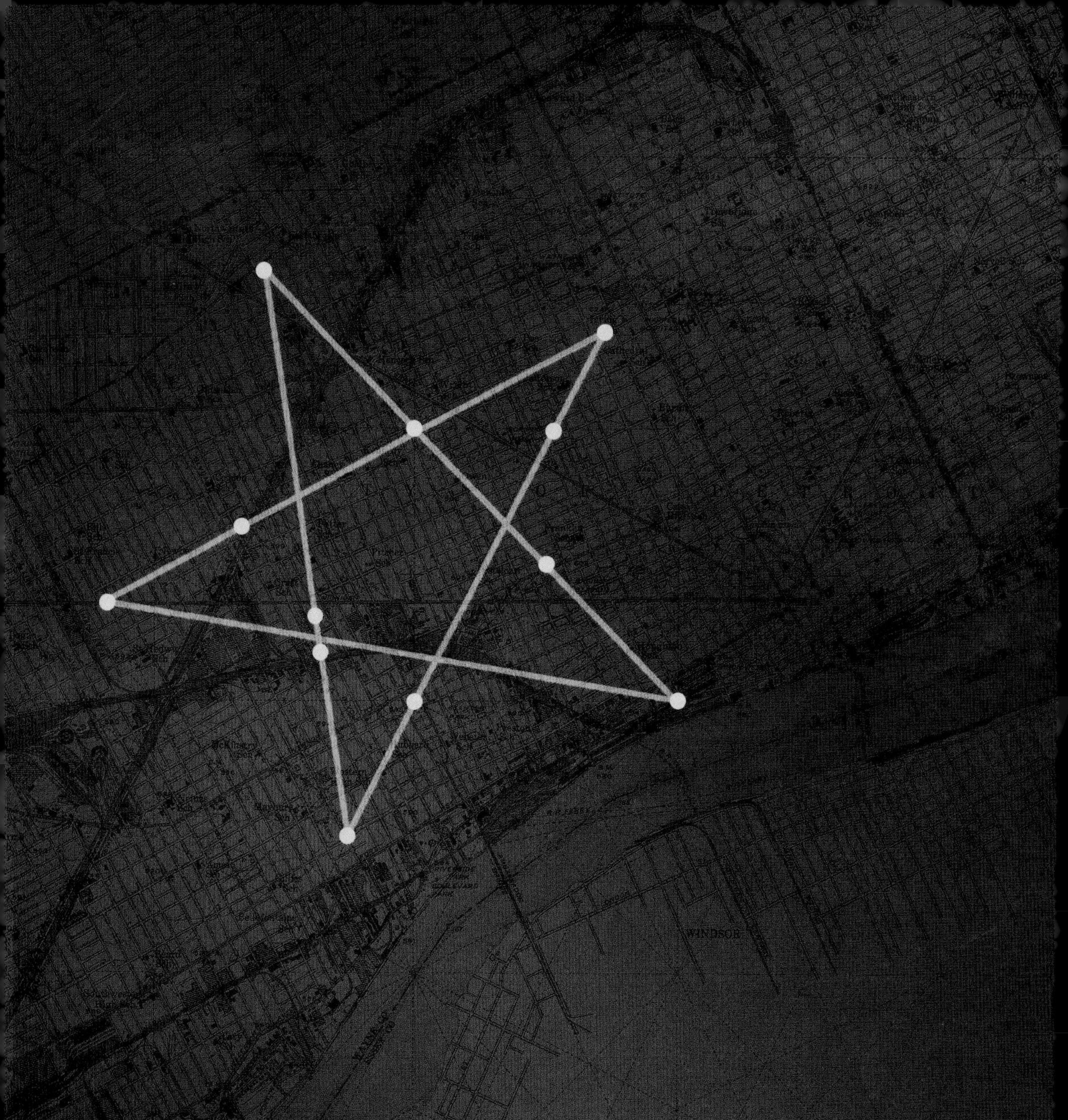

SOMEDAY WE'LL BE TOGETHER

Chapter Five

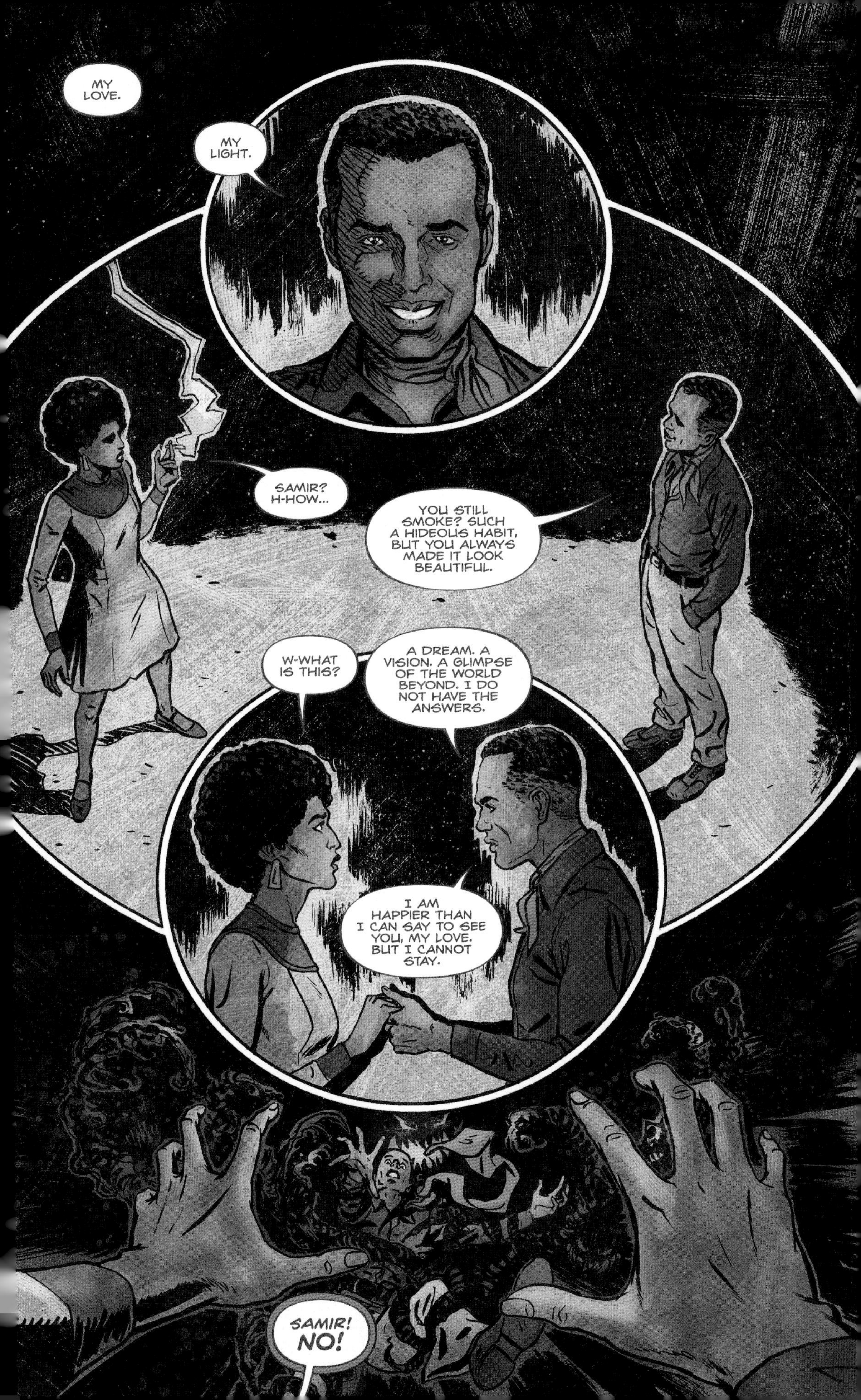
MY LOVE.
MY LIGHT.
SAMIR? H-HOW...
YOU STILL SMOKE? SUCH A HIDEOUS HABIT, BUT YOU ALWAYS MADE IT LOOK BEAUTIFUL.
W-WHAT IS THIS?
A DREAM. A VISION. A GLIMPSE OF THE WORLD BEYOND. I DO NOT HAVE THE ANSWERS.
I AM HAPPIER THAN I CAN SAY TO SEE YOU, MY LOVE. BUT I CANNOT STAY.
SAMIR! NO!

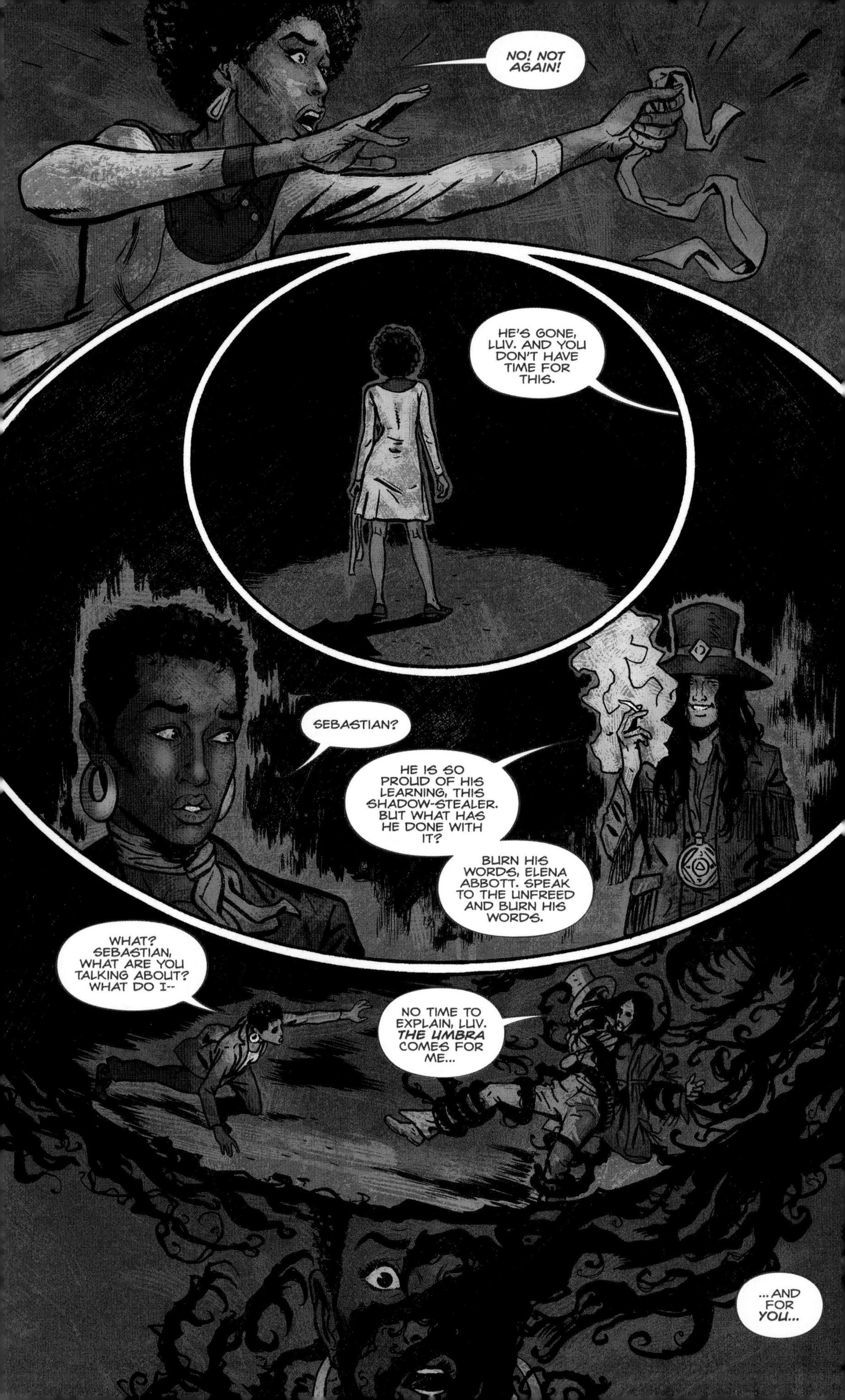
NO! NOT AGAIN!
HE'S GONE, LUV. AND YOU DON'T HAVE TIME FOR THIS.
SEBASTIAN?
HE IS SO PROUD OF HIS LEARNING, THIS SHADOW-STEALER. BUT WHAT HAS HE DONE WITH IT?
BURN HIS WORDS, ELENA ABBOTT. SPEAK TO THE UNFREED AND BURN HIS WORDS.
WHAT? SEBASTIAN, WHAT ARE YOU TALKING ABOUT? WHAT DO I--
NO TIME TO EXPLAIN, LUV. *THE UMBRA* COMES FOR ME...
...AND FOR *YOU*...

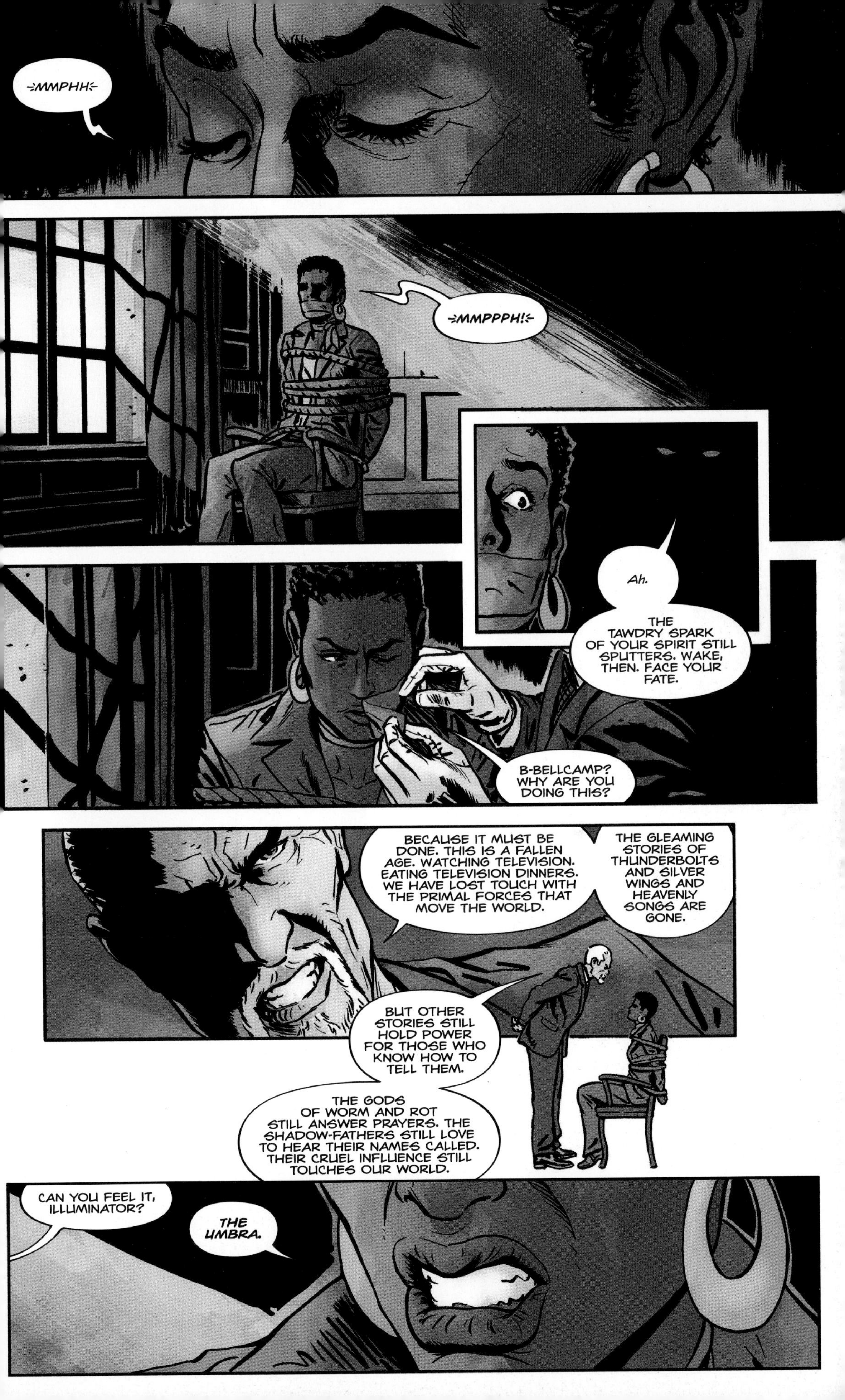
-MMPHH-
-MMPPPH!-
Ah.
THE TAWDRY SPARK OF YOUR SPIRIT STILL SPUTTERS. WAKE, THEN. FACE YOUR FATE.
B-BELLCAMP? WHY ARE YOU DOING THIS?
BECAUSE IT MUST BE DONE. THIS IS A FALLEN AGE. WATCHING TELEVISION. EATING TELEVISION DINNERS. WE HAVE LOST TOUCH WITH THE PRIMAL FORCES THAT MOVE THE WORLD.
THE GLEAMING STORIES OF THUNDERBOLTS AND SILVER WINGS AND HEAVENLY SONGS ARE GONE.
BUT OTHER STORIES STILL HOLD POWER FOR THOSE WHO KNOW HOW TO TELL THEM.
THE GODS OF WORM AND ROT STILL ANSWER PRAYERS. THE SHADOW-FATHERS STILL LOVE TO HEAR THEIR NAMES CALLED. THEIR CRUEL INFLUENCE STILL TOUCHES OUR WORLD.
CAN YOU FEEL IT, ILLUMINATOR?
THE UMBRA.

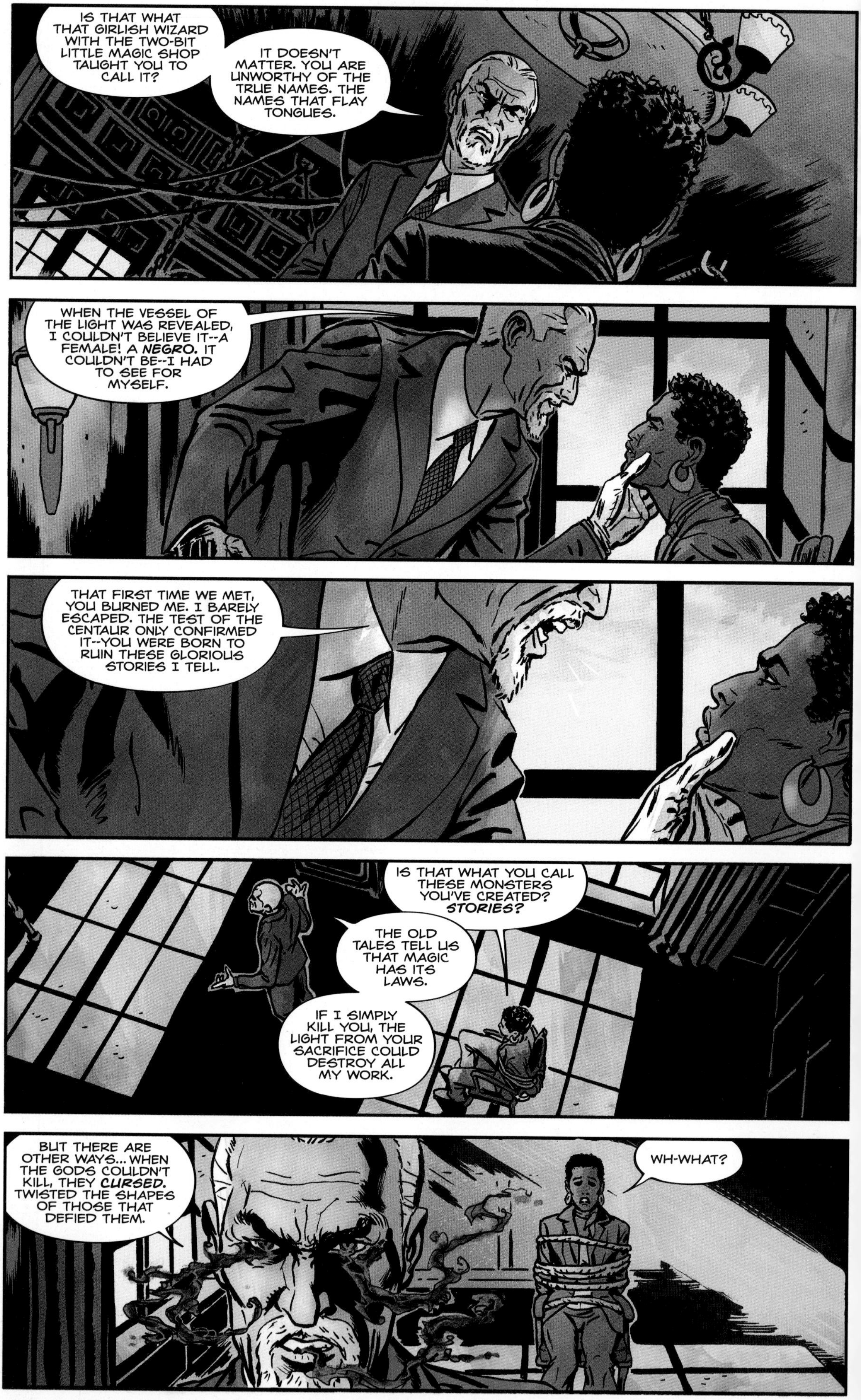
IS THAT WHAT THAT GIRLISH WIZARD WITH THE TWO-BIT LITTLE MAGIC SHOP TAUGHT YOU TO CALL IT?
IT DOESN'T MATTER. YOU ARE UNWORTHY OF THE TRUE NAMES. THE NAMES THAT FLAY TONGUES.
WHEN THE VESSEL OF THE LIGHT WAS REVEALED, I COULDN'T BELIEVE IT--A FEMALE! A NEGRO. IT COULDN'T BE--I HAD TO SEE FOR MYSELF.
THAT FIRST TIME WE MET, YOU BURNED ME. I BARELY ESCAPED. THE TEST OF THE CENTAUR ONLY CONFIRMED IT--YOU WERE BORN TO RUIN THESE GLORIOUS STORIES I TELL.
IS THAT WHAT YOU CALL THESE MONSTERS YOU'VE CREATED? STORIES?
THE OLD TALES TELL US THAT MAGIC HAS ITS LAWS.
IF I SIMPLY KILL YOU, THE LIGHT FROM YOUR SACRIFICE COULD DESTROY ALL MY WORK.
BUT THERE ARE OTHER WAYS... WHEN THE GODS COULDN'T KILL, THEY CURSED. TWISTED THE SHAPES OF THOSE THAT DEFIED THEM.
WH-WHAT?

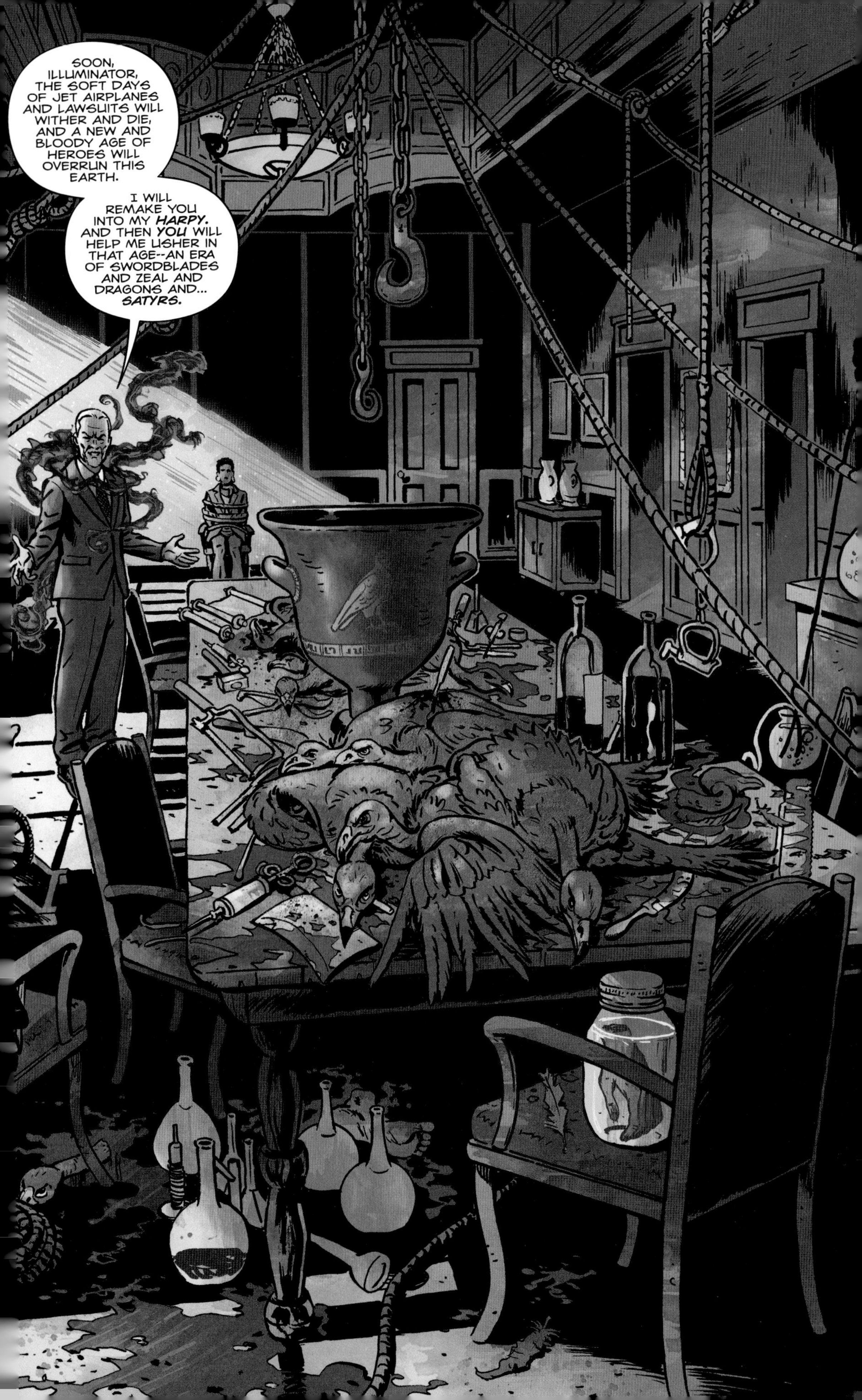
SOON, ILLUMINATOR, THE SOFT DAYS OF JET AIRPLANES AND LAWSUITS WILL WITHER AND DIE, AND A NEW AND BLOODY AGE OF HEROES WILL OVERRUN THIS EARTH.
I WILL REMAKE YOU INTO MY HARPY. AND THEN YOU WILL HELP ME USHER IN THAT AGE--AN ERA OF SWORDBLADES AND ZEAL AND DRAGONS AND... SATYRS.

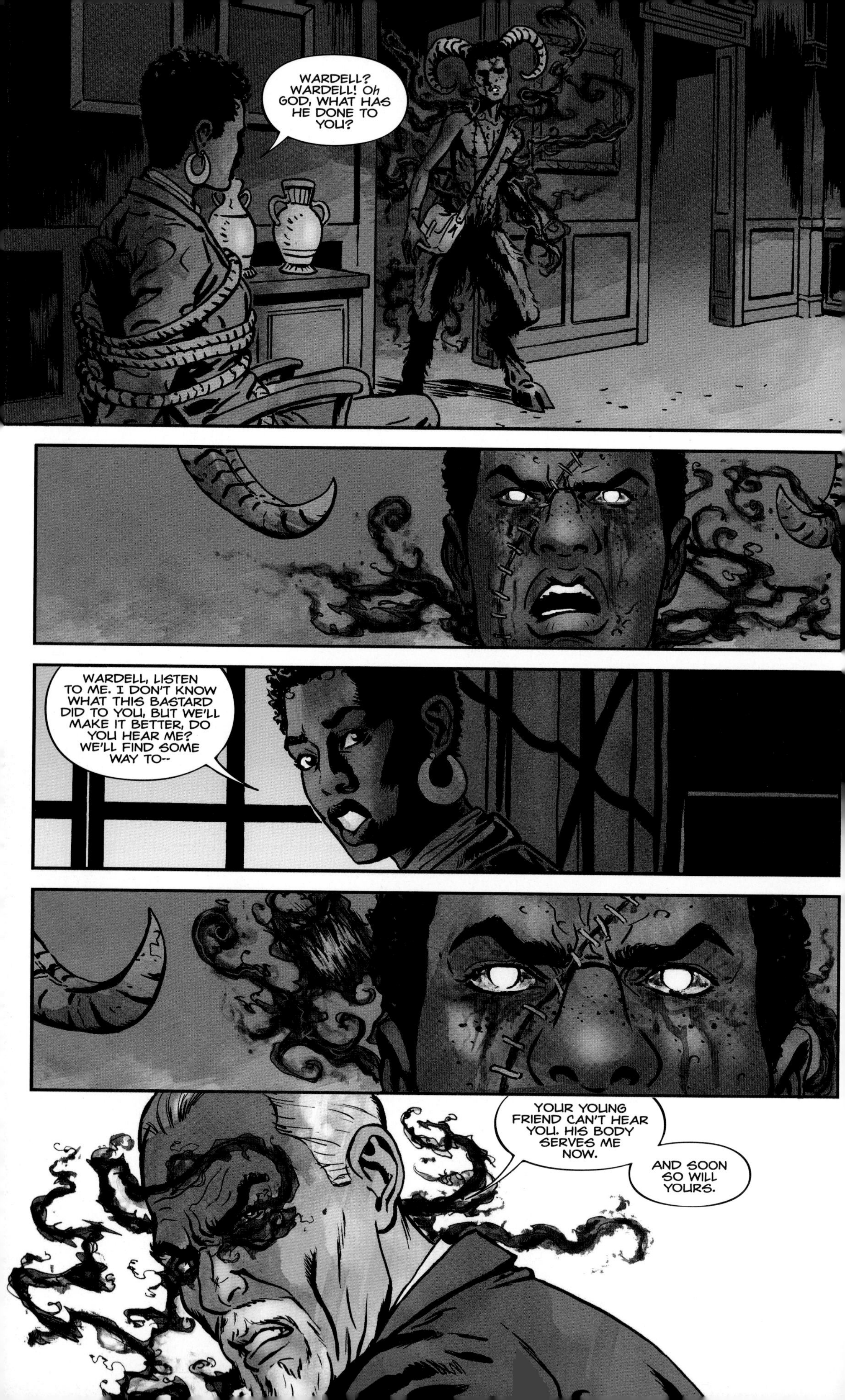
WARDELL? WARDELL! Oh GOD, WHAT HAS HE DONE TO YOU?
WARDELL, LISTEN TO ME. I DON'T KNOW WHAT THIS BASTARD DID TO YOU, BUT WE'LL MAKE IT BETTER, DO YOU HEAR ME? WE'LL FIND SOME WAY TO--
YOUR YOUNG FRIEND CAN'T HEAR YOU. HIS BODY SERVES ME NOW.
AND SOON SO WILL YOURS.

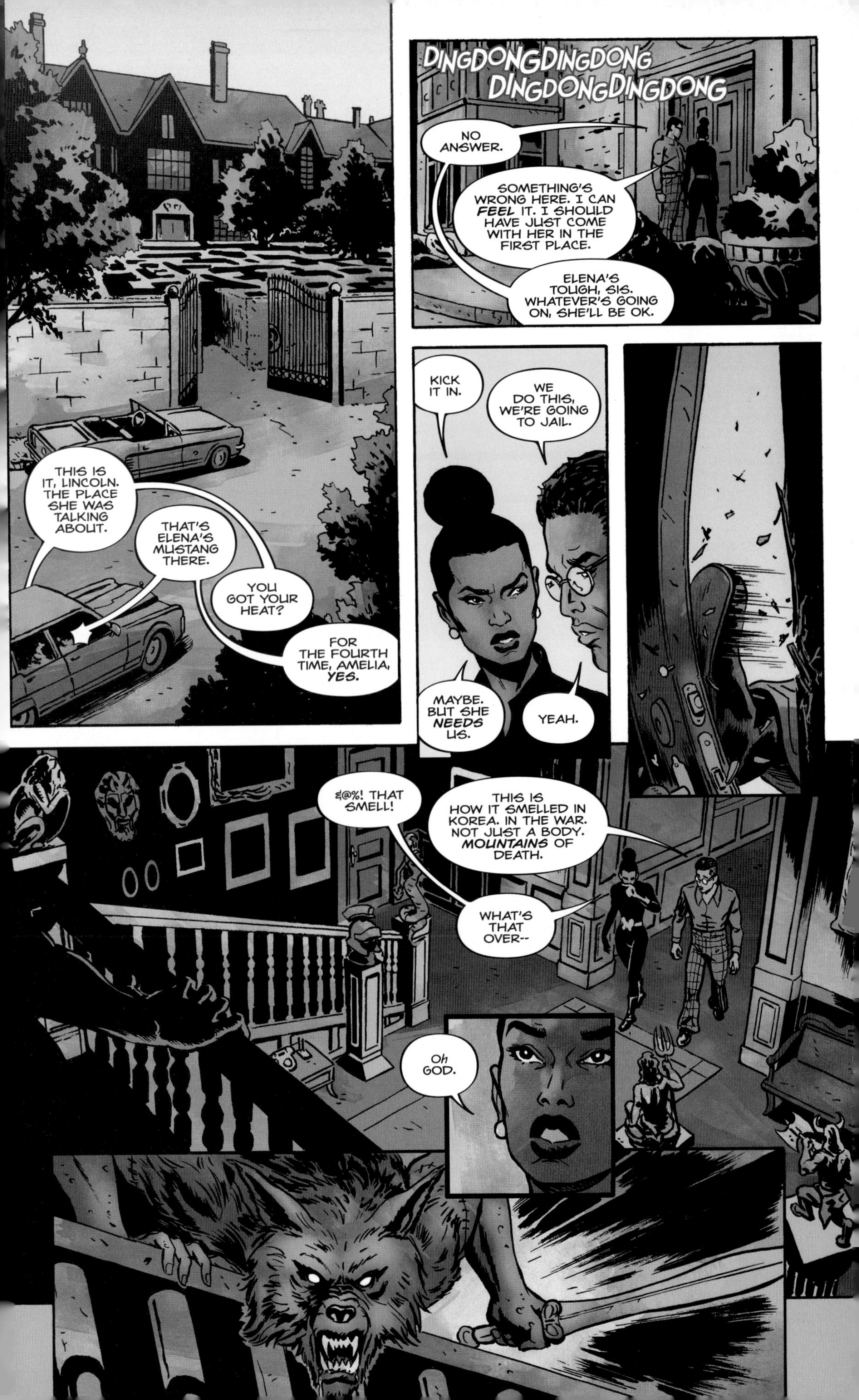
THIS IS IT, LINCOLN. THE PLACE SHE WAS TALKING ABOUT.
THAT'S ELENA'S MUSTANG THERE.
YOU GOT YOUR HEAT?
FOR THE FOURTH TIME, AMELIA, YES.
DINGDONGDINGDONG DINGDONGDINGDONG
NO ANSWER.
SOMETHING'S WRONG HERE. I CAN FEEL IT. I SHOULD HAVE JUST COME WITH HER IN THE FIRST PLACE.
ELENA'S TOUGH, SIS. WHATEVER'S GOING ON, SHE'LL BE OK.
KICK IT IN.
WE DO THIS, WE'RE GOING TO JAIL.
MAYBE. BUT SHE NEEDS US.
YEAH.
$@%! THAT SMELL!
THIS IS HOW IT SMELLED IN KOREA. IN THE WAR. NOT JUST A BODY. MOUNTAINS OF DEATH.
WHAT'S THAT OVER--
Oh GOD.

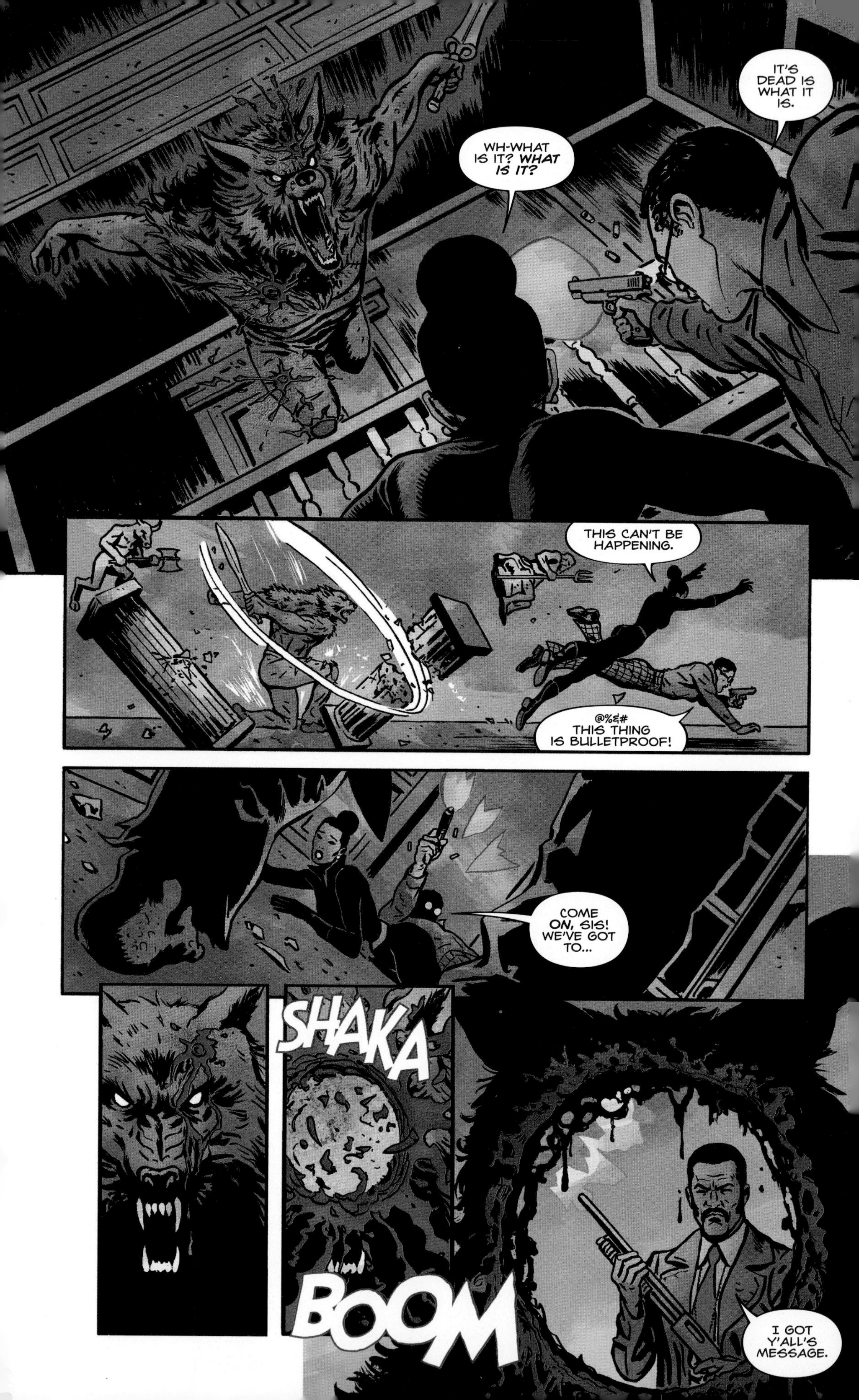
WH-WHAT IS IT? WHAT IS IT?
IT'S DEAD IS WHAT IT IS.
THIS CAN'T BE HAPPENING.
@%&# THIS THING IS BULLETPROOF!
COME ON, SIS! WE'VE GOT TO...
SHAKA
BOOM
I GOT Y'ALL'S MESSAGE.

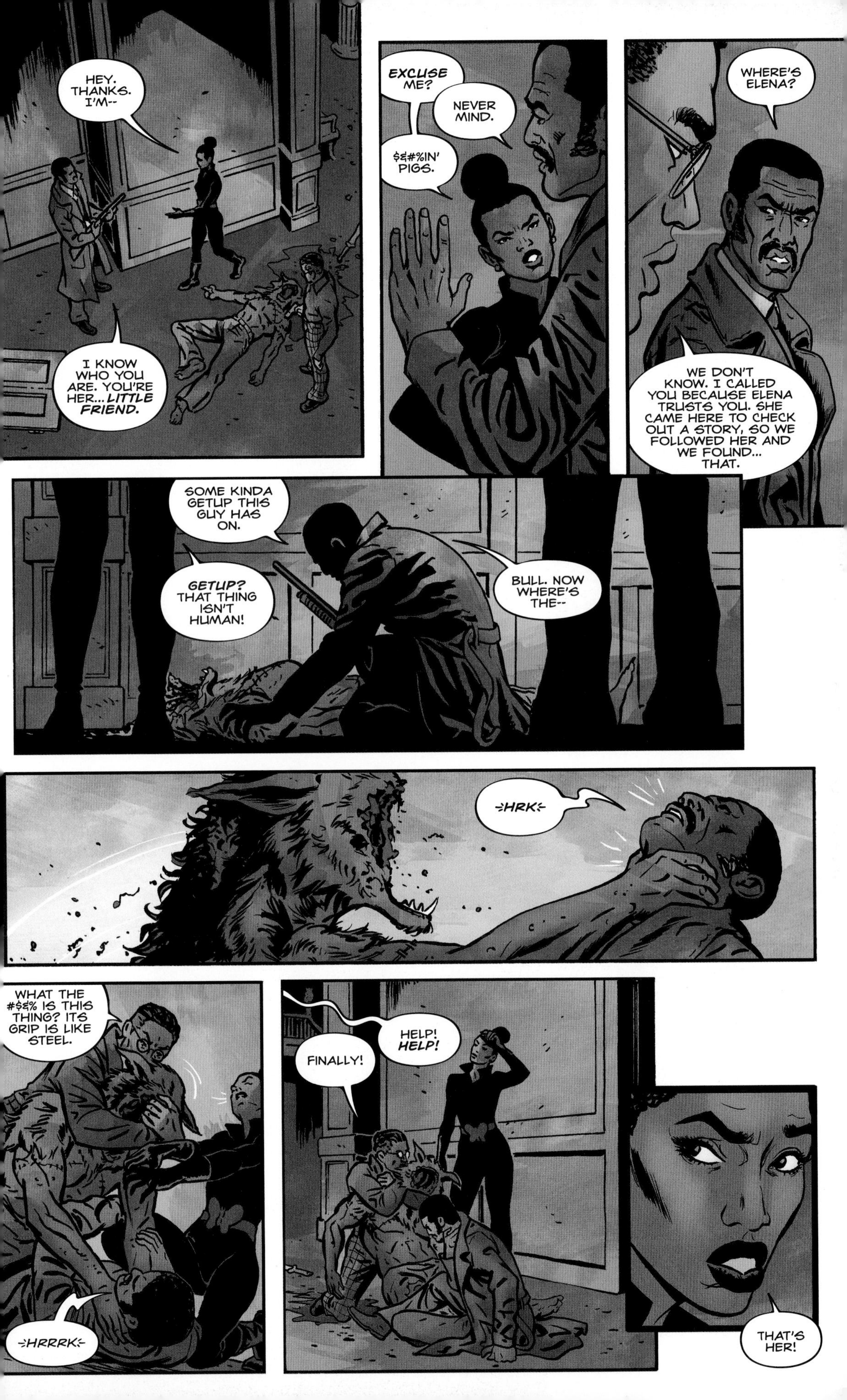
HEY. THANKS. I'M--
I KNOW WHO YOU ARE. YOU'RE HER... LITTLE FRIEND.
EXCUSE ME?
NEVER MIND.
$&#%IN' PIGS.
WHERE'S ELENA?
WE DON'T KNOW. I CALLED YOU BECAUSE ELENA TRUSTS YOU. SHE CAME HERE TO CHECK OUT A STORY, SO WE FOLLOWED HER AND WE FOUND... THAT.
SOME KINDA GETUP THIS GUY HAS ON.
GETUP? THAT THING ISN'T HUMAN!
BULL. NOW WHERE'S THE--
-HRK-
WHAT THE #$&% IS THIS THING? ITS GRIP IS LIKE STEEL.
-HRRRK-
HELP! HELP!
FINALLY!
THAT'S HER!

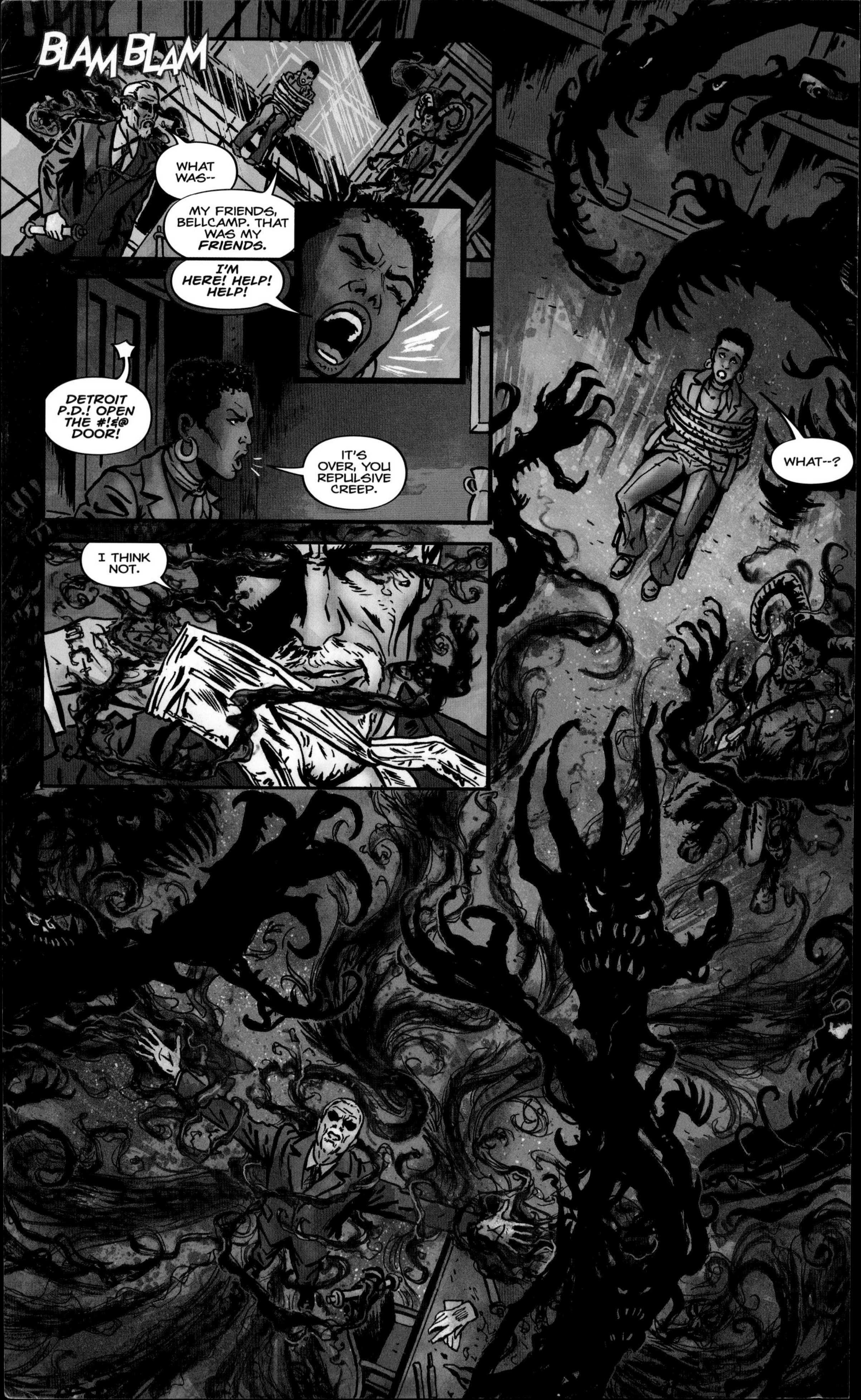
BLAM BLAM
WHAT WAS--
MY FRIENDS, BELLCAMP. THAT WAS MY FRIENDS.
I'M HERE! HELP! HELP!
DETROIT P.D.! OPEN THE #!$@ DOOR!
IT'S OVER, YOU REPULSIVE CREEP.
WHAT--?
I THINK NOT.

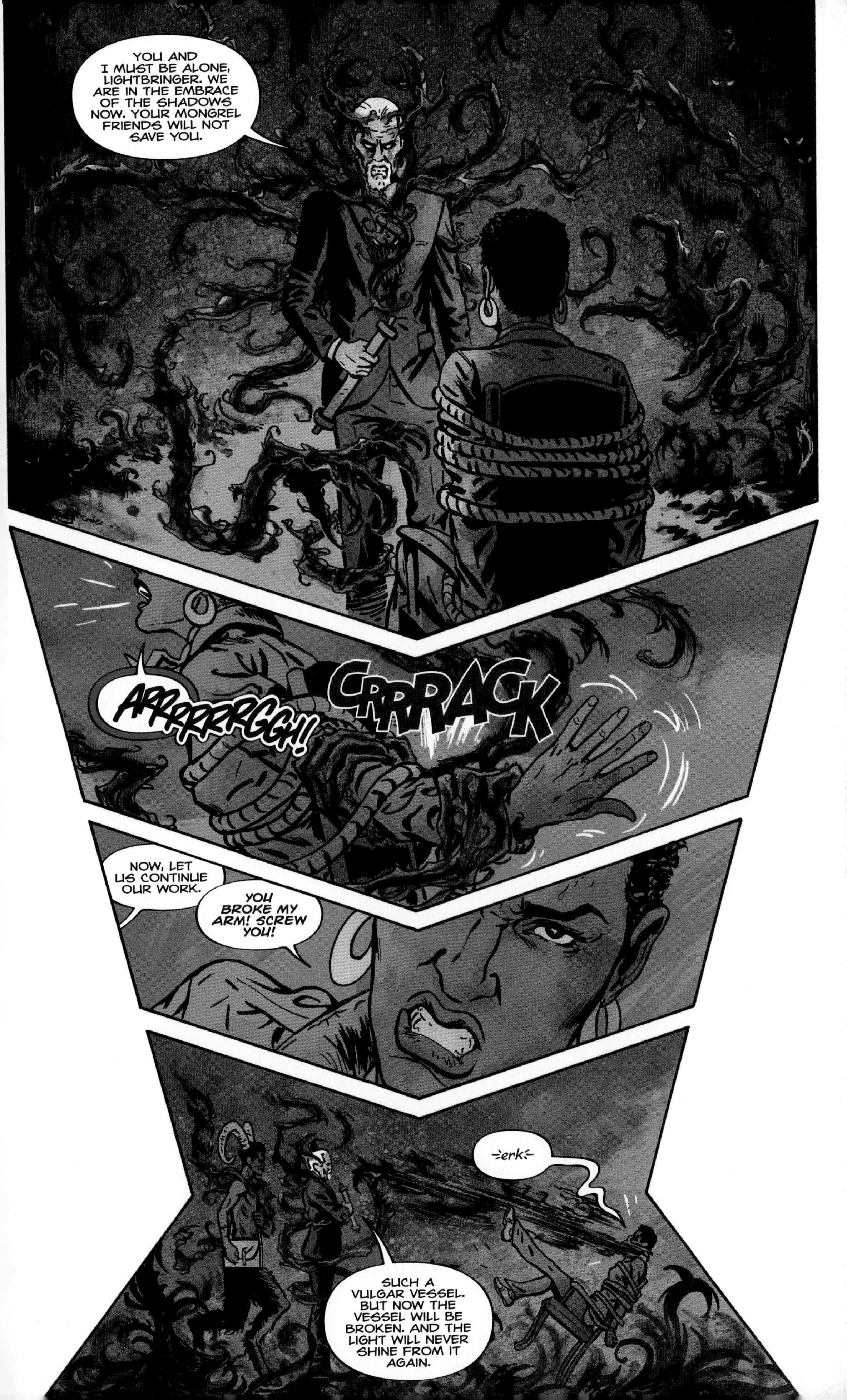
YOU AND I MUST BE ALONE, LIGHTBRINGER. WE ARE IN THE EMBRACE OF THE SHADOWS NOW. YOUR MONGREL FRIENDS WILL NOT SAVE YOU.
ARRRRRRRGGH!!
CRRRACK
NOW, LET US CONTINUE OUR WORK.
YOU BROKE MY ARM! SCREW YOU!
erk
SUCH A VULGAR VESSEL. BUT NOW THE VESSEL WILL BE BROKEN. AND THE LIGHT WILL NEVER SHINE FROM IT AGAIN.

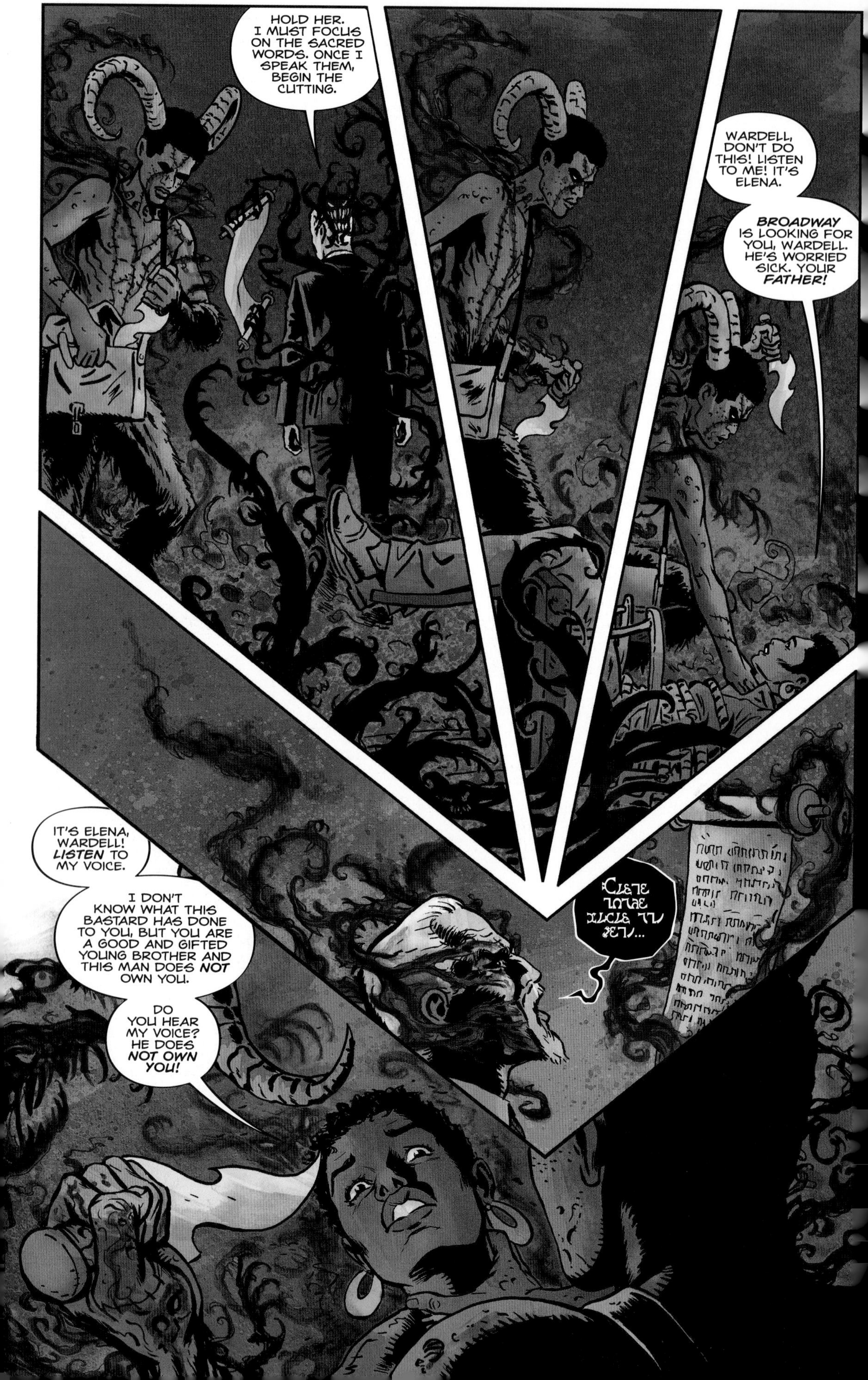
HOLD HER. I MUST FOCUS ON THE SACRED WORDS. ONCE I SPEAK THEM, BEGIN THE CUTTING.
WARDELL, DON'T DO THIS! LISTEN TO ME! IT'S ELENA.
BROADWAY IS LOOKING FOR YOU, WARDELL. HE'S WORRIED SICK. YOUR FATHER!
IT'S ELENA, WARDELL! LISTEN TO MY VOICE.
I DON'T KNOW WHAT THIS BASTARD HAS DONE TO YOU, BUT YOU ARE A GOOD AND GIFTED YOUNG BROTHER AND THIS MAN DOES NOT OWN YOU.
DO YOU HEAR MY VOICE? HE DOES NOT OWN YOU!

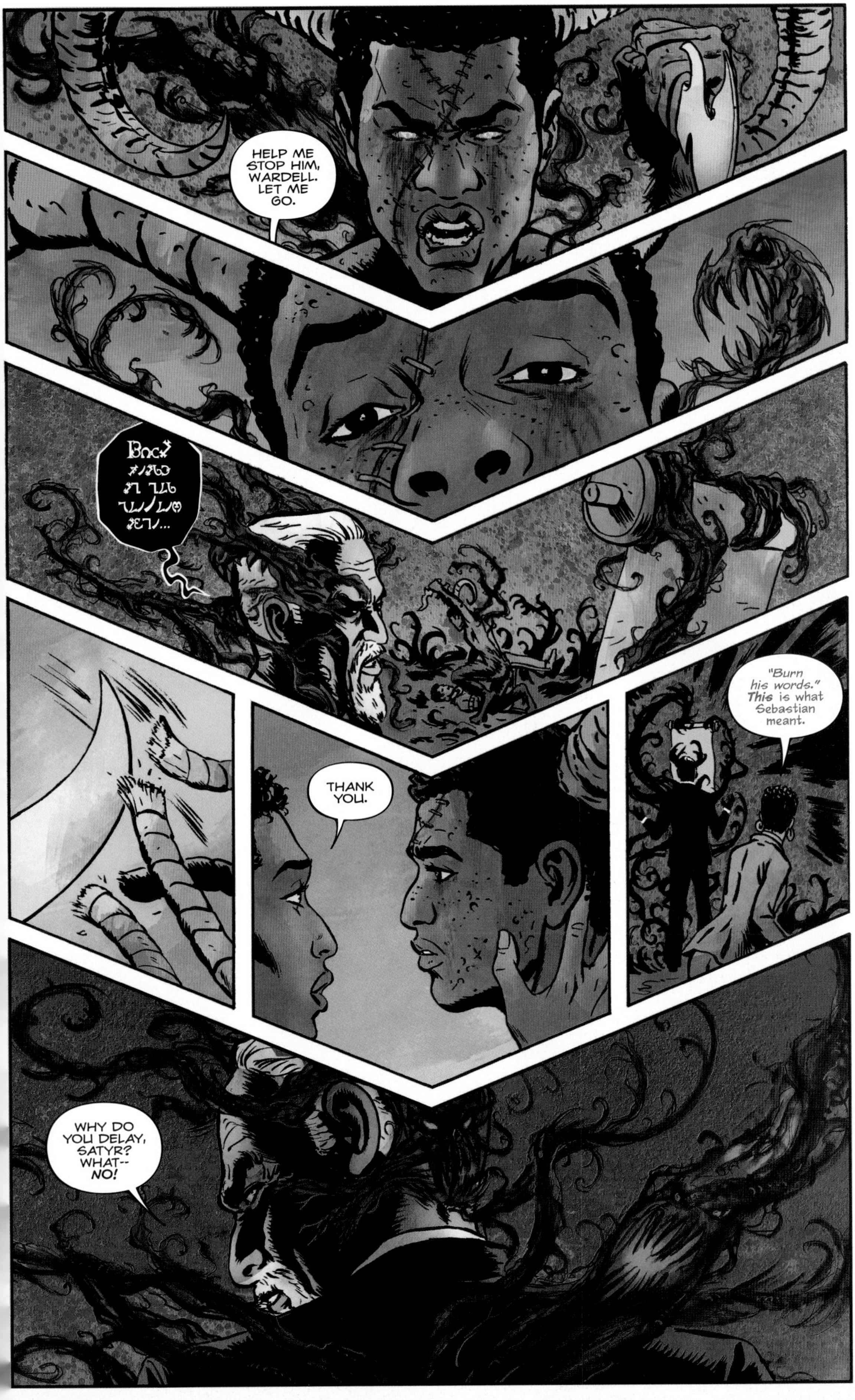
HELP ME STOP HIM, WARDELL. LET ME GO.
THANK YOU.
"Burn his words." *This* is what Sebastian meant.
WHY DO YOU DELAY, SATYR? WHAT-- *NO!*

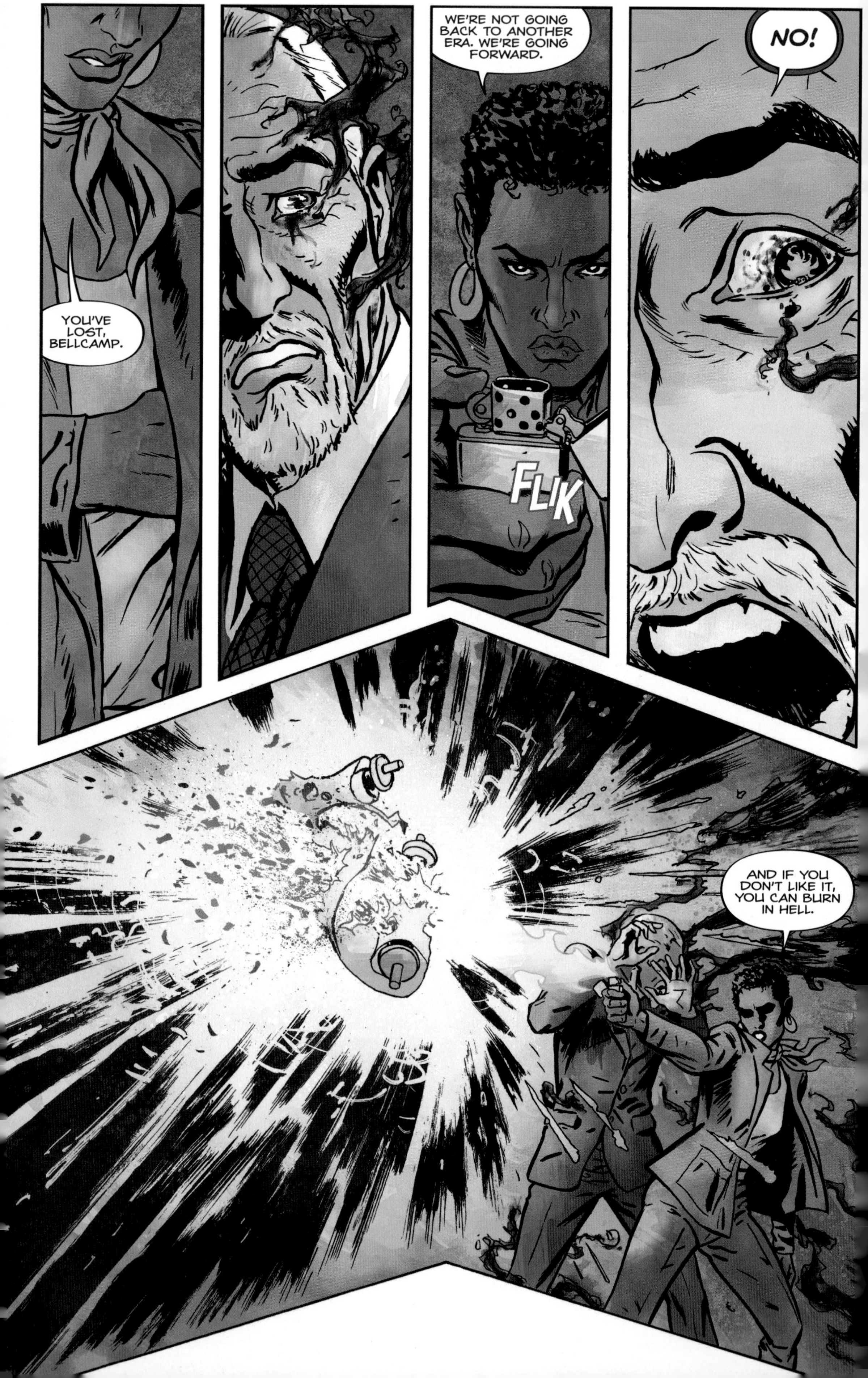

YOU'VE LOST, BELLCAMP.
WE'RE NOT GOING BACK TO ANOTHER ERA. WE'RE GOING FORWARD.
FLIK
NO!
AND IF YOU DON'T LIKE IT, YOU CAN BURN IN HELL.

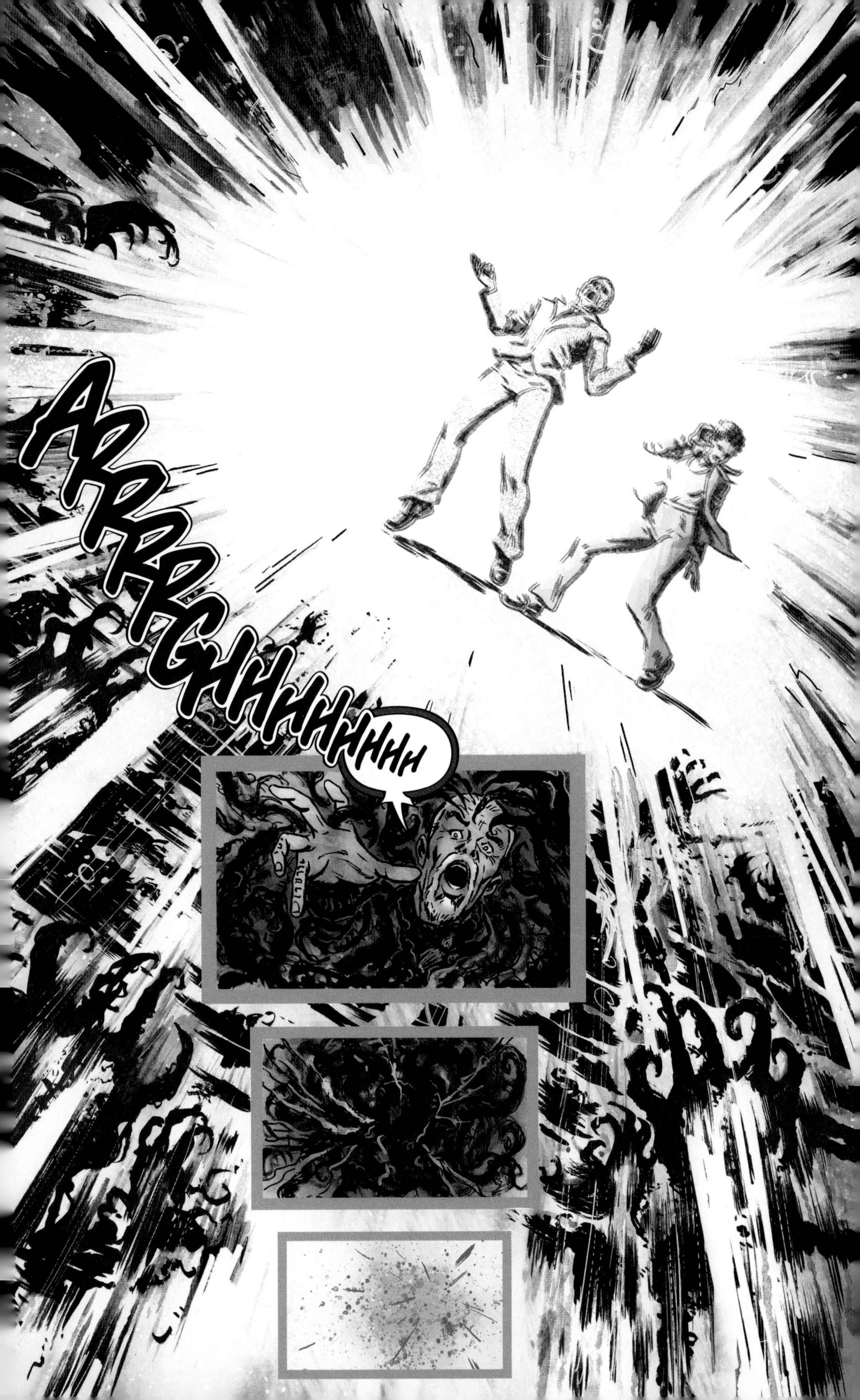
ARRRGHHHHHHHHH

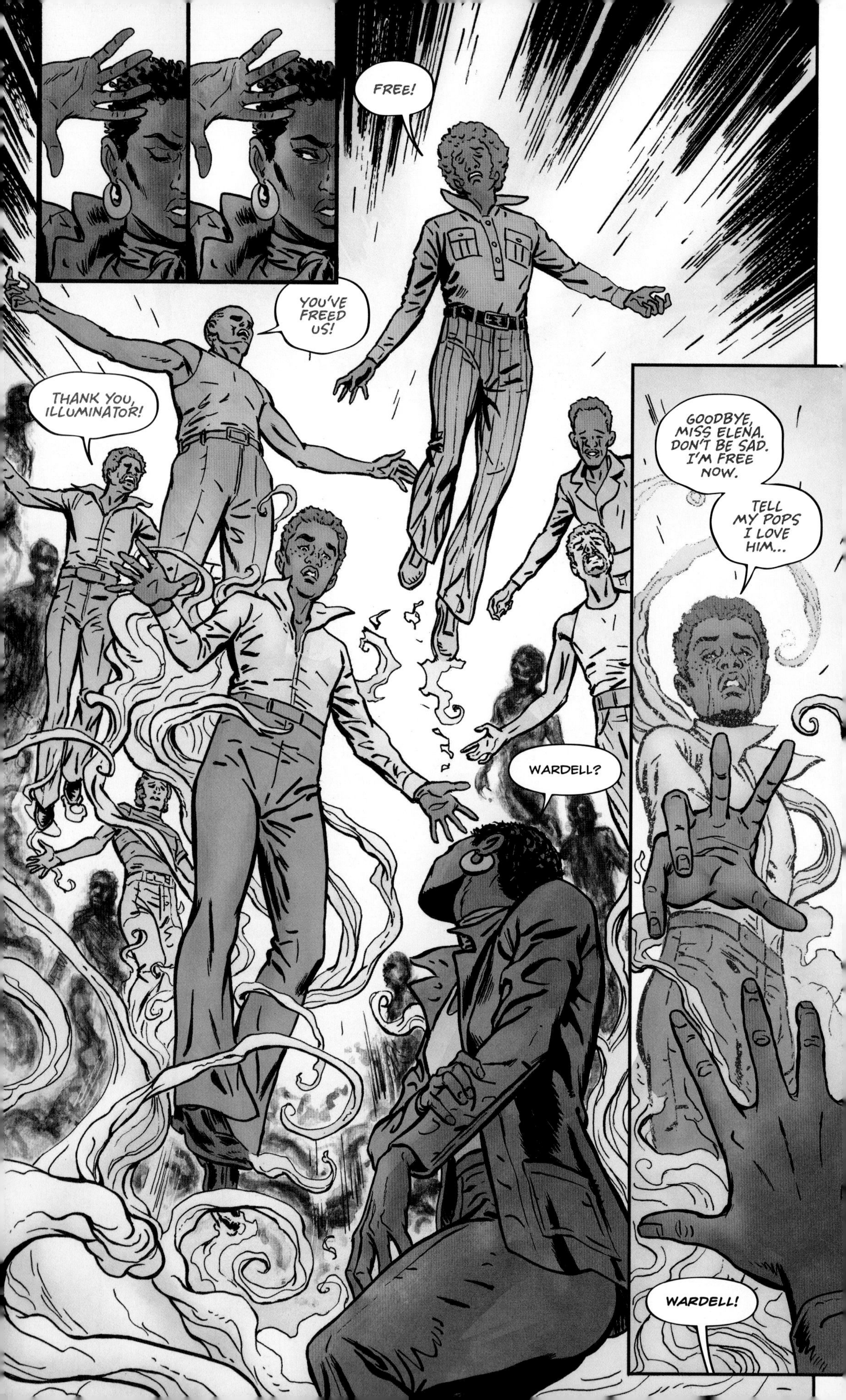
FREE!
YOU'VE FREED US!
THANK YOU, ILLUMINATOR!
GOODBYE, MISS ELENA. DON'T BE SAD. I'M FREE NOW.
TELL MY POPS I LOVE HIM...
WARDELL?
WARDELL!

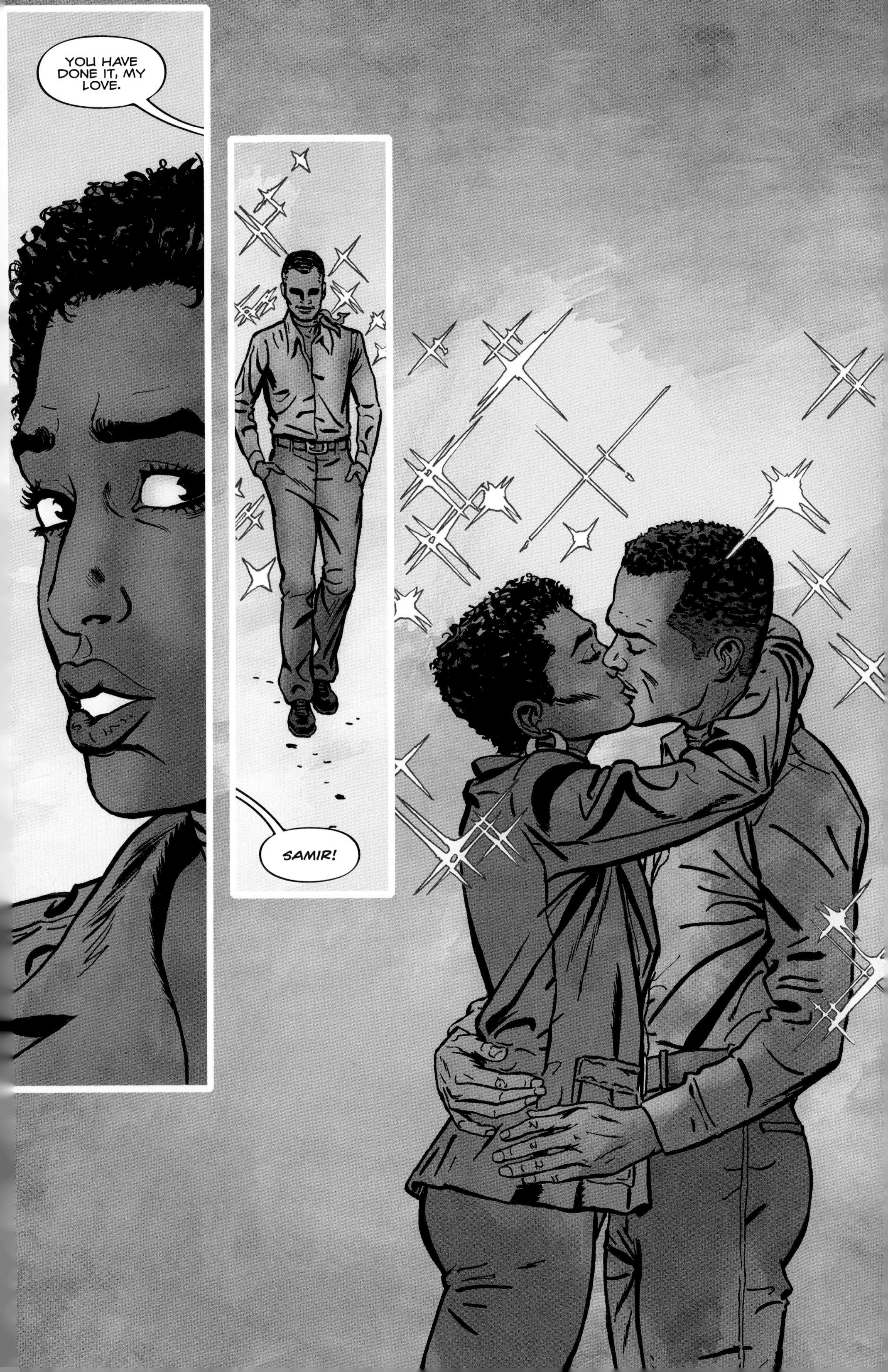
YOU HAVE DONE IT, MY LOVE.
SAMIR!

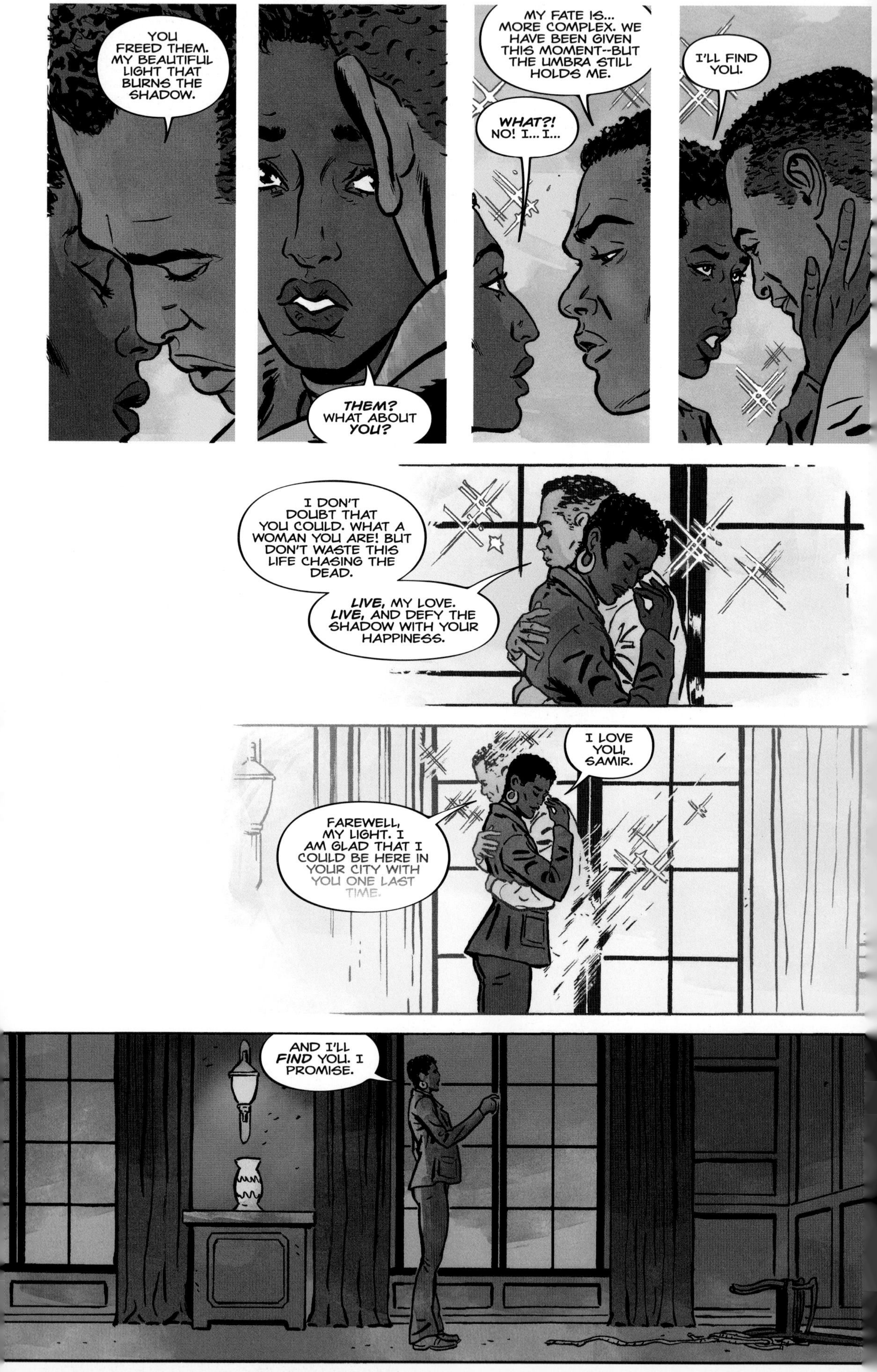
YOU FREED THEM. MY BEAUTIFUL LIGHT THAT BURNS THE SHADOW.
THEM? WHAT ABOUT YOU?
MY FATE IS... MORE COMPLEX. WE HAVE BEEN GIVEN THIS MOMENT--BUT THE UMBRA STILL HOLDS ME.
WHAT?! NO! I... I...
I'LL FIND YOU.
I DON'T DOUBT THAT YOU COULD. WHAT A WOMAN YOU ARE! BUT DON'T WASTE THIS LIFE CHASING THE DEAD.
LIVE, MY LOVE. LIVE, AND DEFY THE SHADOW WITH YOUR HAPPINESS.
I LOVE YOU, SAMIR.
FAREWELL, MY LIGHT. I AM GLAD THAT I COULD BE HERE IN YOUR CITY WITH YOU ONE LAST TIME.
AND I'LL FIND YOU. I PROMISE.

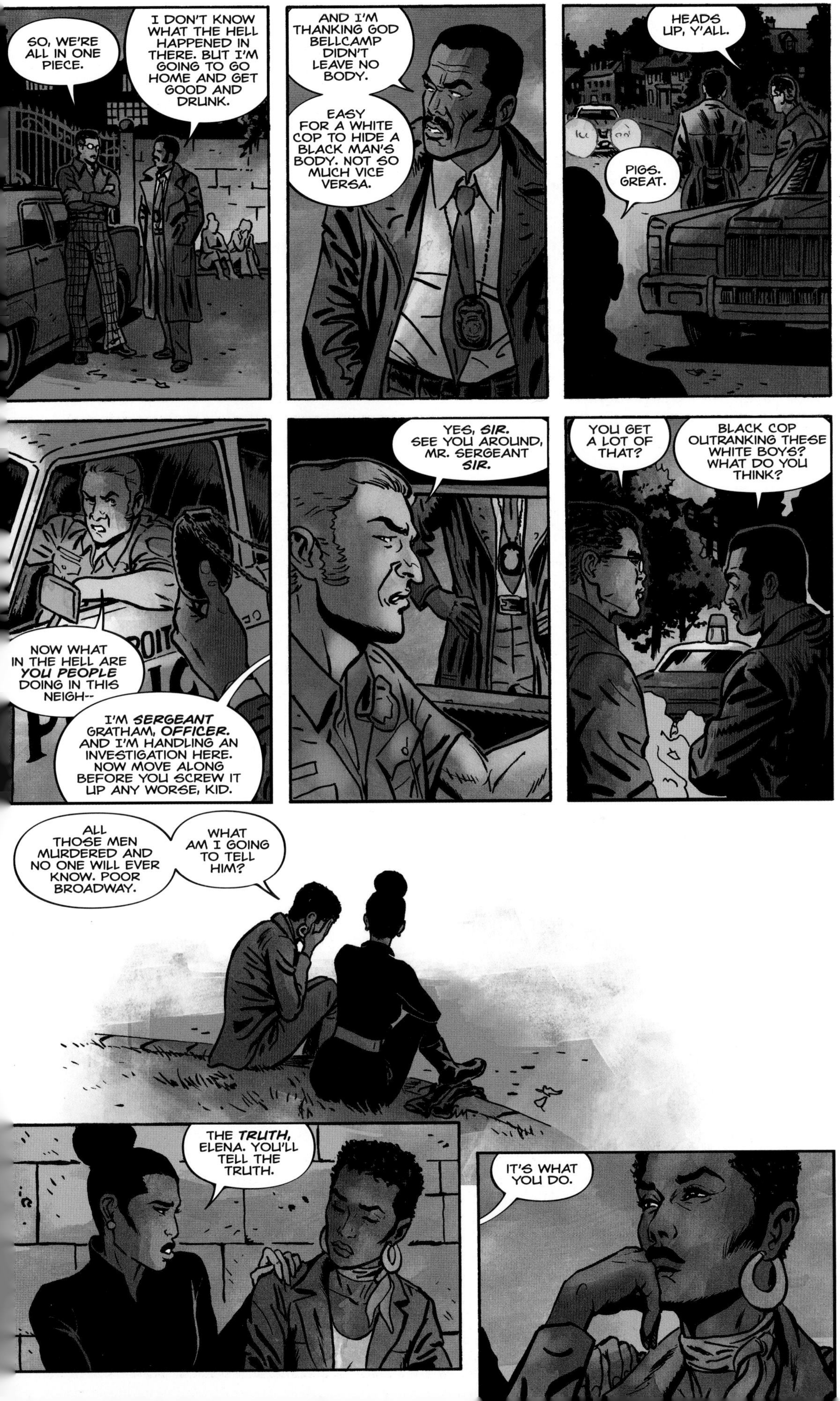
SO, WE'RE ALL IN ONE PIECE.
I DON'T KNOW WHAT THE HELL HAPPENED IN THERE. BUT I'M GOING TO GO HOME AND GET GOOD AND DRUNK.
AND I'M THANKING GOD BELLCAMP DIDN'T LEAVE NO BODY.
EASY FOR A WHITE COP TO HIDE A BLACK MAN'S BODY. NOT SO MUCH VICE VERSA.
HEADS UP, Y'ALL.
PIGS. GREAT.
NOW WHAT IN THE HELL ARE YOU PEOPLE DOING IN THIS NEIGH--
I'M SERGEANT GRATHAM, OFFICER. AND I'M HANDLING AN INVESTIGATION HERE. NOW MOVE ALONG BEFORE YOU SCREW IT UP ANY WORSE, KID.
YES, SIR. SEE YOU AROUND, MR. SERGEANT SIR.
YOU GET A LOT OF THAT?
BLACK COP OUTRANKING THESE WHITE BOYS? WHAT DO YOU THINK?
ALL THOSE MEN MURDERED AND NO ONE WILL EVER KNOW. POOR BROADWAY.
WHAT AM I GOING TO TELL HIM?
THE TRUTH, ELENA. YOU'LL TELL THE TRUTH.
IT'S WHAT YOU DO.

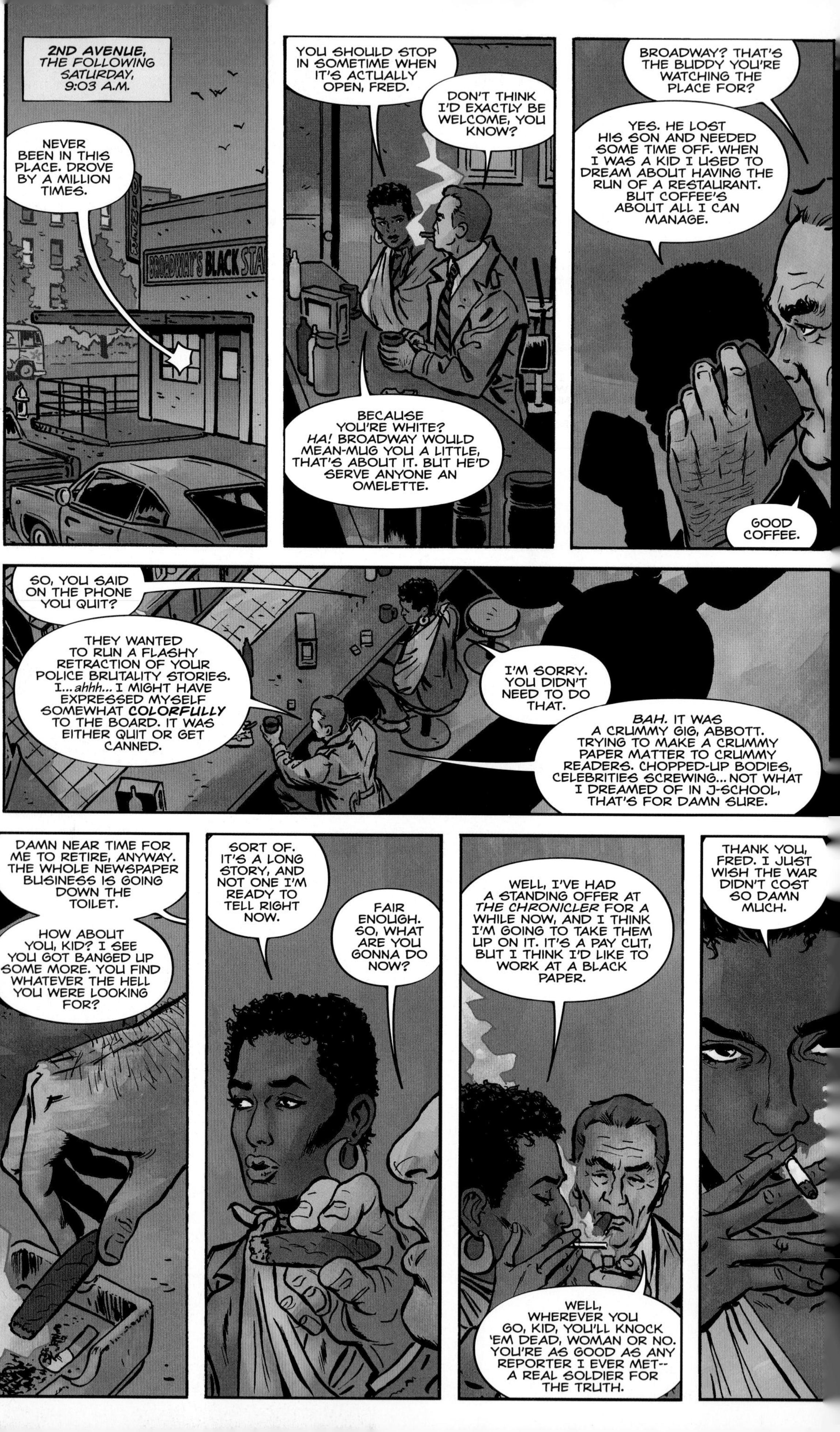
2ND AVENUE, THE FOLLOWING SATURDAY, 9:03 A.M.
NEVER BEEN IN THIS PLACE. DROVE BY A MILLION TIMES.
BROADWAY'S BLACK STA
YOU SHOULD STOP IN SOMETIME WHEN IT'S ACTUALLY OPEN, FRED.
DON'T THINK I'D EXACTLY BE WELCOME, YOU KNOW?
BECAUSE YOU'RE WHITE? *HA!* BROADWAY WOULD MEAN-MUG YOU A LITTLE, THAT'S ABOUT IT. BUT HE'D SERVE ANYONE AN OMELETTE.
BROADWAY? THAT'S THE BUDDY YOU'RE WATCHING THE PLACE FOR?
YES. HE LOST HIS SON AND NEEDED SOME TIME OFF. WHEN I WAS A KID I USED TO DREAM ABOUT HAVING THE RUN OF A RESTAURANT. BUT COFFEE'S ABOUT ALL I CAN MANAGE.
GOOD COFFEE.
SO, YOU SAID ON THE PHONE YOU QUIT?
THEY WANTED TO RUN A FLASHY RETRACTION OF YOUR POLICE BRUTALITY STORIES. I... *ahhh...* I MIGHT HAVE EXPRESSED MYSELF SOMEWHAT **COLORFULLY** TO THE BOARD. IT WAS EITHER QUIT OR GET CANNED.
I'M SORRY. YOU DIDN'T NEED TO DO THAT.
BAH. IT WAS A CRUMMY GIG, ABBOTT. TRYING TO MAKE A CRUMMY PAPER MATTER TO CRUMMY READERS. CHOPPED-UP BODIES, CELEBRITIES SCREWING... NOT WHAT I DREAMED OF IN J-SCHOOL, THAT'S FOR DAMN SURE.
DAMN NEAR TIME FOR ME TO RETIRE, ANYWAY. THE WHOLE NEWSPAPER BUSINESS IS GOING DOWN THE TOILET.
HOW ABOUT YOU, KID? I SEE YOU GOT BANGED UP SOME MORE. YOU FIND WHATEVER THE HELL YOU WERE LOOKING FOR?
SORT OF. IT'S A LONG STORY, AND NOT ONE I'M READY TO TELL RIGHT NOW.
FAIR ENOUGH. SO, WHAT ARE YOU GONNA DO NOW?
WELL, I'VE HAD A STANDING OFFER AT *THE CHRONICLER* FOR A WHILE NOW, AND I THINK I'M GOING TO TAKE THEM UP ON IT. IT'S A PAY CUT, BUT I THINK I'D LIKE TO WORK AT A BLACK PAPER.
WELL, WHEREVER YOU GO, KID, YOU'LL KNOCK 'EM DEAD, WOMAN OR NO. YOU'RE AS GOOD AS ANY REPORTER I EVER MET-- A REAL SOLDIER FOR THE TRUTH.
THANK YOU, FRED. I JUST WISH THE WAR DIDN'T COST SO DAMN MUCH.

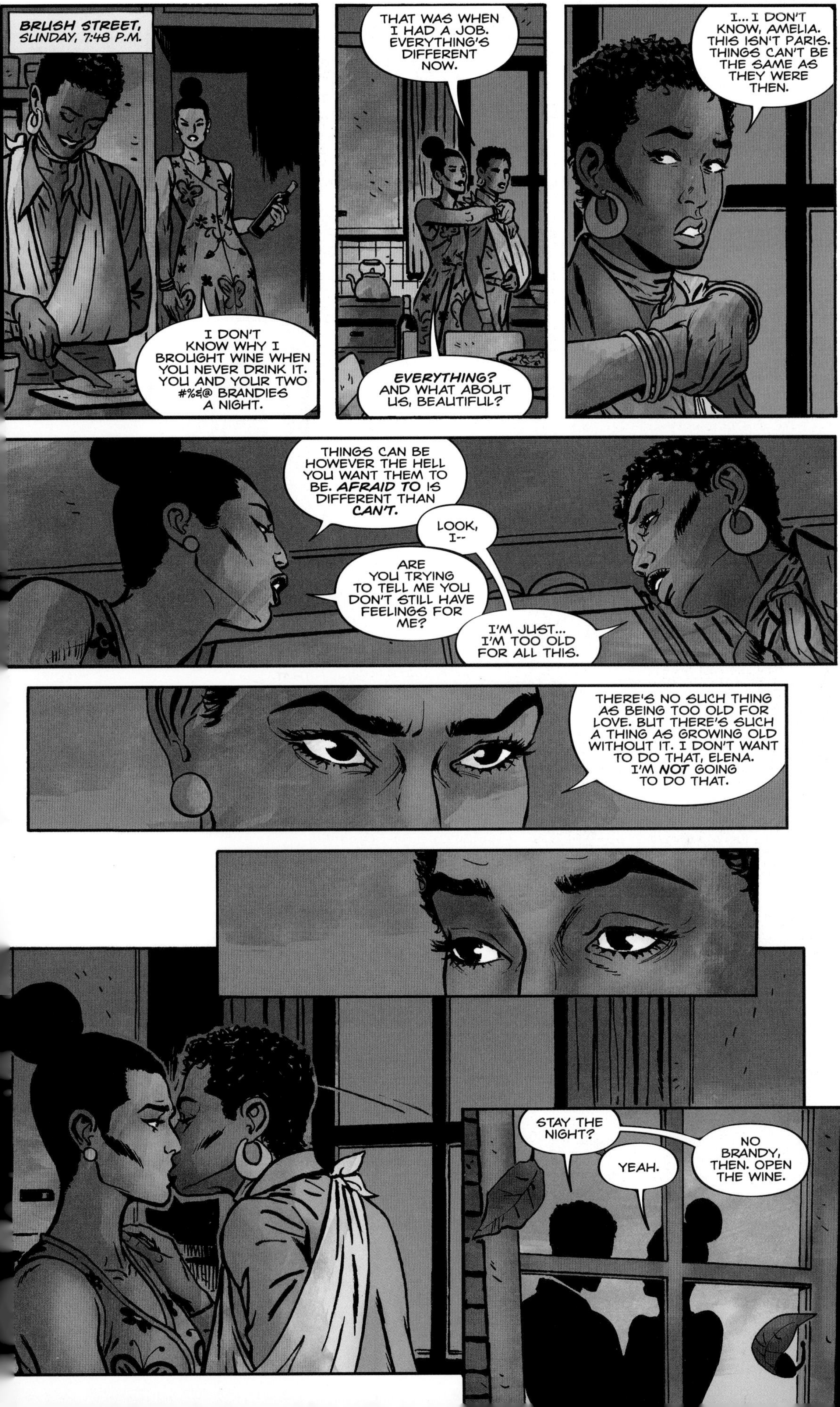
BRUSH STREET, SUNDAY, 7:48 P.M.
I DON'T KNOW WHY I BROUGHT WINE WHEN YOU NEVER DRINK IT. YOU AND YOUR TWO #%&@ BRANDIES A NIGHT.
THAT WAS WHEN I HAD A JOB. EVERYTHING'S DIFFERENT NOW.
EVERYTHING? AND WHAT ABOUT US, BEAUTIFUL?
I... I DON'T KNOW, AMELIA. THIS ISN'T PARIS. THINGS CAN'T BE THE SAME AS THEY WERE THEN.
THINGS CAN BE HOWEVER THE HELL YOU WANT THEM TO BE. AFRAID TO IS DIFFERENT THAN CAN'T.
LOOK, I--
ARE YOU TRYING TO TELL ME YOU DON'T STILL HAVE FEELINGS FOR ME?
I'M JUST... I'M TOO OLD FOR ALL THIS.
THERE'S NO SUCH THING AS BEING TOO OLD FOR LOVE. BUT THERE'S SUCH A THING AS GROWING OLD WITHOUT IT. I DON'T WANT TO DO THAT, ELENA. I'M NOT GOING TO DO THAT.
STAY THE NIGHT?
YEAH.
NO BRANDY, THEN. OPEN THE WINE.

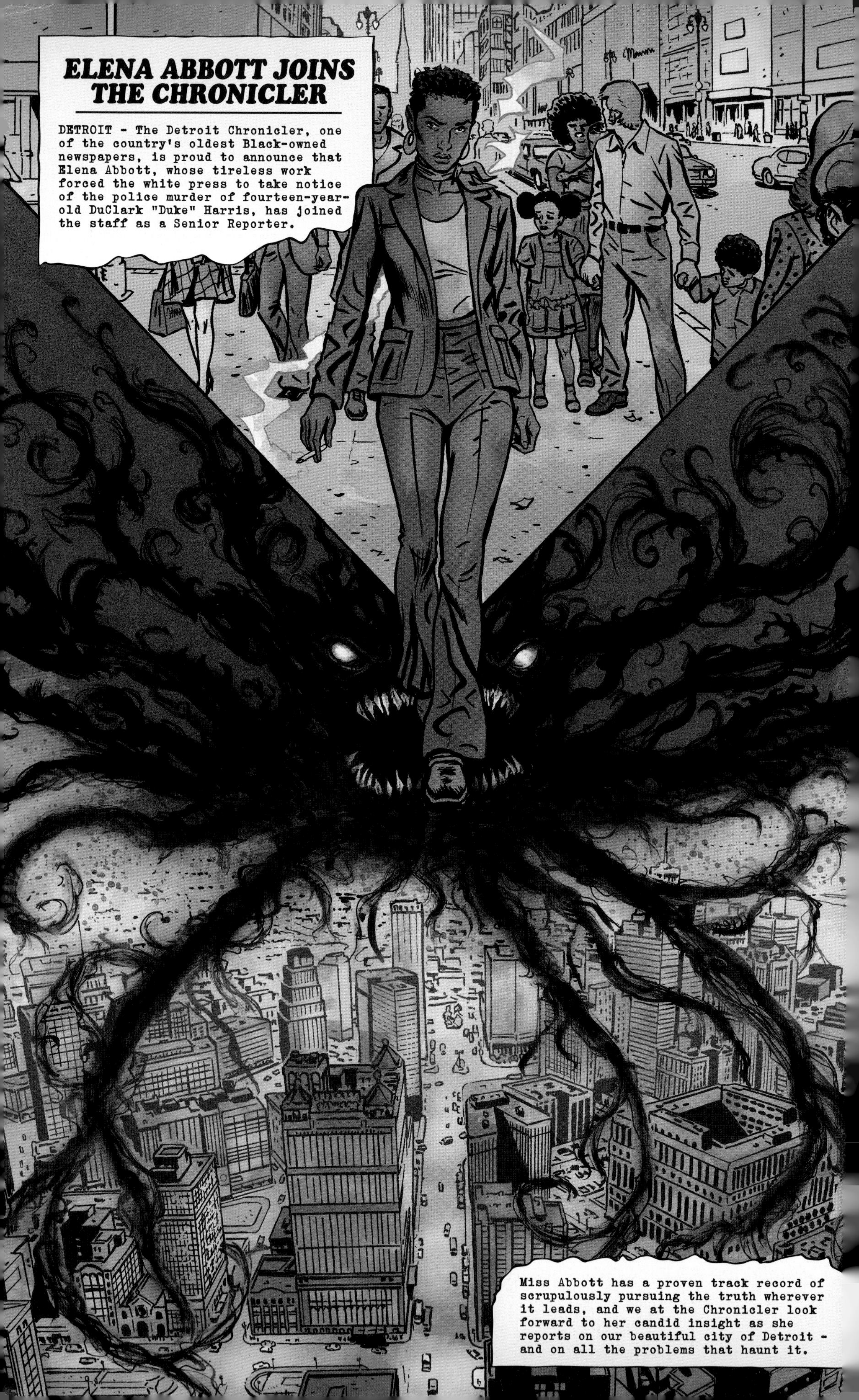
ELENA ABBOTT JOINS THE CHRONICLER
DETROIT - The Detroit Chronicler, one of the country's oldest Black-owned newspapers, is proud to announce that Elena Abbott, whose tireless work forced the white press to take notice of the police murder of fourteen-year-old DuClark "Duke" Harris, has joined the staff as a Senior Reporter.
Miss Abbott has a proven track record of scrupulously pursuing the truth wherever it leads, and we at the Chronicler look forward to her candid insight as she reports on our beautiful city of Detroit - and on all the problems that haunt it.

Issue Five Cover by
Taj Tenfold

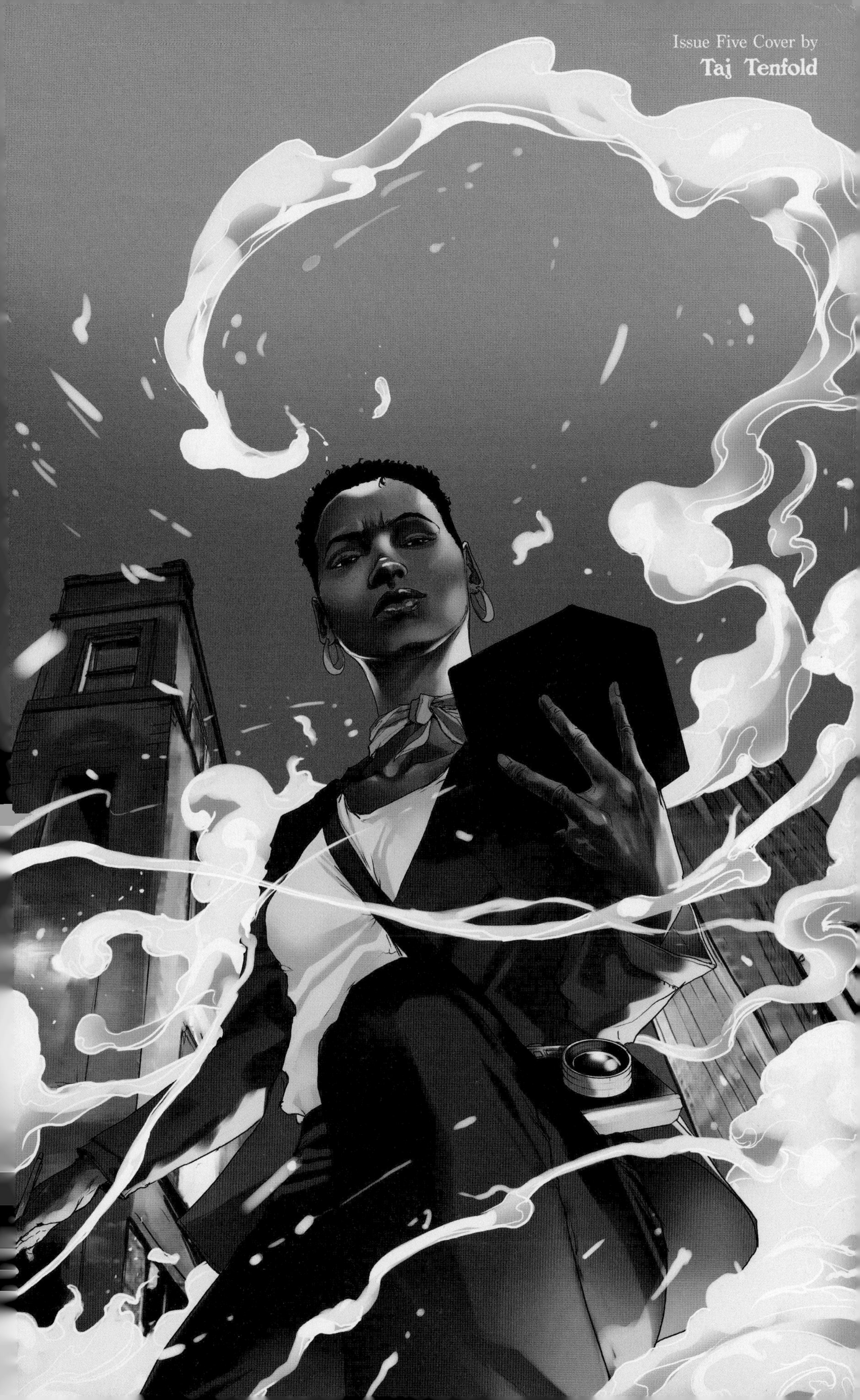

Issue One Variant Cover by
Micaela Dawn

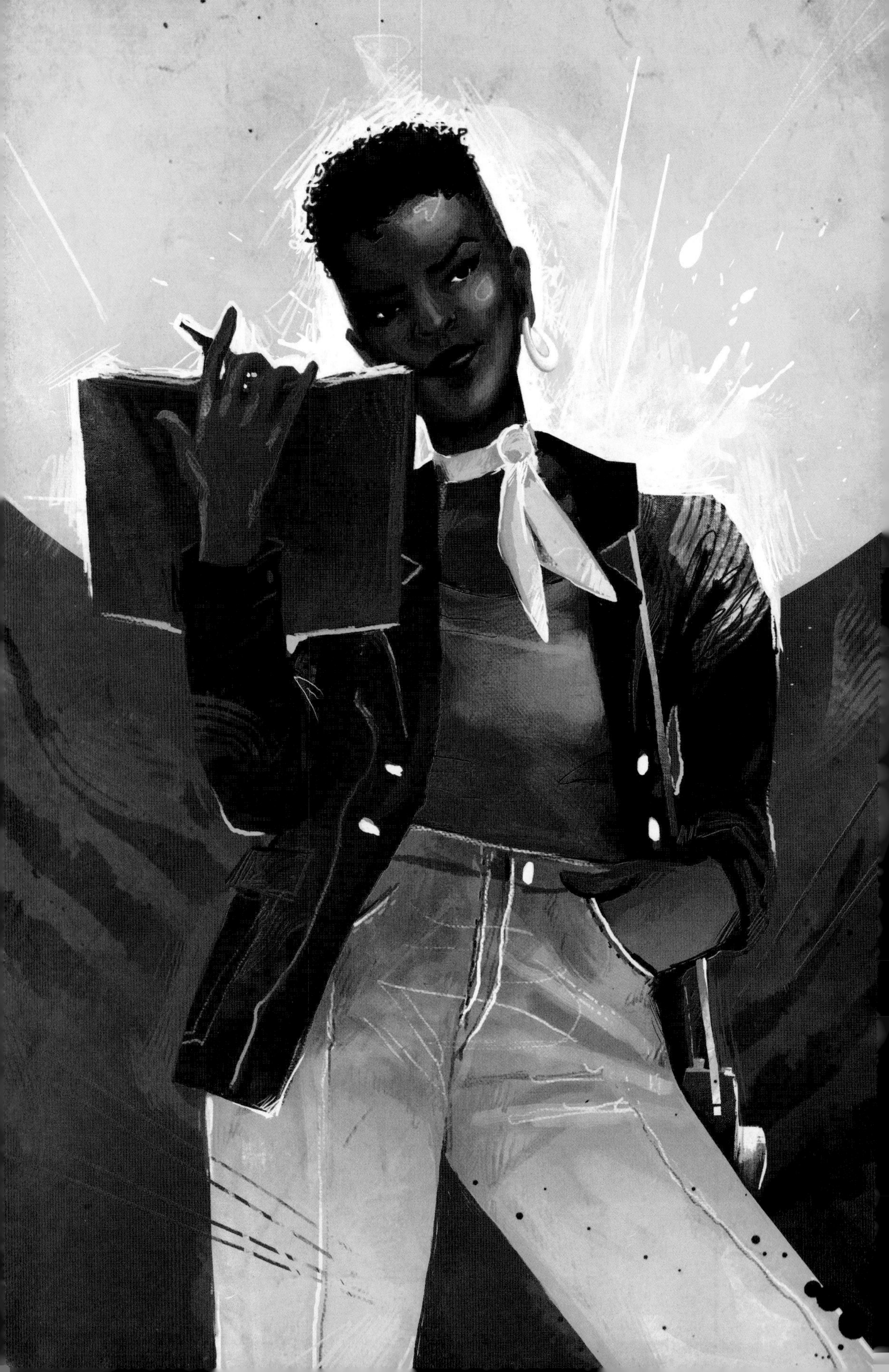

Issue One Unlocked Retailer Variant Cover by
Tula Lotay

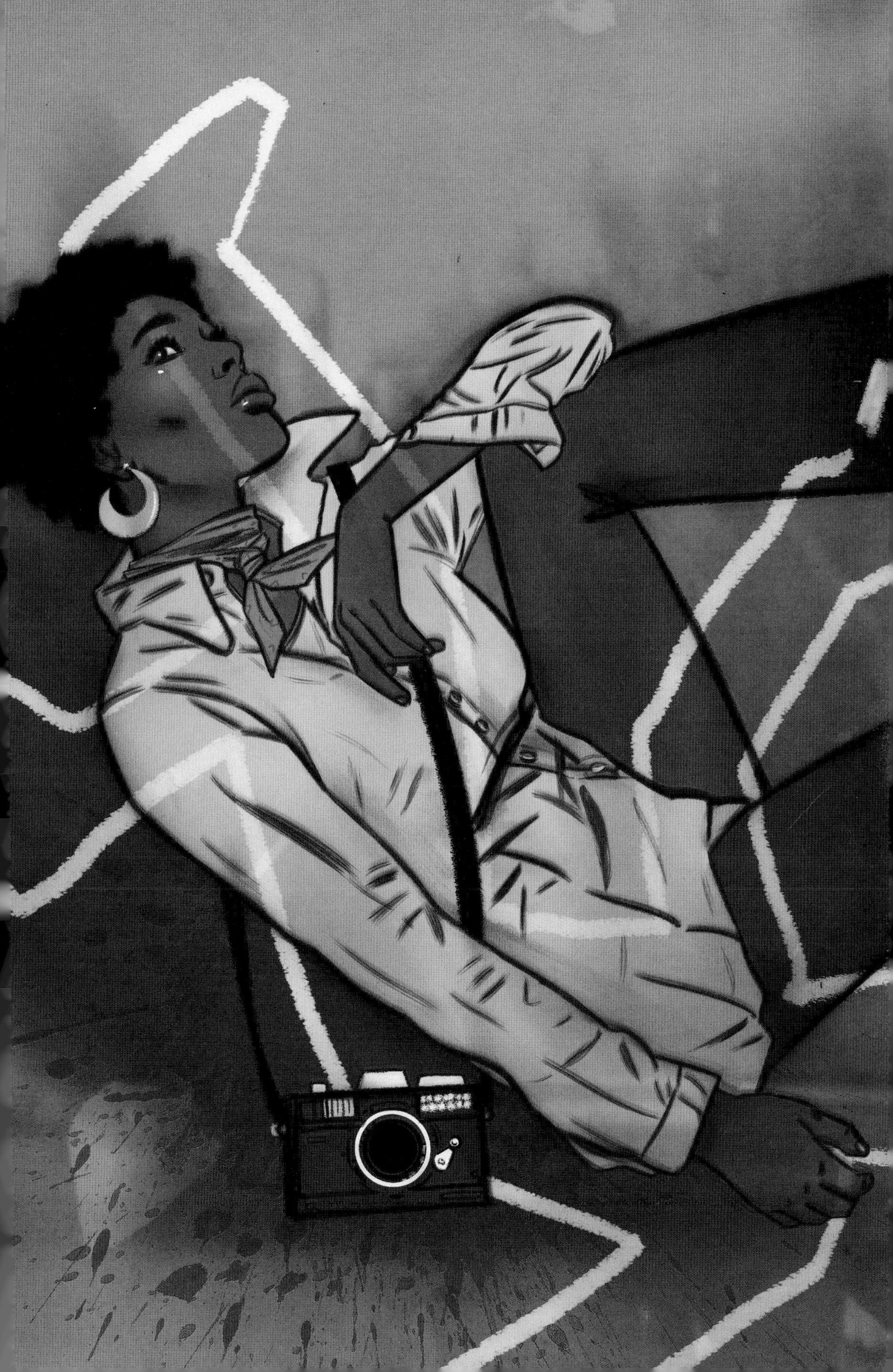

DISCOVER
VISIONARY CREATORS

THE
WOODS
JAMES TYNION IV • MICHAEL DIALYNAS
VOL 1
THE ARROW

THE
SPIRE
SIMON SPURRIER
JEFF STOKELY
ANDRÉ MAY

MARK WAID • PETER KRAUSE
IRREDEEMABLE
AFTERWORD BY
GRANT MORRISON

J.G.
JONES
MARK
WAID
STRANGE
FRUIT
Foreword by
ELVIS MITCHELL

MICHAEL ALAN NELSON
DAN MORA
GABRIEL CASSATA
HEXED
THE HARLOT & THE THIEF VOLUME ONE

ABNETT & CULBARD
WILD'S
END
FIRST LIGHT

James Tynion IV

The Woods

Volume 1
ISBN: 978-1-60886-454-6 | $9.99 US
Volume 2
ISBN: 978-1-60886-495-9 | $14.99 US
Volume 3
ISBN: 978-1-60886-773-8 | $14.99 US

The Backstagers

Volume 1
ISBN: 978-1-60886-993-0 | $14.99 US

Simon Spurrier

Six-Gun Gorilla
ISBN: 978-1-60886-390-7 | $19.99 US

The Spire
ISBN: 978-1-60886-913-8 | $29.99 US

Weavers
ISBN: 978-1-60886-963-3 | $19.99 US

Mark Waid

Irredeemable

Volume 1
ISBN: 978-1-93450-690-5 | $16.99 US
Volume 2
ISBN: 978-1-60886-000-5 | $16.99 US

Incorruptible

Volume 1
ISBN: 978-1-60886-015-9 | $16.99 US
Volume 2
ISBN: 978-1-60886-028-9 | $16.99 US

Strange Fruit
ISBN: 978-1-60886-872-8 | $24.99 US

Michael Alan Nelson

Hexed The Harlot & The Thief

Volume 1
ISBN: 978-1-60886-718-9 | $14.99 US
Volume 2
ISBN: 978-1-60886-816-2 | $14.99 US

Day Men

Volume 1
ISBN: 978-1-60886-393-8 | $9.99 US
Volume 2
ISBN: 978-1-60886-852-0 | $9.99 US

Dan Abnett

Wild's End

Volume 1: First Light
ISBN: 978-1-60886-735-6 | $19.99 US
Volume 2: The Enemy Within
ISBN: 978-1-60886-877-3 | $19.99 US

Hypernaturals

Volume 1
ISBN: 978-1-60886-298-6 | $16.99 US
Volume 2
ISBN: 978-1-60886-319-8 | $19.99 US

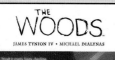

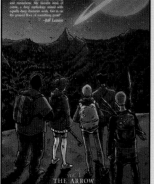

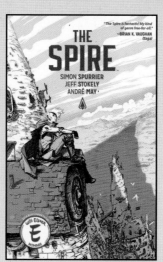

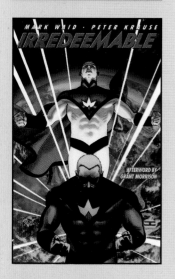

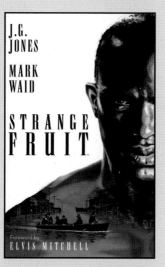

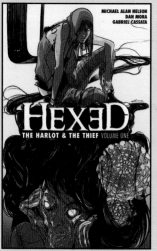

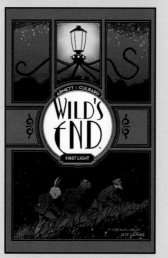

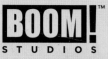